Overcoming Obstacles

A *Memoir of*
Ann DiMare's Life

Ann R. DiMare

Title ID: 3605756

ISBN: 1461141443
ISBN-13: 978-1461141440
LCCN: 2011910718
CreateSpace, North Charleston, South Carolina

DiMare, Ann
Overcoming Obstacles – 1st ed.

Nonfiction Memoirs

Prologue

This book is an accounting of my life, based on my experiences and perceptions from as far back as I can remember. I hope it may inspire readers to believe that despite an overwhelming number of obstacles, there is the possibility of achieving a fulfilling, successful life. It is not my intention to hurt anyone with the contents of this memoir. Since I wasn't privy to what was inside some people's hearts, I can only record what happened, the obstacles I overcame, what I learned, and the ways in which the knowledge I gained helped me to thrive.

As my life was unfolding, many people suggested I write a book. I started writing this book while I was recovering from surgery and undergoing radiation and chemotherapy treatment for endometrial cancer, so that in the event of my untimely passing, my decendents would have an appreciation of our family history and understand that lifes obstacles can be overcome.

I want my decendants to know that my love of people and my trust in God have been the driving forces in my life. I learned about love and faith from my grandmother Anne and hope I have passed my beliefs onto them.

I dedicate this book to my daughters Cara and Deana, and my grandsons Logan and Mason, who have enriched my life with their unconditional love. I also dedicate it to my fiancé Dick who encouraged my physical and mental strength throughout my battle with cancer.

I would like to thank my editor Beverly Ballaro, my cousin Attorney Carla DiMare, my Godfather Judge (retired) Domenic Russo, my nephew Jacob DiMare and my friends Marco Renda and Karen Mustone for their valuable assistance in helping me to make this book a reality.

May God bless you all.

Contents

MY
FAMILY

*T*his section covers my ancestors and their decendants, my father's story, my mother's story, my parents' courtship and marriage, my siblings, our family's medical history and traditions.

The research I carried out to write this book gave me unexpected insights into what a truly amazing woman my mother was! Her faith in God and her love of family are what sustained her. Her life was filled with sadness yet also with joy. From the expression on her face on the day she died, I knew she had seen Jesus and was going home to be with Him in heaven.

I pray that readers of this book will find something in it that will help them overcome life's struggles and realize they are not alone.

Ann DiMare's Ancestors

Ann DiMare 1953-

Salvatore DiMare 1929-

Carmela Faro 1929-1994

Charles DiMare 1897-1983

Anne Fazio 1906-1960

Domenic Faro 1902-1985

Josephine Noe 1909-1997

Domenic DiMare 1875-?

Rosa Fazio 1878-?

Salvatore Fazio 1875-1949

Carmela Silvestro 1885-1975

Angelo Faro 1876-1950

Ventura Intagliata 1873-1951

Santo Noe 1883-1969

Carmela Bianco 1892-1973

ANCESTORS and DECENDENTS

*M*y ancestors immigrated to America from Italy in the early 1910s. With the exception of my paternal grandmother Anne Fazio, who was born in Boston, MA, my paternal and maternal grandparents all grew up in the town of Augusta on the island of Sicily. Both the DiMare and Faro clans were fishermen in Augusta. Initially, the men came to America seeking work. They sent a portion of their wages back to Sicily to support their families. Once they became U.S. Citizens, they were permitted to bring two people to America each year provided they could guarantee work and housing for them. I can recall family members arriving by ship, over the years, at the port of New York City. They were processed at Ellis Island and then released to the sponsoring family member.

As a child, I remember my grandmother reminiscing about Via X Ottobre, Via Principe Umberto and Via Megara in Augusta, Sicily. My grandparents' family members had lived on those streets.

Josephine Noe's home (1972)   Domenic Faro's home (1972)
Via Megara, Augusta Sicily   Via Principe Umberto, Augusta, Sicily

I never knew my father's and mother's paternal grandparents so I have only included their names and available pictures in the ancestors family tree. My only memories of my father's and mother's maternal grandparents are their names and where they lived. We referred to them as "Big Nana" and "Big Nano" to distinguish them from our grandparents, whom we called Nana and Nano.

My paternal great-grandparents, Salvatore and Carmela Fazio lived in Belmont, where I remember visiting their home in the late 1950s. On the left is a picture of Nana and Nano Fazio taken in May 1927. My maternal great-grandparents, Santo and Carmela Noe, lived in East Boston. I have memories of holidays spent with them and visits to their house on Havre Street. They died in 1969 and 1973 respectively. On the right is a picture of Nana and Nano Noe taken on February 10, 1951.

My paternal grandfather, Charles DiMare, was born on July 10, 1897 and my paternal grandmother Anne Fazio, was born on October 22, 1906. They were married on July 4, 1922 in Boston, MA. They had four sons: Domenic Joseph "Joe" DiMare (born May 12, 1927); Salvatore Robert DiMare (born December 1, 1929); and twins Charles J. DiMare, Jr. and James Francis DiMare (born March 31, 1932).

My uncle Joe DiMare founded a crab-fishing business, Charles DiMare & Sons, in 1947. Joe funded the business but put his father's name on it as a gesture of respect. The business was located at the former T-Wharf in Boston. In 1958, Joe expanded the business and renamed it the DiMare Lobster Company. Together with his father, my uncle Joe ran DiMare Lobster Company until 1971. In the early 1960s, my father Sal, worked alongside his brother Joe. In the mid 1960s, Sal founded his own business, which he named the Boston Lobster Company.

For a brief time, Charles Jr. worked for the DiMare Lobster Company. After graduating college however, he got a job at the Stone and Webster Engineering firm in Boston, where he remained until his retirement. Charles' twin brother, James, worked for the New England Telephone Company (AT&T) until his retirement. Charles, Sr. and Anne raised their sons initially on Green Street and Hale Street in Boston's West End. In February 1941, they moved to 100 Yeomans Avenue in Medford. My grandmother Anne was a devout Catholic and attended mass daily. She died on August 26, 1960 of Hodgkin's lymphoma. Her widower returned to his native Augusta, Sicily to find a bride. Less than one year later, Charles married Bianca Ruggiero on July 4, 1961. They remained married until Charles died on November 13, 1983. They lived in Charles's home in Medford.

Anne & Charles July 4, 1922   *Charles & Bianca July 4, 1961*

My uncle Joe DiMare married Mary Albaro on May 6, 1951. They had four children: Richard; Donna (Cody); Joseph; and Paul. They have 13 grandchildren: Elizabeth; Jennifer; Katy; Jonathan; Christopher; Bryan; Matthew; Jaclyn; Francesca; Andrew; Abigail; Colin (deceased); and Madelyn. They also have five great-granddaughters: Rebecca; Maeve; Eleanor; Julia; and Vivienne and another great-grandchild due in November 2011.

I took this photo on May 12, 2007 at Uncle Joe's 80th Birthday Party in Danvers, MA.

Julia Marie

Rebecca

Maeve Jennifer

Ella Marie

Vivienne Noelle

Matthew, Jaclyn, Bryan & Francesca

My father, Salvatore DiMare married Carmela Faro on February 25, 1951. They had three children: Charles "Chucky"; Ann (me); and Domenic. They had six grandchildren: Jenna; Carina; Cara; Deana; Jacob; and Maximilian. They also had two great-grandsons, Logan and Mason both born after Carmela died.

My father also had three sons with Frances Whiting Horgan: Robert (whose adoptive parents renamed him Philip Vaden); Salvatore; and Anthony. Dad and Frances had seven grandchildren: Stefanie; Courtney; Andrew; Alexander; Abraham; Michael; and Zachary. They have three great-grandsons: Devin; Jordan; and August, all born after Frances died.

On July 1, 1965, my father married Shirley Palermo Sullivan. Shirley had two daughters (Lori and Julie) from her previous marriage.

My uncle Charles J. DiMare, Jr. married Carmela "Bella" Albano on May 8, 1955. They had three children: Charles III "Chipper"; Christina; and Charlene (Costa). They have two granddaughters, Shanna and Carlie.

My uncle James DiMare married Margaret Fidaleo on February 15, 1958. They had five children: James; Carla; Christopher; David; and Catherine. They have seven grandchildren: Anthony; Tianna; Nicholas; Chloe; Kyle; Zachary; and Derek.

Steven Costa, Charlene, Charles Jr., Bella and Christina, Chipper is missing.

James and family taken in 2009 (Carla is missing)

My maternal grandfather, Domenic Faro, was born July 16, 1902 and my maternal grandmother, Josephine Noe, was born September 23, 1909. They were married on March 25, 1925 in Augusta, Sicily. They had five children: Ventura "Winifred" Faro (born July 10, 1926); Angelo Faro (born March 11, 1928); Carmela C. Faro (born December 29, 1929); Santo Faro (born September 11, 1933); and Josephine Marie "Joann" (born April 14, 1941).

Domenic Faro worked at the Bay State Lobster Company on Commercial Street in Boston, which was founded by his father Angelo Faro. When Angelo died on May 23, 1950, Domenic's brother, Sebastiano "Jimmy" Faro took over and operated the business. Winifred was a homemaker. Angelo and Santo worked at Bay State Lobster Company. Carmela (my mom) worked at the Kennedy's Men's Clothing Store in Boston. Joann died of toxemia during childbirth on January 6, 1963, at 21 years of age. Domenic and Josephine raised their children at 352 Shirley Street in Winthrop. The house was a six-family apartment dwelling. Family members occupied three of the apartments. The other three apartments were rented out.

Winifred Faro married Salvatore Paci on August 31, 1941. They had five sons: Domenic "Dicky"; James; Joseph; Salvatore (deceased at age 17 of cerebral palsy); and Paul. They had eight grandchildren: Christine; Domenic; Kimberly; Lori; Joseph; Brett; Carly; and Sam. They had six great-grandchildren: Danielle; Jenna; Domenic; Layla; Max and Karina.

Angelo Faro married Lillian Famolare on October 22, 1950. They had three children: Joan; Domenic; and John. They had six grandchildren: Nicole; Domenic (deceased at birth); David; Richard; Gregory; and Jamie. They also had two great-grandchildren: Chloe and Eli and another great-granddaughter due in August 2011.

Carmela Faro married Salvatore DiMare on February 25, 1951. They had 3 children: Charles "Chucky"; Ann (me); and Domenic.

They had six grandchildren: Jenna; Carina; Cara; Deana; Jacob; and Maximilian. They also had two great-grandsons, Logan, (born March 30, 2009) and Mason (born June 3, 2011), both born many years after Carmela died. In 1969, Carmela married Joe Sicuso. Joe had a daughter, Teresa from a previous marriage.

Santo Faro married Sarah Capodilupo on January 20, 1957. They had 3 daughters: Joann; Louise; and Gina. They have 4 grandchildren: Sarah; Alexander; Anthony; and Brianna. Joann Faro married Frederick Battista on November 19, 1961. They had a baby girl who remained nameless as Joann died giving birth and the baby died the next day.

This photo was taken in March 1975 at my Faro grandparent's 50th anniversary party
Included are: 1st Row: Gina Faro, Sarah Faro, Carmela DiMare, Josephine Faro,
Domenic Faro, Winifred Paci, Lillian Faro
2nd Row: Santo Faro, James Paci, Domenic DiMare, Joseph Paci, Chucky DiMare,
Domenic Faro, Ann DiMare, Louise Faro, John Faro, Joann Faro, Joan Faro, Paul
Paci, Angelo Faro, Domenic "Dicky" Paci and Salvatore "Sam" Paci.
Joann Faro (mom's sister) and Sammy Paci (my cousin) were missing from the photo
as they were both deceased. The great-grandchildren are also missing as none of
them were born yet.

FATHER'S STORY

1930   *September 12, 1952*

Salvatore Robert DiMare

Salvatore Robert DiMare (Dad) was born on December 1, 1929
to Charles C. DiMare and Anne Fazio DiMare in the New England
Hospital in Boston. Dad was a middle child and told me he had
lived an unhappy childhood. His mother was often sick and it
took all her energy to keep herself healthy and take care of dad's
younger twin brothers. As a child, my father posed a challenge
for his parents. Dad told me one day his father became so angry
with him that he took him out to sea on one of their fishing boats
and tried to drown him in the ocean by entangling him in the
fishing nets! When I asked my uncle about this incident, he said it
never happened. Dad must have had a vivid imagination! Dad ran
away from home at the age of 15 but soon returned. He attended

Medford High School from September 1943 to June 1946, but never graduated. He attended Medford Vocational School for one year at night taking the automobile mechanics course.

Dad served in the Navy Reserves from his induction on October 26, 1949 to his honorable discharge on October 25, 1953. His service number was 415 75 34. His rank was SR/SA US Navy Reserves. He was stationed at the United States Naval Training Center (USNTC) in Bainbridge, Maryland from 1/13/1952 until 1/26/1952, at the Office of the Secretary of Defense (OSD) in Boston from 1/28/1952 until 4/12/1953 and on the USS Provincetown (PCS) 1378 from 4/12/1953 until 5/13/1953.

Pictured are dad's birth certificate and US Navy Reserves discharge certificate.

In 1947, Salvatore met my mother, Carmela. My parents were married from February 25, 1951 until December 14, 1966. While married to my mother, dad had relationships with other women ultimately leading him to seek a divorce from my mother. First, he met Frances Whiting Horgan around 1953. With her, he had three sons: Robert Charles (born May 4, 1955), Salvatore Robert (born July 5, 1958) and Anthony Francis (born December 28, 1961). Frances had a daughter Kathy from a previous relationship. Frances gave both Kathy and Robert up for adoption. Robert's adoptive parents renamed him Phillip Charles Vaden. Kathy's adoptive parents renamed her Karen. Frances gave them up because dad promised her he would divorce my mother and marry her if she did.

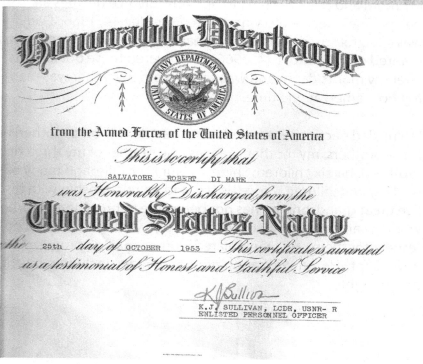

In 1955, dad experienced financial problems that compelled him to file for bankruptcy. The bankruptcy was granted on January 30, 1956. By1964, dad again found himself mired in financial problems, thanks to his obligations toward his five remaining children, none of whom he adequately supported. He abandoned my mom, Frances and all the children and entered a relationship with Shirley Palermo Sullivan. Dad started a refrigeration and air conditioning company with financial support from Shirley's dad. He named it Highland Refrigeration and Air Conditioning. Dad and Shirley moved to Haywood Avenue in Melrose Highlands. They got married on July 1, 1965, over a year before he was divorced from my mother! Dad and Shirley's union forever changed the complexion of our family.

My mom and dad's decree nisi and final divorce decrees are shown below. Their decree nisi was granted on June 14, 1966. Dad was cited for "cruel and abusive treatment." The final decree was granted on December 14, 1966. I discovered these documents after my mom's death and was sad to learn my father was married to two women at one time.

I think dad's actions wounded many people: his own mother; his three brothers; my mother; Frances (the mother of my three half brothers); his six children; Shirley's daughter Julie; and many of his 13 grandchildren. Since he has had no relationship with his five great grandsons, he has not been able to hurt them. Hurting women came easy for dad, because from what I saw, he had no respect for them. He manipulated women making promises he never kept. He was a disappointment to many including me, his only daughter.

Commonwealth of Massachusetts

Suffolk County

Registry of Probate

No. 73852

Re DIMARE

Dear Sir:

Boston, June 14, 19 66.

Decree Nisi for the cause of cruel and
abusive treatment. $25. weekly ~~support~~
support for libellant and $16.66 weekly
for each minor child. (J.V.M.)

IF INQUIRING BRING THIS CARD WITH YOU. McD Louis F. Musco, Register

[A.C. (Divorce) 8]

COMMONWEALTH OF MASSACHUSETTS.

SUFFOLK, ss. PROBATE COURT. CASE No. 73852

I, ~~Louis F. Musco,~~ Arthur A. Kelly, Asst. Register of Probate for said County of Suffolk, hereby certify, that a Probate Court held in and for said County, on the fourteenth day of June in the year of our Lord one thousand nine hundred and sixty-six a divorce from the BOND OF MATRIMONY — Nisi — was decreed by the Court, between Carmela DiMare also called Carmela C. DiMare of Winthrop, in the County of Suffolk, libellant, and Salvatore DiMare also called Salvatore R. DiMare of Malden, in the County of Middlesex, libellee, in favor of said libellant, for the cause which is fully set forth in the decree on file in said Court. Cruel and abusive treatment on the part of the said libellee. Libellant have custody of the minor children, Domenic James, Charles Joseph and Ann Rosemarie DiMare. Libellee pay to said libellant the sum of twenty-five (25) dollars weekly hereafter towards support of libellant and sixteen dollars and sixty-six ($16.66) weekly hereafter towards support of each minor children.

Said decree of divorce to become absolute after the expiration of six months, unless the Court shall have for sufficient cause, on application of any party interested, otherwise ordered.

And on the fourteenth day of December 19 66 the said six months having expired, and the Court not having otherwise ordered, said decree became absolute.

IN WITNESS WHEREOF, I have hereunto set my hand and affixed the seal of said Court, this eighteenth day of September in the year of our Lord one thousand nine hundred and seventy-three

Arthur A. Kelly
Register.

General Laws, Ch. 208, Sec. 21. "Decrees of divorce shall in the first instance be decrees nisi, and shall become absolute after the expiration of six months from the entry thereof, unless the Court within said period, for sufficient cause, upon application of any party interested, otherwise orders. After the entry of a decree nisi, the libel shall not be dismissed or discontinued on motion of either party except upon such terms, if any, as the Court may order after notice to the other party and a hearing, unless there has been filed with the Court a memorandum signed by both parties wherein they agree to such disposition of the libel."

Sec. 24. "After a decree of divorce has become absolute, either party may marry again as if the other were dead."

17

Since the rest of my dad's life has included Shirley, I have included the history of their marriage and its impact on our family here.

I first met Shirley when I was 11 years old. Dad introduced her to me as his cousin. He told me that her two daughters, Lori and Julie, were my cousins. My earliest memories of Shirley were extremely unpleasant. She gave me the feeling she did not want my father spending time with me.

On July 1, 1965, when I was 12 years old, dad married Shirley in New Hampshire. The wedding took place despite the fact that his divorce from my mother would not become finalized by the Massachusetts courts for another year. As a result, it's still not clear that his marriage to Shirley was ever legally valid. They nonetheless lived as man and wife for many years. My "cousins" Lori and Julie became my step-sisters. I never formed a close relationship with Lori. Julie and I get along and have gotten together at least once a year since 1996.

From the beginning, Shirley made it clear I wasn't welcome in "her" house so I stayed away. She often criticized me to my relatives. She let them know she didn't like me. Because of the way she treated me, I knew to stay out of her path. When I couldn't manage to avoid her completely, I did all I could to be kind to her.

It wasn't easy though. On several occasions, Shirley experienced emotional outbursts that made those present extremely uncomfortable. At my Aunt Mary's fiftieth birthday party in 1980, Shirley started screaming hysterically and insisted my father take her home. Later he claimed that Shirley had mistakenly thought he had given me a ring as a gift. He had handed me a ring – it was the friendship ring my ex-husband had given me when we were dating. At the party, my father returned it to me after I had given it to him to have his friend, a jeweler, repair it for me.

During the many years in his "marriage" to Shirley, dad had strained relationships with his brothers, his children and his grandchildren.

He has only seen one of his five great-grandsons and the visits with him stopped in July 2009.

Dad didn't attend most of his nieces' and nephews' weddings because Shirley felt uncomfortable with the DiMares. She confessed to me that she hated "anything DiMare". She even said some nasty things to me about my grandmother Anne, even though she never met her!

Shirley skipped numerous family functions I invited her to, including my confirmation, my high school graduation, and my bridal shower. In 1974, she attended my wedding and caused a scene in the church and at the reception. Shirley's actions toward me were that of a jealous woman.

Shirley may have thought she knew where my father was, but, Dad was well practiced at deception. During my high school years, dad "secretly" showed up at different events. He attended my confirmation and my basketball games, although he didn't attend my high school graduation or either of my college commencement ceremonies.

When I worked in Cambridge, dad sometimes invited me to meet him for lunches at the Rusty Scupper Restaurant, which was owned by one of his air conditioning clients. Shirley kept the books for the company. Dad introduced me as his "friend" lest someone reveal to Shirley that he was spending time with his daughter.

When I was in my twenties and at home raising my daughters, dad occasionally visited us, never staying too long. Dad kept reminding me not to tell anyone about his visits. I found his behavior weak, sneaky and less than honest. Dad tried to justify his weakness by telling me that Shirley was insanely jealous of me. I don't know if that was true. According to him, she was fat and I was skinny; she was uneducated and I had a college degree;

she was incapable of taking care of herself and I could – and did – take care not only of myself but also my children. "Shirley favors underdogs", he told me, "like her and her daughters". "If you fail at something," my father told me, "she will grow to accept you too." He went so far as to suggest I sell my house and rent an apartment that wasn't as nice! When dad claimed that Shirley was hoping to see me fail at something, it made me all the more determined to succeed. Dad would often say vicious things about people including my brothers, Shirley's daughter Julie, Julie's children Alicia and Lucas, and even Shirley, but I didn't trust what he said so I formed my own opinions about them.

When I had my children, neither my dad nor Shirley acknowledged them. In December 1978, when my younger daughter was four months old and my older daughter was almost two years old, I called my dad and asked him if he had any interest in meeting his granddaughters. After checking with Shirley, he invited me to visit their home with my daughters. We went and, despite Shirley expressing her belief to me that "girl babies" were evil, we all agreed to make another try at maintaining a family relationship for the sake of the children.

After that, I invited dad and Shirley to events such as my children's birthday parties, religious celebrations, graduation parties, engagement parties, bridal showers and weddings. Shirley rarely attended. My father came to some events – Cara's high school graduation, Cara and Deana's college graduation party, Cara's wedding and family Christmas parties.

In the fall of 1988, Deana was at the Hilltop Steak House soliciting money for Saugus Youth Sports. My father and Shirley went there to dine and my father walked past Deana, not recognizing her. Shirley called him back and asked Deana if she knew who they were. She told them she did. That prompted my father to get back in touch with me after a five year absence from my life.

Despite Shirley's continued lack of respect for me and my children, I continued to try and try again and again and again. I remember on one visit, Shirley asked probing questions meant to drive me and my daughters apart. She asked why I wouldn't give my daughter Deana the money she wanted to go to the college of her choice. I explained that I treated my daughters equally and I wasn't going to give more to one than I gave to the other.

She also worked at destroying the relationships between me and my brothers. After my mother's death, she made a point of reading me a letter my brother Chucky had sent our father. In the letter my brother accused me of stealing from my mother's estate. My hearing that letter made it difficult for me to trust my brother as it appeared he was angry and out to hurt me too since he had no basis for his accusations.

From the mid-1960s until the early 1990's, dad owned and operated his air conditioning company. In 1990, he closed his business and moved to Bonita Springs, Florida with Shirley. I felt bad about him leaving but I was also somewhat relieved as this meant I no longer had to worry about dad getting caught visiting me. By then, Shirley's aunt (her mom's sister) was a neighbor of mine, as was Shirley's cousin. Neither of them had a good relationship with Shirley but they did talk to her mother.

In March 1992, Dad came to Boston for medical appointments. Since Shirley stayed in Florida, dad was able to see his children without her objection. We had dinner at the Old Mill in Westminster. Chucky's family came from Amherst. Dom and Laura came from Webster. Cara, Deana, Jacob and Max drove together and Richard drove dad and me there. On our way home, dad asked, "If I could give you anything you wanted in life what would you choose?" I immediately responded, "A family who loves me and wants to be with me and my children". His response was "It is never too late. One never knows what the future will bring."

21

March 1992
Seated: Ann, Jenna, Chucky,
Dad and Dom
Standing: Richard, Max, Jacob,
Deana, Joan, Carina, Cara and
Laura

In 1994, shortly after my mother died, Shirley called me and told me she understood that all I had left was my dad. She invited me and my daughters to their Florida home. I decided to try and put the past behind me and give her yet another chance even though both my daughters and I were truly afraid. We didn't know what she was capable of doing because of her history of anger and hatred toward all of us.

We went to Bonita Springs for three days and although we felt extremely uncomfortable going there because of her past outbursts, we walked away with a hope the future would be different. Over the next year I was reminded that nothing changes if nothing changes – and since Shirley didn't change, her negative behavior started again.

During my visit to dad's house (November 1997), he slipped a manila envelope and a white envelope in my suitcase and told me not to open them until he died. He told me they contained his original will, his trust and some old coins. He went on to say that everything he owned would be left to me and that I should share my inheritance with anyone who had treated me well through the years. He then asked if either of my brothers had been good to me. I told him they hadn't. "You see what I mean", he said, "in that case, keep it all for yourself".

I told dad I would most likely share it with my half brothers as they had been kind toward me. To my surprise, he said he didn't want me sharing it with "those bastards," as he called them. I asked him, "Who made them bastards?" and told him he was sticking me in a no-win situation. My brother Chucky was already angry with me about my probating my mother's will and now my father was putting me in the same position with his will. He then told me Chucky and Shirley's daughter Lori, are the trustees of his trust.

In November, 1999, my daughter Deana, her friend Kristy and I celebrated Thanksgiving with my dad in Florida when Shirley was in Massachusetts celebrating Thanksgiving with her family. Dad took us for a boat ride and enjoyed our company. On another occasion, I met dad at a rest stop along Alligator Alley in Florida as Shirley was in town and thus I couldn't go to their house.

In early May 2000, after I bought my condo in Fort Lauderdale, my brother Dom offered to come help me update the electrical outlets in the unit. I accepted his offer – and accepted him back into my life. I thought we too could start anew.

When Dom came to Florida, I asked him if he had spoken to our dad lately. He said he had and planned, in fact, to visit with him later that week. He mentioned that each time he spoke to our father, dad would ask him if he was in touch with me.

Why I did so, I will never know but I told my brother Dom about the envelopes and suggested to him that perhaps dad was giving him a chance to be kind to me so he could inherit some of dad's estate too. I then explained the estate instructions dad had given me to be carried out upon his death.

Three days later, when Dom arrived in Bonita Springs to see my dad, he told Shirley about the envelopes. Shirley started screaming. Dad was furious with me. I was disappointed in my brother Dom for helping to create all this drama. In his anger, dad took back the envelopes when he came to Boston for my daughters' college graduations (using an airline ticket I paid for). I was relieved to be rid of the envelopes. I learned through court documents that my dad subsequently appointed Chucky's wife Joan in charge of his trust. I've always felt if I couldn't have dad's love I didn't want his money anyways.

In November 2001, Dad came to me as he wanted help while visiting a lawyer in Florida. He was finally ready to divorce Shirley. Dad and I went to see Chucky's attorney friend, Mayer Gattegno, in Coral Springs, FL to discuss potential terms of Dad's and Shirley's divorce agreement. Even though dad had been careful to put everything in his name alone, because he was a Florida resident, he was legally obligated to give Shirley half of what he owned. Dad sold his beautiful home and boat on a canal in Bonita Springs and gave Shirley half his money (approximately $300K).

Dad helped Shirley return to Massachusetts to live with her mother. He then bought a new condo in Naples close to his brother Jimmy. Once Shirley was no longer a part of his life, I called my dad almost every day. I hated to see him be alone. I encouraged him to get on with his life and try to meet someone else. I kept hoping and praying he would. Deep down though, I knew Shirley would be back as she would want the rest of his money just to be sure my brothers and I didn't inherit anything.

After Shirley spent a winter in Malden living with her mother, in the fall of 2002, she returned to the warmth of Florida and my dad's welcoming arms and open wallet. Dad was extremely lonely during their time apart. He was 72 years old and several of his friends had died so he had no one to pass the time or to go fishing with. She moved into dad's condo although she and my dad never remarried. But they told people they had, as Shirley did not want to be perceived as living in sin. This struck me as peculiar, given their marriage may not have been valid from the onset.

During a visit with them in March 2003, they revealed to me they weren't married. When Shirley announced to me in front of my father that she was only living with him to serve as his nurse so when he died, she would get the rest of his money, I wasn't surprised. When they first got divorced, I predicted Shirley would be back. I believed she never loved my father. Instead I felt she loved the life he provided her (i.e., vacations, nice cars, nice homes).

My father told me that Shirley worked part time jobs to pay for her cigarettes, her gasoline, and have money to send to her daughters, who needed financial support. I was fine with dad and Shirley's new living arrangement as it would relieve me of any responsibility for taking care of a man who never took care of me. As his only daughter, I was sure I would eventually experience the injustice of having to care for and support him in his old age.

Since some of the family believed my father and Shirley had remarried, they sent wedding cards and gifts. I didn't acknowledge their "re-marriage" as I knew it wasn't genuine. My lack of celebration led Shirley's mother Mary to call to reprimand me. At the time she was nearly 90 years old. I let her rant and rave on the speaker phone for about ten minutes as I continued getting ready for a date. She accused me of being the cause of the breakdown of dad and Shirley's marriage and also the reason why her daughter had such a miserable life. She told me she hated me as much as her daughter did.

Before she had finished screaming at me, my date arrived. I let him listen to her accusations. When she finally stopped and asked, "So what do you have to say for yourself?" I replied, "Thank you for calling. Have a good evening." And I hung up the phone. Mary's verbal abuse was nothing compared to the emotional abuse I took from her daughter.

Indeed after the "re-marriage" nothing had changed. During a
visit with dad and Shirley in 2004, when Shirley met my girlfriend
Roberta for the first time, she badgered Roberta into telling her
what I had said about her on the way to visit with them. Roberta
insisted I hadn't said anything. Shirley didn't believe her and called
Roberta a liar. I knew Shirley's actions would show Roberta who
she really was so I didn't have to say a word. When Roberta and
I went to bed, Shirley continued screaming at my dad for quite
some time. Roberta and I were uncomfortable so we left the next
morning, despite our original plan to stay for two days.

In March 2006, Dad and Shirley came back to live in Massachusetts
despite my father' insistence he would never return. He said
he returned as he didn't want to be alone. They moved into a
condo my dad purchased in Ipswich. I decided to try once again.
I tested Shirley by telling her something in confidence. She
immediately exploited the information in an attempt to destroy
the relationship between me and my cousin. I was blessed in that
instead of allowing Shirley to come between us, my cousin called
me to tell me what she was up to. Over the years I kept promising
myself to keep her out of my life but since she was pretending
to be "married" to my dad, this was difficult to do if I wanted a
relationship with him.

In May 2008, I invited dad and Shirley to my retirement party at
the Marriott Hotel in Cambridge. They came and sat with my
brother Chucky, my daughters and their spouses. After the party,
my daughters told me that Shirley mimicked me and criticized
everything I said in my speech. She also insulted my dad by telling
him my success was "no thanks to him."

On May 31, 2008, Shirley attended my daughter Deana's wedding.
She said she liked Deana because she and Deana were alike.
Deana's birthday is August 1st and hers is August 2nd. She doesn't
even know my daughter! Thank goodness, Deana is nothing like
Shirley.

In June 2008, we were invited to my Aunt Margie and Uncle Jim's 50th anniversary party. Shirley's daughters were also invited. At the party, I told Shirley I was planning a family retirement party at my house and wanted her to save the date. She asked me to invite her daughters and I agreed to do so. When I sent out the invitations, I did as I had promised, adding 11 people to the original guest list by inviting her daughters and their families. None of them responded to the invitation and none of them came to the party. My dad arrived alone and said Shirley would be joining him later. She never showed. Since Shirley had always told many of my relatives how much she hated me, it would have been difficult for her to have the rest of the family see her there to honor me

Sal and Shirley June 22, 2008

In September 2008, I moved to a new home in Saugus. My dad came over quite often. I invited Shirley to come too but she never did. She let me know she wanted nothing to do with me.

In February 2009, I was limited to inviting ten people to Deana's baby shower. I eliminated Shirley thinking I would be doing her a favor. Including Deana's friends, Sean's family, Deana's dad's family and my guests, we invited 44 people to my home. We kept the guest list to Deana's closest friends and relatives. Shirley was neither. She thus found the ammunition she needed to start a new rampage against me.

In March 2009, when my first grandchild was born, I called my dad to tell him he had another great-grandson. Shirley screamed at me on the phone, demanding to know why she hadn't been invited to the baby shower. I quietly kept asking for my dad and explained to her that I had been limited in the number of people I could invite. As she handed the phone to my father, I could hear her in the background screaming, "She's a liar, she's a liar!"

In April 2009, Shirley went with my dad to Deana's house to meet my grandson, Logan. I was there too, as my daughter asked me to be. Shirley refused to talk to me except to keep ordering me to "give the baby to his mother". We were able to get a picture showing four DiMare generations. However, based on what transpired shortly thereafter, it is doubtful Logan will ever know his great-grandfather.

In May and June 2009, dad visited quite often to see Logan and hold him in his arms. He was enjoying spending time with his great-grandson and told me he would continue coming to see Logan. He claimed he wanted to be a part of Logan's life and was even willing to babysit for Logan.

On one of his visits, I mentioned I was planning to remodel my kitchen. Dad asked me for some of my old appliances. I suggested he take just the refrigerator as the other appliances weren't in good working order. On the Friday before Father's Day, I called dad to tell him I'd arranged to have the refrigerator delivered to his house later that afternoon. He was thankful and said he would talk to me later. On Father's Day, I called him to wish him a happy day. I asked if he received the gift I sent him, a Home Depot gift certificate, and if he liked the refrigerator. He said he and Shirley liked it a lot and had decided to use it in their house and put their old refrigerator in their garage.

One month later, in July 2009, Deana invited Shirley and my dad to Logan's christening. My dad showed up in dungarees and stayed two minutes, hastily explaining to Deana that he was too busy and had to leave. He also told Deana he wanted to meet her for lunch without me because he wanted to talk to her alone.

In August 2009 they met for lunch. Dad told Deana he wanted a relationship with her and Logan but not with me because Shirley forbade it. He told my daughter that I was the "plague" of the DiMare Family. When Deana pushed him to know more about who thought I was a plague, my father admitted it was just him and Shirley. At first he insisted that my brothers felt that way too but Deana assured him my brothers and I were okay with each other.

Dad told Deana that Shirley is the person who takes care of him, washes his clothes, cleans his house and feeds him and that she will leave him if he ever reestablishes a relationship with me. Deana responded that she was old enough to see how both he and Shirley had treated me though the years and frankly, she couldn't understand why I had anything to do with either of them. That day was the last Deana saw or heard from her grandfather.

The day of Logan's Christening (July 12, 2009) was the last time I saw my father. When I underwent endometrial cancer surgery in November 2009, I didn't hear from him, although my brother Tony told me he had informed him about my cancer and my brother Chucky called me as my dad had called him to tell him about my cancer. In 2010, I suffered through radiation and chemotherapy, blood clots and kidney surgery as well, without a word from my father. Friends and family have encouraged me to let him go. He and Shirley are meant for each other.

Four generations: Dad, Ann, Logan and Deana

I have remained friends with Shirley's daughter Julie and her grandchildren Alicia and Lucas. When Shirley's mother Mary died in December 2009, my brother Dom emailed me asking if I would be going to the funeral. My response on December 23, 2009, was,

"Since dad has not acknowledged his only daughter had cancer recently and said the day our mother died was the "happiest day of his life", I would have a difficult time showing respect to someone (Mary) whose daughter has hated me for over 45 years when I have done nothing to deserve it. R.I.P. Mary!"

At a very young age, I learned to expect bad behavior from both my father and Shirley. I overcame them as an obstacle by not allowing them to inflict pain and stress on me. Today, I consider them both deceased. They can continue to play their games with each other. They can continue to pretend they are married. It's healthier for me to have them out of my life. My father has lost his daughter, two of his granddaughters and two of his great-grandsons, while Shirley keeps her family close to her. It amazes me what my dad is willing to sacrifice to keep her in his life.

From my many years of trying to please both my dad and Shirley, I learned to only go where I am wanted. There was nothing I could do to change what is in either of their hearts. I don't need to continue to be emotionally battered. Shirley can control my father's life. But, she can't control mine. I wish them both the best and will continue to pray for them. I have forgiven them many times over for their actions towards me and my daughters and will continue to do so as I vowed to keep love in my heart. From my relationship with my father, I learned that love is meaningless when it is forced. You can't make someone love you.

1935   *1947*

Carmela Concetta Faro

Carmela Concetta Faro was born on December 29, 1929 to Domenic and Josephine Noe Faro. She was born at 352 Shirley Street in Winthrop, in a six family house owned by her father. Mom was the third of five children. As a middle child, my mother was extremely obedient. She was a people pleaser and would have done anything to help anyone. Family was the most important element in my mother's life and she remained close to her loved ones until she died.

Carmela was baptized at Sacred Heart Church in Boston, MA on February 1, 1930. Her Godparents were Giuseppe and

Maria Stamato, friends of my grandparents. Carmela attended Winthrop Public Schools and graduated from the commercial program at Winthrop High School in 1947. She was a member of the school chorus in her sophomore and senior years. She was an outstanding typist and had the ability to type 90 words per minute. That was an incredible speed given the old Royal Typewriters used in those times. Carmela was the first in her family to graduate from high school. Here are mom's birth certificate, graduation photo and her high school diploma. Mom should have been extremely proud of her accomplishment considering the obstacles she overcame.

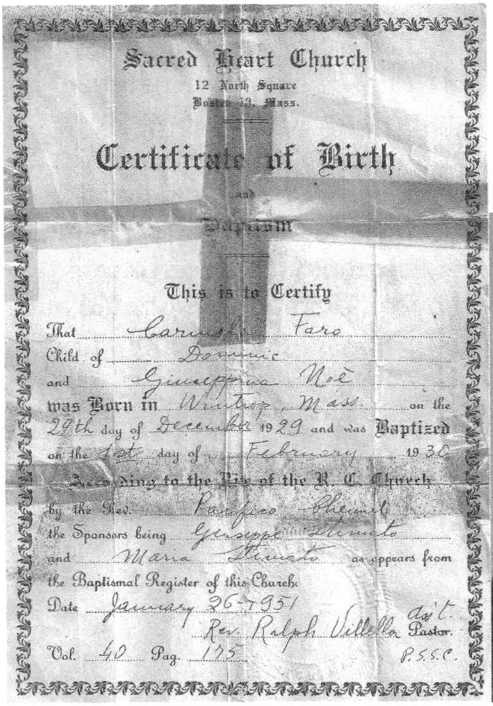

Sacred Heart Church
12 North Square
Boston 13, Mass.

Certificate of Birth
and
Baptism

This is to Certify

That Carmela Faro
Child of Dominic
and Giuseppina Noè
was Born in Winthrop, Mass. on the
29th day of December 1929 and was Baptized
on the 1st day of February 1930
According to the Rite of the R. C. Church
by the Rev. Pacifico Chenuil
the Sponsors being Giuseppe Stimato
and Maria Stimato as appears from
the Baptismal Register of this Church
Date January 26-1951
Rev. Ralph Villella ast. Pastor.
Vol. 40 Pag. 175 P.S.S.C.

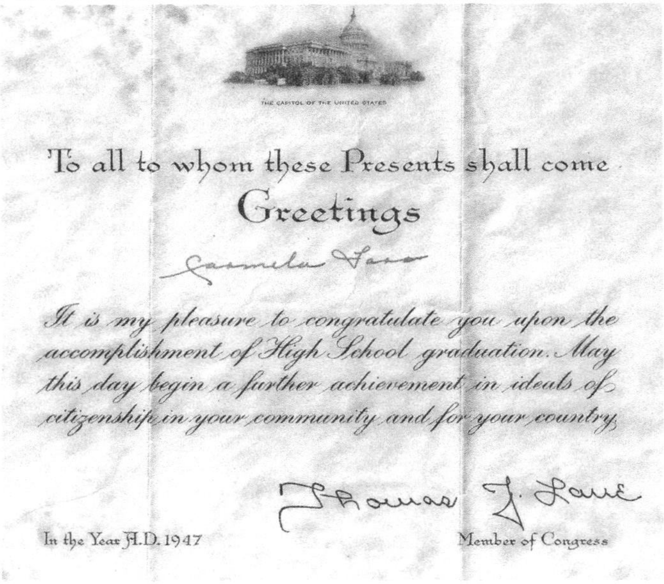

THE CAPITOL OF THE UNITED STATES

To all to whom these Presents shall come
Greetings

Carmela Faro

It is my pleasure to congratulate you upon the accomplishment of High School graduation. May this day begin a further achievement in ideals of citizenship in your community and for your country.

Thomas J. Lane

In the Year A.D. 1947 Member of Congress

My grandmother Josephine was an extremely demanding woman. My mother, perhaps out of fear and perhaps out of appreciation, helped in any way she could. My mother became my grandmother's slave. By doing most everything for her mother, she learned to be an outstanding cook and great homemaker. Carmela had a big heart and was a loving and caring lady, always smiling and giving of her time and herself to others. She loved to throw parties and cook for people. Her way of showing love was through her food.

After graduating high school, Carmela met Sal. They were married from February 25, 1951 until December 14, 1966. After her divorce from my dad, mom seemed desperate for companionship as my brothers and I were growing up and away from home a lot. Mom worked full time at Kennedy's, a men's clothing store in Boston. She spent most of her evening and weekend time alone.

In 1968, mom met Joseph Sicuso. Joe lived in East Boston and worked at the Federal Reserve Bank in Boston. Joe's wife had died years earlier. Joe had one daughter Teresa. Teresa was busy either working or going out with her friends. Joe was as lonely as mom. Mom and Joe were good companions; however Joe wanted to be married. In early 1969, he proposed to mom. On March 22, 1969, they got married and we moved to 206 Orient Avenue in East Boston. How could they do that to us? We went to Winthrop High School. We didn't want to live in East Boston.

Joe Sicuso & Carmela DiMare March 22, 1969

Joe's daughter Teresa became my third step-sister. She was 22 years old at the time. I was 16. We got along well and enjoyed shopping together. Within a few short months, though, Joe and my brothers were fighting with each other. My brothers were experimenting with growing marijuana plants in their bedroom in Joe's house. When Joe discovered what they were up to, he went ballistic. He pretended he had a gun and told one of my brothers he would shoot him if he didn't get rid of the plants.

On another occasion, a cop came to the front door and delivered my brother Dom, who was drunk on cough syrup and had fallen asleep on a lawn at the bottom of the hill where we lived. When growing weed didn't work out, my brothers, like so many others of our generation started having marijuana shipped to them. So, I wasn't surprised when federal marshals showed up because they had intercepted a package at Logan Airport. Mom and Joe were away on vacation so I handled the situation as best I could on their behalf. I remember my mother calling my Godfather, an attorney, for help. When they returned from their vacation and learned what had taken place in their absence, Joe made it perfectly clear to my mother he wanted my brothers out of his house – and my brothers were more than happy to oblige him.

By the end of that summer, both Chucky (age 17) and Dom (age 15) had moved to an apartment on Shore Drive in Winthrop. They used the money they made from part time jobs to pay their rent and living expenses. Chucky never returned to live with mom. Dom returned briefly when mom moved to Saugus. When my brothers moved out, I was left living with mom and Joe. I was only 16 years old. Mom cried constantly over my brothers. Both were getting into trouble at the time. Both were smokers. Both were doing poorly in school. Mom always praised me as being a good girl, who always did the right thing. By then, though, I was becoming angry and so I started doing some wrong things too.

In early 1971, Joe began needling my mother for being overweight. Joe bet mom the doctor would tell her she was overweight. Mom bet he wouldn't. She thought something else was wrong with her. Mom went to a doctor for the first time since my brother Dom was born in 1954, 17 years earlier. She was not surprised by what she learned. The excess weight was a tumor growing in her stomach accompanied by cervical cancer. In March 1971, mom had a radical hysterectomy at the Beth Israel Hospital in Boston. For the next five years, my mom's biggest fear was the cancer would recur.

Prior to mom coming home from the hospital, I went on a pre-scheduled vacation to Fort Lauderdale, Florida. I was a high school senior and the trip had been planned long before I learned about my mother's health problems. I would be returning home a couple of days after mom's release from the hospital. I knew caring for her would be one of the assignments I would have in addition to going to school, doing homework, working and playing softball. A couple of my uncles were upset with me for leaving town and called to chastise me for my decision. As expected, when I returned, mom needed a lot of care and I was the provider. I never understood how ill she felt until I myself had cancer and a radical hysterectomy in November 2009, some 39 years later.

On August 15, 1973, 4 ½ years after mom and Joe married,
Joe had a heart attack at work and was taken to Massachusetts
General Hospital's intensive care unit, where two days later, he
died. Mom was fearful about being single again even though
mom and Joe fought constantly about my brothers.

Joe hadn't prepared a will. When he died, Teresa inherited half her
father's estate and she wanted to sell the house. After the house
was sold, mom and I moved back to Winthrop in an apartment
at 12 Locust Street. We lived like friends instead of mother and
daughter confiding in each other about almost everything.

Soon after moving back to Winthrop, I became engaged to Joseph
Anthony Fulchino, Jr. and in October 1974, we were married. Mom
continued to live in Winthrop for two more years. In October 1976,
I suggested she move to Saugus as I was pregnant and intended
to settle permanently there. In December 1976, mom bought her
very first and only house at 71-73 Essex Street in Saugus.

Mom worked at Kennedy's Men's clothing store in downtown
Boston. She was in charge of their print shop and operated
their multi-graph printing machines. She produced all the
advertisements sent by their stores throughout the country. She
stayed working there until her retirement in 1989.

After leaving Kennedy's, she worked at several part-time jobs. One
was in a bakery in Cliftondale Square, Saugus. She also worked in
the bakery at our local Stop and Shop supermarket. In 1992, she
retired permanently. From then until her untimely death in 1994,
mom concentrated most of her energy on her six grandchildren.
Mom adored her grandchildren and was always eager and excited
to have them visit her and babysit them. She loved to cook for
them. Mom used cooking delicious food as a means to show her
love for people.

Mom was always happy to throw parties and she always enjoyed family gatherings. She hosted Christmas Eve in her house every year. My brothers would come with their families. My daughters spent Christmas Eve with their father's family after our divorce so I would go alone. On our last Christmas Eve together, in 1993, mom declared, "This is the happiest Christmas Eve of my life because my whole family is here!" Those words struck a nerve since the whole family wasn't there; Cara and Deana couldn't be there.

Later that evening, after my brothers had left and I helped my mother clean the dishes and the house, she said, "Annie, you have been a good daughter. You always do the right thing and I love you very much". Then she kissed me. That was the one and only time I remember my mother telling me she loved me. I left her house crying and went home to wait for my daughters to return.

Jacob, Deana, Carina, Jenna, Max and Cara

Mom had many girlfriends and played bingo, went shopping and vacationed with them. She also had a few boyfriends from time to time: Charlie T., Joe F., and Jim M. Jim had never been married.

He was a disabled veteran who lived in Medford. Mom met him at Wonderland Ballroom in Revere. Jim wined and dined mom in the beginning of their relationship. Later he found comfort in simply eating at her house, and just watching television. When mom complained about their changed relationship, Jim broke it off and she never saw him again.

Jim died soon thereafter without having changed his will. At the time of his death, Jim still had everything he owned willed to my mother. Since she knew the circumstances of their relationship, she met with his lawyer and signed everything over to his niece and nephew. I was shocked she didn't accept at least a portion of the money Jim willed to her to cover the costs of feeding him and caring for him throughout their relationship. Mom wouldn't hear of it.

Mother was a sensitive and giving person. She had a beautiful smile. She spent many years extremely frustrated by the way she was treated by men: her father, her husbands, her sons and her boyfriends. Based on her reasonable frustrations, she instilled in me the belief that men were users and takers and weren't to be trusted. She had experienced it firsthand and because she was a people-pleaser, as most middle children are, she didn't know how to stop it. Mom died alone on February 8, 1994.

MY PARENTS COURTSHIP AND MARRIAGE

My parents were introduced to each other by my mother's aunt Antoinette Faro and my father's mother, Anne DiMare, in 1947. Antoinette and Anne were best friends for many years. When Antoinette married my grandfather's brother Jimmy, Charles and Anne were their best man and maid of honor. Antoinette and Anne thought it would be wonderful if Sal and Carmela met and married so they would then be related to each other.

Sal and Carmela were the same age and both came from families originally from Augusta, Sicily. Mom was an introvert but was extremely friendly and giving once she knew and trusted someone. Sal came highly recommended and was so handsome!

On their first date, my parents went to the old "Ship" restaurant in Lynnfield. My mother's brother Angelo and his fiancée, Lillian, went with them. My mother told me she should have known something was uncouth about dad as he forgot his wallet that evening. My uncle Angelo had his and bailed dad out. That night was the first of many times uncle Angelo would rescue dad from problems he created for himself.

By 1950, mom and dad were engaged. On February 10, 1951, they attended their bridal shower and on February 25, 1951 they were married at St. John's the Evangelist Church in Winthrop. Their reception was a buffet style dinner that took place at the Winthrop Elks on Washington Street. Their marriage joined two competitor "fishing" families.

41

February 10, 1951

Charles, Anne, Sal, Carmela, Josephine and Domenic
February 25, 1951

My parents' marriage was rocky from the start. They lived on Forest Street in Winthrop, around the corner from mom's parents on Shirley Street. During their marriage, dad held various jobs. He filled vending machines, was a meat cutter for the Elm Farm Grocery store in Medford, and worked as a lobsterman in a business he started: Boston Lobster Company. Mom worked for Cinderella Shoe Company.

Shortly after their marriage, mom became pregnant with the first of their three children. Charles Joseph DiMare was born on March 1, 1952. A year later I (Ann Rosemarie DiMare) was born, on March 14, 1953. My brother Domenic James DiMare came along a year later, on May 8, 1954. My father was not there for both my birth and my brother Dom's birth. He was busy working – or at least that is what he told my mom. The truth emerged much later. When they were married, dad had not yet grown up. He hadn't finished sowing his wild oats. Mom was ready to be a wife and mother but dad was still playing the field.

Shortly after I was born, Mom and Dad moved to 352 Shirley Street, as one of the apartments in Nano Faro's home became available. It was the apartment directly above the one my grandparents lived in. Our move into our grandparents' home might have been the onset of the demise of my parents marriage or it might have been my mother's salvation because my father was neither physically or emotionally available to her.

Mom and dad fought constantly. Dad would call her a nag and other nasty names. Mom complained constantly because of dad's irregular schedule. Mom was wise beyond her years. She saw signs that dad wasn't being faithful to her (lipstick on his collar, calls from females, dad not sleeping at home) despite his insistence that he was working.

As a side job, dad delivered food to the various lighthouse keepers in Boston Harbor. On one of his harbor visits, he met Frances Whiting Horgan. She was an extremely attractive woman and caught dad's eye. In a short time, they became intimately involved. Their relationship lasted from the early 1950s until at least 1963. I know this because my brother Tony showed me pictures of times spent with our dad.

I also have memories of my dad visiting Frances in her apartment on Winthrop Avenue in Revere's Beachmont section. This was about three miles away from where we lived in Winthrop. Dad left my brothers and me locked in his black Rambler station wagon. My brother Dom cried as he was scared and thought we had been abandoned. I hugged him and assured him dad would come back and he always did. I, too, was petrified but put on a brave act for Dom's sake. I don't know how long each visit lasted. For me each time dad left us in the car felt like an eternity.

In 1958, my parents separated for a short time. Dad moved to California and said he was living with priests in a rectory, in an attempt to reform himself. He had been cheating on my mother since the early 1950s and his promiscuous life style was catching up to him.

During their separation, my mother corresponded with my dad's cousin, Father Domenic Silvestro. After my mother died, I found Fr. Domenic's letters. My mother had an elastic around the letters with a message that read, "Please don't throw away. Read these." And so I did. They validated the stories my mother told me about my father. I have included some of them as Appendix A along with a letter my Grandmother Anne wrote my mother regarding her marriage to my father. It was heart wrenching for me to read them and realize the pain my mother lived with. My mom always said my dad was "her cross to bear", perhaps because initially Fr. Domenic encouraged her to be patient in order to keep her marriage intact.

After reading the letters, I felt guilty because, for so many years, I had insisted to mom that she just needed to get over my dad and get on with her life. I also wasn't willing to blame him entirely for their divorce; I'd always thought it took two people to make a marriage work. After having read the letters, I was convinced my mother had done everything she humanly could do to save the marriage. The outside forces (other women) were just too strong for dad to live without.

Mom had always insisted that dad had a child out of wedlock as she had once discovered a picture inscribed in my father's distinctive hand writing as "my son Robert." Dad's middle name was Robert. After six months of dad's living with the priests in California, dad thought he was ready to resume his marriage to my mom. He asked her to bring my brothers and me and come live in California so they could get a fresh start in their marriage away from both his and mom's family. My mother told me he thought her family had too much of an influence on them.

Mom did as dad asked. In late August 1958, she packed up three children, ages 6, 5 and 4, and we traveled across country by train to meet dad. Upon arriving in California, dad presented mom with a male infant child and asked her to adopt him! When mom inquired as to the birth mother, dad confessed that it was Frances's child. Mom had known that Frances was pregnant as Frances had phoned mom to tell her that she was pregnant with dad's child. Frances also told mom that my dad had promised to divorce Carmela and marry her. Mom refused to adopt the child and told dad to give the child back to his mother, Frances. We later learned the baby was my half-brother Sal. Then, who was "my son Robert"? We learned "Robert's" identity 34 years later. Who wouldn't be emotionally disturbed by all this?

We lived a fantasy life at 4034 West Boulevard apartment D, in Los Angeles for less than one year. The area we lived in is now known as Watts. Chucky and I went to public school. I was in the first grade. We visited Disneyland in Anaheim, Knottsberry Farms, and Forest Lawn Cemetery in Glendale, where the movie stars are buried, Grauman's Chinese Theatre in Hollywood, Hillcrest Drive Playground, and Ghost Town in Buena Park, Marine Land, and mom's Godmother Connie who lived in San Diego. By March 1, 1959, mom and dad agreed we should return to Massachusetts. We returned to living in

Anne, Fr. Domenic Silvestro, Mom
June 1960

4034 West Boulevard, Los Angeles, CA

our grandparents' house on Shirley Street in Winthrop. I wasn't allowed to continue in the first grade as the age requirement was different in Winthrop. I had to wait until September 1959

45

to re-start the first grade. It was traumatic for me but as I had everything else in my life, I learned to get over it.

Once back in my grandparent's house, dad resumed his cheating ways. Dad always insisted on privacy as he was always hiding something. He was living a double life. Unbeknownst to mom, Frances had also moved back from California to live in Revere. Dad was always there for breakfast in our house but never there for dinners, birthday parties, holiday gatherings or other important events. Our mother became extremely frustrated and deprived of affection.

I realize now that mom did the best she could under the circumstances. She was constantly challenged by her love for dad and her lack of self-respect, which led her to tolerate his behavior. He would tell mom he had to work late. Mom wasn't stupid. She put up with his bad behavior to keep the marriage intact. Mom was left at home to raise three children while dad played the field. When I was 39 years old, I learned just how much of a double life dad was living.

Over the years, Mom became extremely introverted, insecure and angry. Often she took out her anger on my brothers and me with a wooden spoon. Dad was physically violent too. When he was home, if our mother complained about anything we did wrong, dad would beat us with a thick, black, leather strap he had hanging on a hook in the kitchen. I specifically remember one time when he kicked me and my brother Dom clear across the kitchen and into the bathroom where we were both left bleeding and hugging the toilet. For some reason, Chucky escaped that beating.

I also remember my dad throwing dishes and eggs at my mother. I never quite understood why, if they hated each other so much, they didn't just get divorced. I knew the way they treated each other was not considered a good marriage and since neither of them set a good example for me, I grew to hate them both as much as a child could hate at that young age. I sought out the love of other people in the family who showed me the kind of affection I craved. Those people were my grandmother Anne and my Aunt Joann and Uncle Freddy.

I remember dad at home playing his guitar in the living room. In August, 1960, I remember him violently banging on the washing machine when we got a phone call telling us his mother had died. I remember him coming to my Aunt Joann and Uncle Freddy's wedding in November 1961. On March 14, 1963, I remember dad being at home when we got a call telling us that Auntie Mary had given birth to a baby boy. At the time I cried because I didn't want anyone else to have a birthday on my birthday! Today, I am thrilled to share my birthday with my cousin Paul.

Mom and dad were named Godparents to my cousin Sammy, (born on September 13, 1951), my cousin Paul, (born on March 14, 1963) and my cousin David, (born on May 22, 1963). It was shortly after David's christening that dad packed his stuff in green plastic trash bags and left for good. Dad had stayed for four more years after our return from California. I remember crying for him to stay even though I was relieved to see him go as his departure meant I would no longer have to take physical beatings and mom would no longer have to take emotional beatings – or so I thought. The woman dad met this time offered him something neither my mother nor Frances could. Her name was Shirley. She offered dad an escape from his children and from two women vying for his attention.

Mom and dad had been separated for a year when dad filed for divorce. Mom refused to divorce him as she was Catholic and didn't want to be excommunicated from the church. Dad fought long and hard for the divorce promising to pay child support and alimony. Mom finally relented based on the advice she received from Father Domenic. Mom and Dad's decree nisi and final divorce decrees are shown in the section on Dad. Their decree nisi was granted on June 14, 1966 and final decree granted on December 14, 1966. When I found these documents, after my mom's death, I asked my father to verify when he and Shirley had married. He told me July 1, 1965. I learned then my father was married to two women at one time! In an email communication I had with my dad in June 2008, he told me July 1st was his and Shirley's 45th anniversary which would mean they were really married in 1963, almost three years before he and my mom divorced and right after dad stopped living with us.

The court granted mom meager alimony and child support for three children, which Dad seldom, if ever paid. When my mother died, I found a log with the checks listed that Dad had sent. He would send mom checks that would bounce causing mom more problems than the checks were worth. At one point, she did have him picked up and incarcerated in the Suffolk County jail located at Deer Island for non-support.

Mom was forced to resort to Aid for Dependent Children (AFDC). This was a form of welfare where the social worker would see to it that we had food on the table and a limited amount of clothing in the closet. We were allowed two pair of shoes a year, one for school in the fall and one in the springtime. We were not allowed to have sugar in the house so we only had fruit for dessert unless visitors brought something containing sugar. The welfare department had a key to our house so mom never knew when they would show up to check on her. Mom lived in fear during those days.

As children, we loved peanut butter and jelly for lunch. Jelly wasn't allowed as it contained sugar. Our time on welfare didn't last long. Mom worked harder to get pay raises and longer hours to make more money.

Mom spent much of her life taking care of everyone else so she took little care of herself. She cared for her parents, her children and her second husband Joe. When I was 15 years old, she finally got her driver's license and became more independent. She didn't need to rely on her siblings to take her grocery shopping. She no longer needed to rely on the Rapid Transit Bus System in Winthrop to take her to the Orient Heights Subway station so she could go to work. She relied more on herself and seemed happier for a short while. I believe mom's caring for everyone but herself shortened her life by many years.

These are the only pictures I have that include our family. The photo on the left was taken on February 14, 1955. The photo on the right was taken on November 19, 1961 at my aunt Joann Faro and uncle Fred Battista's wedding.

*I*nitially, the siblings consisted of two brothers and me. Later through remarriage of both our parents, we acquired three step-sisters and thanks to an investigation done by my brother Chucky, we found our three half-brothers. In this section I will speak only of the children of Sal and Carmela. In a later section, I will discuss the children of Sal DiMare and Frances Horgan. I will not include any more about the step-sisters.

Chucky 1970   Ann 1971   Dom 1973

Charles ("Chucky") Joseph DiMare was born on March 1, 1952 and was named after our paternal grandfather and his Godfather Joseph Fazio (dad's uncle). Chucky graduated from Winthrop High School in 1970. He attended Massachusetts Bay Community College in Waltham, MA for two years and then transferred to the University of Massachusetts at Amherst from which he graduated in 1974. He then attended Vermont Law School in South Royalton,

Vermont graduating with a Juris Doctorate Degree in 1977. He moved to the San Francisco Bay area for one year and returned to live in the basement apartment in my home in Saugus in the summer of 1978. I charged Chucky $200 a month rent while the going rate was $500 per month. Chucky and I rotated cooking responsibilities. I was getting the brother back that had been taken away from me nine years earlier. Until Chucky was able to afford a car, I bought him an orange Volkswagen bug, for which he paid me back in about a year's time. At Chucky's request, I became a notary public to help him with his legal work. Chucky lived with me for two years. He then moved to the Amherst area and took a position with the University of Massachusetts as the Director of their Legal Services Office. He still holds the position today. There Chucky met Joan Antonino. They married on August 1, 1982. Their daughter Jenna Noel Antonino DiMare was born on March 14, 1987 (my 34th birthday) and their daughter Carina Ariel Antonino DiMare was born on January 21, 1991. Since Chucky ended up raising his family in the Amherst area, our children did not know each other well as they were growing up.

Ann Rosemarie DiMare was born on March 14, 1953 and was named after our paternal grandmother Anne and her Godmother Rosemarie Maiolino Russo. Ann graduated Winthrop High School in 1971. She then attended Boston State College. This college eventually merged with the University of Massachusetts Boston. She graduated cum laude in May 1975. In May 1972, while a student at Boston State, Ann started work at the Transportation Systems Center (TSC) in Cambridge. Ann married Joseph Anthony Fulchino, Jr. on October 13, 1974. Their daughter Cara Ann Fulchino was born on January 4, 1977 and their daughter Deana Marie Fulchino was born on August 1, 1978. Ann went to Northeastern University in Boston and graduated with a Master of Science Degree in Civil Engineering in June 1982. Ann continued working as an Operations Research Analyst at the TSC (renamed the Volpe Center) until June 2008 when she retired. Ann continues to work at her income tax business which she started in February

1982. Ann's daughter Cara married David Silipigni on May 5, 2001 and her daughter Deana married Sean McGovern on May 31, 2008. Deana and Sean had a son Logan Anthony McGovern, born on March 30, 2009 and a son Mason Kevin McGovern born on June 3, 2011.

Domenic James DiMare was born on May 8, 1954. He was named after our maternal grandfather Domenic and his Godfather James DiMare (dad's brother). As a child, I remember Dom getting hit by a bus on Shirley Street in Winthrop. We were playing hide and seek. Dom ran across the street into the path of the oncoming bus. Dom graduated from Winthrop High School in 1973. Dom married Mary Lynn Trippe on March 22, 1974. They had two sons. Jacob Gerard DiMare was born on February 25, 1975. Maximilian DiMare was born on October 7, 1977. Dom and Mary Lynn were divorced. Dom married Laura Pease on February 15, 1992 and was divorced from her in 2009. Over the years, Dom struggled with substance abuse. From time to time, I attended Narcotics Anonymous meetings with him. I thought I could help him. I later learned he was the only one who could help himself overcome his addiction. To his credit, he did but it took many years of counseling. As the youngest child, he was often known as "Dommy Baby" and was protected and enabled by our mother. Once Dom's sickness was in remission, he successfully owned and operated several restaurants. He was an incredible cook (taking after our mother). One restaurant was named DiMare's Deli and featured luncheon specials named after our grandmother and our mother. Dom was a hard worker and always had a good heart but was lost without the guidance and love of a father.

March 1975
Nana & Nano's 50th Anniversary
Mom, Nana, Nano
Chucky, Ann, Dom

May 20, 2000
Cara & Deana's College Graduation
Dom, Dad, Ann, Chucky

February 2000
Dom, Max, Jacob

March 1992
Jenna, Dad, Joan, Carina, Chucky

I grew up in a time when people didn't discuss their medical issues with one another. Medical issues were considered "private". The only way I knew about some of the conditions in my family was by my asking questions and finding medical documents when my mother died. The limited information contained below is all I know about our family's medical history.

Salvatore		
ILLNESS	**WHEN**	**DESCRIPTION**
Kidney Stones	Multiple	
Melanoma	Approx. 2008	Removed right thumb
Carmela		
Appendix	unknown	Removed appendix as a teenager
Hysterectomy	March 1971	Radical hysterectomy to remove cervical cancer
Foot Surgery	December 1976	Removed fungus toe nail.
Gall Bladder	January 28, 1994	The surgery caused peritonitis which ultimately caused mom's death on February 8, 1994
Ann		
Heart Murmur	Diagnosed when I was in Grade 4	Irregular heart beats

54

Scoliosis	Diagnosed when I was in Grade 7	Curvature of the spine
Dental work	Starting in childhood through adulthood	11 Rotted teeth pulled by the time I was 12 years old due to no money for dentist visits, multiple periodontal surgeries; three mouth bridges
Kidney Stones	multiple	Underwent at least 6 lithotripsy procedures over the years; passed many stones on my own as well. I started having kidney stones in 1977. My last two stones were in June 2010 and August 2010, both in my left kidney.
Parotid Gland Tumor	October 1999	Dr. Richard Bowling removed the tumor at Melrose Wakefield Hospital (MWH). I was in the hospital for seven days.
Ovary Removal	January 2000	Dr. Steven Dakoyannis removed my left ovary at MWH. I was in the hospital for two days.
Rosacea	2003	Redness of the checks and dilation of the blood vessels in the face

Hysterectomy	11/13/2009	Dr. Adel Hamid performed a radical hysterectomy to remove endometrial cancer at MWH. I was in the hospital for five days.
Endometrial Cancer	11/13/2009	Dr. Anthony Russell, performed three rounds of High Dose Brachytherapy radiation therapy at the Massachusetts General Hospital (MGH) on January 4th, 11th and 20th, 2010. Dr. Nashima Khatoon performed chemotherapy at the Commonwealth Hematology and Oncology Center on Montvale Ave in Stoneham, MA on January 5th and 26th and February 16th, 2010 (Taxol and Carboplatin); lost my hair
Blood Clot	3/12/2010	CT scan was performed at MGH revealing a blood clot in my stomach. I was put on Coumadin for 5 months to thin my blood and abdominally injected 6 needles of Levenox to break up the clot.

Neuropathy	5/25/2010	Numbness and tingling in my feet and hands. Side effect of Taxol chemotherapy drug.
Renal Stent	8/9/2010	Dr. Sidney Rubenstein inserted a renal stent to eliminate the blockage in my left kidney.
Tendonitis (left foot)	12/24/2010	Dr. Edward Mostone treated with a cortisone injection and Flector patches.
Deana		
Sarcoidosis	2009	Multisystem inflammatory disease characterized by small inflammatory nodules. The cause of the disease is still unknown. Virtually any organ can be affected; however, they most often appear in the lungs or the lymph nodes.

FAMILY TRADITIONS

As a young child, I remember visiting my DiMare grandparents at 100 Yeomans Ave in Medford. We celebrated portions of some holidays with them. My cousins lived next door so we visited them when at my grandparents' house. These visits ended for the most part in 1960 when my grandmother Anne died. A year later my grandfather Charles remarried. We visited him and Bianca from time to time. Those visits stopped when my parents divorced in 1966. However, my mother continued our visits with my DiMare cousins helping to bond my relationship with them into the future.

Since we lived with my Faro Grandparents, we spent most of our holidays with them. Families create traditions over time. Our traditions originated in Sicily. My grandparents continued them in America. On the eve of each holiday, my grandmother Josephine and my mother cooked for the entire family. For Christmas and New Year's, they cooked two days ahead as we celebrated the holiday eves as well as the holidays. The entire Faro family including my cousins (24 people) got together to eat food, have dessert and play an Italian card game. The holidays we celebrated in my grandparent's house with an incredible amount of food were New Year's Eve, New Year's Day, Saint Joseph's Day (March 19), Palm Sunday, Easter Sunday, Thanksgiving, Christmas Eve and Christmas Day. I loved holidays and being with my aunts, uncles and cousins.

On Christmas Eve, the Italian tradition was to have seven fishes. Typically, we ate lobster, shrimp, scallops, squid (calamari), eel, scrod, and octopus. On Christmas Day, we would usually have lasagna, followed by meatballs, *braciole* (rolled steak usually with

58

egg inside), sausage, and vegetables. On Palm Sunday, we would eat ham and on Easter Sunday we would have lamb. On Saint Joseph's Day, we ate bean soup and a special Italian dessert called *zeppole*, a Sicilian dessert. Each holiday also included some kind of pasta dish (i.e., lasagna, ravioli, manicotti, spaghetti).

Each family would host the birthday parties for their family members and Auntie Winnie would host the Fourth of July celebration as she had a swimming pool in her back yard at 183 Somerset Avenue in Winthrop, MA.

At most of these gatherings, lunch would be at noon time or 1:00 PM, followed by dessert and an Italian card game called *"scangu".* *Scangu* was a game any number of people could play at one time and it cost only $.25 to play. Since many of us played, the pot of money the winner got was usually close to $10.00. That was a lot of money in those days and everyone was excited about the possibility of winning! I remember my grandfather Domenic always trying to peek at the cards of the people sitting on either side of him. My mom used to warn us to hold our cards close to our chest so Nano couldn't peek. Each person had three chips and you could continue playing until you lost all three. I used to get nervous when I was down to one chip as I was always desperate to win the money. After playing a few games of *Scangu*, dinner would be served.

Everyone would go home bloated. Fortissimo wine was served with all holiday meals. The only time any other alcohol was served was at midnight on New Year's Eve. The adults had a shot of a *liqueur* as a toast to the New Year. The children were allowed to stay up on New Year's Eve and use noise makers or bang pots and pans together at midnight. We went to bed early on Christmas Eve as the adults needed to get the gifts ready from Santa Claus.

When my aunts and my mother were cleaning the dishes after each meal, the cousins played in the hallway or upstairs in our apartment. This always led to someone crying from being roughed up or getting hurt and usually, the DiMare children were to blame. Since we lived in my grandparents' house, it was easier to blame us than to blame the children they saw less often.

Being raised Sicilian and Roman Catholic also meant our fair share of celebrations for religious rites of passage and other events. These included yearly birthday parties for everyone, baptisms, first communions, confirmations, graduations, engagement parties, bridal showers, weddings and funerals. With a family as large as ours, someone was always receiving one of the sacraments or celebrating another event. The hosting family had a gala celebration in their home or a function hall. Sometimes these events were catered and at other times we had home-cooked food.

Based on my having good times with our family, I vowed to always put my family first whenever I became blessed to have children of my own. I wanted to instill in my children the same family traditions I grew up with.

Ann's Story

This part of the book tells the rest of my story. It gives information on Ann's life growing up in Winthrop from childhood through adolescence and her adult years. It contains details about Ann's descendents (i.e., Cara, Deana, Logan and Mason), their family gatherings, weddings, vacations, and other important events. It also tells about my half brothers and the special relationships I have had through the years.

I hope the beginning of this book has laid the ground work for showing obstacles can be overcome. The rest of the story will tell how I dealt with various obstacles to arrive at a successful outcome and a life filled with joy and peace. If I could do it, anyone can.

J, Ann Rosemarie DiMare was born on March 14, 1953 to Salvatore Robert DiMare and Carmela Concetta Faro. Since Dad was absent for my birth – as he was for much of my life, my Uncle Angelo took my mother to the Revere Memorial Hospital in Revere. She gave birth to me in a hallway since there were no birthing rooms available for us. I weighed 8 lbs 2 ounces and was 19 and ½ inches long. I was the second child born to Carmela and Sal.

I was born on Albert Einstein's 74th birthday and Billy Crystal's 5th birthday. Dwight D. Eisenhower was the President of the United States. Richard Nixon was Vice President. Pope Pius XII was Pope at the time. Maurice J. Tobin was the Governor of Massachusetts. John F. Kennedy (D) and Leverett A. Saltonstall (R) were U.S. Senators from Massachusetts. Jonas Salk announced the polio vaccine on March 26, 1953. Queen Elizabeth II's coronation took place at Westminster Abby in June 1953. John Kennedy married Jackie Bouvier in September 1953 in Newport and the Boston Braves moved to Milwaukee.

The average cost of a new house was $9,550. The average wage was $4,000 a year. Minimum wage was $.75 an hour. Gasoline was $.29 a gallon and the average price of a new car was $1,650. The first color televisions went on sale for $1,175 and cigarette smoking was reported as causing lung cancer.

I was baptized at St. John's the Evangelist Church in Winthrop on March 29, 1953. My Godparents are Rosemarie Maiolino Russo and Judge (retired) Domenic J. Russo.

When I was an infant of only 11 months, my mother fell down a flight of stairs with me in her arms. When she pulled me tightly into her chest so I wouldn't fall to the ground, she broke my leg. At 11 months, I was already walking. My mother told me that when the cast was removed I got up and immediately walked again. I guess nothing was going to keep me down as an infant. Perhaps this was the first obstacle I overcame and from the picture on the next page, it appears I did it all with a smile.

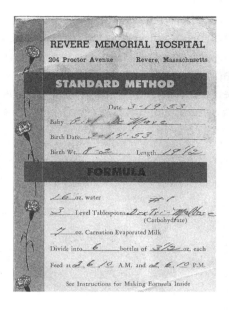

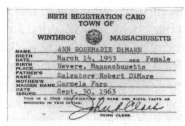

Winthrop is a peninsula town located northeast of Boston. It's a seacoast community with seven miles of shoreline offering beautiful beaches for summertime relaxation. To get to Winthrop, one goes through the Beachmont section of Revere or the Orient Heights section of East Boston. When I was a child, Winthrop was a military town, the home of Fort Heath, an Air Defense Radar Station in the Highlands section of the town as well as the US Army's Fort Banks, complete with underground bunker and a fort built to protect Boston Harbor during the World Wars. As a youngster, I remember uniformed people and businesses that serviced them throughout the town.

Winthrop was largely settled by immigrants of Irish and Italian decent. Many people of Jewish ancestry also settled in Winthrop. For the most part, the different ethnic groups settled in different sections of the town (the Highlands, the Center, Point Shirley "the Point" and the Beach). We lived in the Winthrop Beach section. Winthrop Beach started at the Highlands and contained Shore Drive and the parallel road Shirley Street and all the streets between the two. Initially, Winthrop Beach had a green wrought iron barrier separating the beach from the adjacent sidewalk. Later, a cement wall was constructed that ran the length of the beach. "The Wall" was a popular spot for teenagers to meet, play cards and hang out.

Over the years, the Jewish people transformed their homes in our area from summer cottages to year-round residences. We were one of the few "goy" families living in the area. Yes, I learned some Yiddish as a child! My mother always suggested we make friends with the Jewish people since they had the same values as the Italian people. Mom said the Jewish people loved their families, friends, food, and festivals. She said they valued an education and were extremely hard working people. She also said they would be willing to help anyone that helped themselves. As far as marriage went, though, she made it clear she wanted me to "marry Italian" so we wouldn't have religious issues and would celebrate the same holidays. The Jewish people also had the "Jew Wall" which was located on Shore Drive at the top of Pearl Avenue. That is where I hung out as a young teenager.

Since my childhood friends were mostly Jewish girls and boys, I went to the Temple Tifereth Israel on Saturday and St. John's the Evangelist Church on Sunday. If it was a Jewish holiday, I couldn't go to Temple since I hadn't paid for a seat. I attended many bar mitzvahs and bat mitzvahs through the years and always felt honored to be invited as these were gala events beyond anything I could have imagined given my humble background. To attend these events, one had to dress in fine clothing, of which I had none. The parents of my friends loaned me an outfit or bought me a dress and accessories so I was properly dressed.

Since my grandfather worked at Bay State Lobster Company, we often ate lobsters and fish for dinners. My mom made lobster salad sandwiches with the left over lobster. I traded these sandwiches (at school for lunch) with my Jewish girlfriends as they didn't have lobsters in their homes.

I grew up in a strict Sicilian household at 352-254 Shirley Street Winthrop, MA. My grandparents lived on the first floor of the left side of the triple-decker, six-family home. My mother raised my two brothers and me on the second floor of the left side. Above us were various renters through the years. The right side of the building housed tenants on the first two floors and my Uncle Santo and Aunt Sarah lived on the third floor with my three cousins: Joann, Louise and Gina.

352-354 Shirley Street Winthrop, MA

My bedroom in our five room apartment was next to the kitchen. It was a room 4' by 6' and had a twin bed, bureau and dresser in it. There was no walking space except for a one foot wide path my two brothers used to get to their bedroom. There was no such thing as privacy in our apartment. From my bed, I could see the kitchen clock. I spent hours watching it to see what time dad came home. Usually he would arrive at 5:00 AM and be home for breakfast. As a child, I remember my mother and father constantly yelling and screaming at each other. Dad was physically violent hurling things at my mother. As a child, I often wondered why, if he was miserable there, he didn't just leave? I learned why later on.

Since we lived in my grandparents' house, quite often the rest of the family came on Sundays for dinners. My mother worked full time for minimum wages so my grandparents provided our food and disciplined us as best they could, given they spoke little English. As children, when my brothers and I made too much noise, my grandfather used a broomstick to bang on the pipes.

That meant to settle down or he would use the boom stick on us next.

Growing up Sicilian meant adhering to old fashioned values as practiced in Sicily in the early 1900s. Growing up Roman Catholic meant constantly having guilt trips put on me for anything I did that wasn't what my mother or grandparents wanted me to do. I had three parents once my father left: my mother, grandmother and grandfather. Sicilian women existed to serve their men. Men were responsible for bringing home money to run the house. Women were second-class citizens and weren't allowed to speak unless spoken to. Everything good went to the men first…food… opportunity …clothes…money…education, etc.

Women did the cooking, served the food, cleaned the table, washed, dried the dishes and did the laundry and housekeeping. Since my mother worked full time, these became my chores. My brothers ate dinner and disappear to do as they pleased. Sometimes, I burned the food or broke dishes "accidently" out of anger. I was always given smaller portions of food than the boys and always had to clean up after them.

My relatives spoke Italian to each other. However we were told not to listen and not to ever tell anyone we were Italian as they would treat us differently. We were to profess that we were proud to be American and speak only English when we left the house so that is what we did. How unfortunate we weren't brought up bi-lingual! This was my first experience with discrimination.

My mother's frustration with her marriage manifested itself in her being unhappy and anxious. She was serving her parents, working full time at Kennedy's and caring for her three children. This was an almost impossible task given how demanding my grandmother Josephine was of my mother's time and energy. As far as she was concerned, my mother should have been grateful for her taking us in and my mother's first obligation was to her and my grandfather.

My mother was stifled and told me she was forced to accept her lot in life.

In my early childhood, we had no telephone and no television. I took dancing lessons at Miss Irene's School of Dance and was a member of the American Veterans (AMVETS) Drum and Bugle Corp. I only had one toy that wasn't handed down from my brothers or cousins. It was a doll named Ina Sue. Ina Sue was four feet tall. She wore the same size clothes I wore. Every day, I dressed Ina Sue and talked to her as if she could help me. She was a great listener.

During our early childhood, I remember my mother packing lunches for us in the summer and our having picnics on Winthrop Beach with our friends and relatives. I remember picking periwinkles off the jetties at the beach and going out to the Breakers at low tide to get mussels and clams. I remember mom taking us to Daw Playground at Lewis Lake to ride on the swings, the merry-go-round and the see-saw.

I remember going to Fenway Park to watch the Red Sox play ball. Each year the Winthrop Elks took a bus load of children for $.25 each. I remember going to the movie theatre in Winthrop Center for $.10 on a Saturday afternoon.

I also remember my brothers taking swimming lessons at Winthrop Beach. Perhaps there was not enough money for me to take lessons too as I never learned how to swim. So despite my last name meaning "of the sea" and my birth sign being a Pisces "fish", I still have not overcome the obstacle of the water.

Since my father was totally unavailable and my mother was emotionally unavailable to give me the love I needed, I turned to my grandmother Anne, my Aunt Joann and Uncle Freddy for love.

My grandmother Anne DiMare was a loving, kind, gentle, petite lady. She was a devout Roman Catholic who attended mass on a daily basis. On our many visits to her in Medford, she talked about God to my brothers and me and called us her "little angels". Since she had all sons and I was the first born granddaughter and named after her, she would tell me I was special. Knowing my grandmother as I did, she probably told my cousins they were special too because to her, we were all little angels sent from God.

Nana taught me a lot about the church and told me that God was always with me and if I trusted in God and believed in him, he would help me through life. Now, I bring my grandson to church to try to pass on Nana's teachings about God. I want my grandsons to remember me as having a steadfast love of God and know He will help them to get through life's hard times.

Nana told me that I should love my mother and my father the same even though they treated me differently. She told me I should not resent either one of them as they both had their own problems. This was a lot for a child to comprehend but I listened intently when she talked. She was soft spoken and always spoke with love.

Nana DiMare died in 1960 when I was just 7 years old. I was devastated. She was the love of my life. I always knew she would hug me and show me love and affection when others didn't. As a youngster, I always knew that Nana wasn't very healthy but I never knew what her medical issues were. My uncle Joe later confirmed for me that Nana died from Hodgkin's disease or lymphoma cancer. Nana is buried in the Forest Lawn section of Oak Grove cemetery in Medford.

This is a letter Nana DiMare wrote to me and my brothers when we lived in Los Angeles, CA. It was written on November 7, 1958. When Nana DiMare died, I was forced to look elsewhere for the love she provided. Fortunately for me, it was nearby. In 1959, my aunt Joann started dating Freddy Battista, from East Boston.

Joann & Freddy's wedding
November 1961 – I am the flower girl.

AUNTIE JOANN and UNCLE FREDDY

*A*untie Joann lived with my grandparents on the first floor of our house in Winthrop. Auntie Joann was 12 years older than I was so I looked up to her. I remember her as a fun loving teenager always singing and dancing to Elvis Presley songs. Auntie Joann graduated Winthrop High School in 1958. I admired her, as she was very pretty and so sweet. I remember her dressing for her senior prom. She looked like an angel in her yellow party dress and open toed shoes.

Whenever I had a problem with my mother or father, I talked to Auntie Joann about it and somehow, magically, the problem went away. As a youngster I was dealing with issues many people don't deal with in a lifetime.

In those days, girls weren't allowed to date without a chaperone being present. Auntie Joann and Freddy got permission to have me be their chaperone. They took me everywhere with them. My grandmother told me it was my responsibility to watch them to be sure they didn't kiss. That is what I did! We went to stores, restaurants, the beach, bowling and the drive-in theatre together. They loved taking me to the drive-in movies as they knew I would fall asleep as soon as it got dark. I wonder if they kissed once I was asleep! Auntie Joann and Freddy treated me as if I was their child. They seemed to love having me around and I loved being with them. When they decided to get married, they asked me to be their flower girl. I was overjoyed. Freddy was going to become my uncle. I knew they both loved me dearly.

Soon after they were married, they moved to New Jersey as Uncle Freddy was in the U.S. Army and stationed at Fort Dix. My grandparents and I drove to visit with them nearly every other weekend. In a short time, Auntie Joann was pregnant with their first child. She was due in early January 1963. On her due date, Auntie Joann was taken to the hospital for what was supposed to be the happiest day of her life. Instead, she passed away from toxemia at 22 years of age. My cousin, their daughter died the next day.

For a short time, I had the love I needed but now, my grandmother Anne and my Aunt Joann were both dead. There I was alone again as was Uncle Freddy. At the time, he was the closest person in the world to me. Uncle Freddy became my father, my friend and my teacher. He was 23 years old. I was 9 years old. When he came to visit Nana and Nano, I would hug and kiss him. He returned my affection.

For the next five years, Freddy was my best friend and was there for me as a father would have been. He came to my dance recitals, my birthday parties and my Confirmation ceremony and party. When I was 12 years old, Freddy pierced my ears for me. He helped me with my math homework throughout my school years and when I was in college.

When I was a little over 14 years old, Freddy was banned from visiting because my grandmother feared he would try to become intimately involved with me. My grandmother hoped he would take an interest in my mother. He didn't. My mother was 10 years his senior. I was 14 years younger.

When Freddy remarried, I was invited to his wedding. I was happy for him but sad for me. I lost my best friend again. In later years, Freddy and I reconnected. He visited me and my daughters when he was in Boston on business. I helped his daughter get a co-operative position with the Department of Transportation when she was a student at Northeastern University. Each year for my birthday, Freddy would send me flowers or a gift.

I admired Freddy and was thankful for having him in my life. He set an example for me that few other adults had. He helped me to see what was important when I was raising my daughters often reminding me to "choose my battles" if the girls were messing up the house with their toys!

Freddy died on March 13, 1996 while on a business trip in Washington D.C. He was just 57 years old. I knew he loved me up until the day he died and was devastated when his sister Lalia called to tell me of his passing. Freddy is buried in Hackettstown Union Cemetery in New Jersey. A few years after his passing, I tried to find his gravestone but to no avail.

SHIRLEY STREET SCHOOL

I don't quite remember how I met Paula, but I know I met her while at the Shirley Street School. Our friendship started in the third or fourth grade and has lasted through the years. Paula's mom, Frances, treated me as if I was her daughter. She invited me to family gatherings and took me along with her five children wherever they went. I was fully integrated into their family and loved every minute of being with them.

Paula's family's house overlooked Winthrop Beach and had a beautiful picture window and front porch. We spent hours watching the cars going by Shore Drive in Winthrop. I slept over Paula's house as often as possible. We studied, played cards on "the Wall" at the beach, went to church together and hung out together on Perkins Street near her house. Paula and I became part of the Perkins Street crowd. To be part of the crowd you had to have a boyfriend so we all did. We sat around talking about sports and sex as we understood it. We gossiped about our parents and our teachers. Sometimes we played spin the bottle and kissed in our friend Jill's cabana. Paula and I are still friends today. She came to both my daughters' weddings and is my closest friend from Winthrop and my childhood.

In grammar school, I was outstanding scholastically. I never missed the honor roll and had a sincere interest in academics. I decided at an early age to become a schoolteacher as my teachers were the people I admired the most. The only truly intelligent people I knew at that time were my Uncle Freddy and my teachers. At home, my mother and grandmother made it clear they expected me to get married and have babies. At school, I was encouraged to study hard so I could go to college.

I was also one of the more popular kids in school so I rarely had troubles with my peers. I loved being with my friends. They and their families gave me the love and understanding my family didn't. When I received awards at school, my friends' families clapped for me along with my teachers. My family didn't attend academics award ceremonies. School activities were not important to them.

Miss Louise Auger was my third grade teacher and my first lifetime mentor. Miss Auger saw a needy child longing for love and provided what I needed. She favored me even though I was a constant chatterbox in her class! She invited me to her apartment at 90 Shore Drive on Winthrop Beach on the weekends. I helped her clean her apartment. Then we walked the beach and gathered seashells. She knew I came from a "broken" family and that I longed for attention.

Miss Auger and I stayed friends long past my school years. I invited her to my wedding and brought my children to meet her when they were toddlers. Every year after her retirement, I sent her birthday cards and Christmas cards with pictures of my daughters and updates about my life. One day in December 1991 I arrived home from a business trip to find a very large manila envelope with Miss Auger's return address. I knew immediately that she had passed. I cried for days. The message enclosed stated, "Dear Ann, My sister, my beloved Louise died October 10, 1991. She died peacefully in her bed with her sisters near her. I have been sorting through her memorabilia and came on her cards from friends which she kept from year to year. I am sending these precious loving cards back to you as I know you will treasure them. Much love, Francois A. Whitman"

The Shirley Street School was later renamed to the Preston L. Chase School after its former principal, Mr. Chase. Mr. Chase was the principal when I was in the first and second grades but once I was in the third grade, Robert Duke became the principal at the Shirley Street School. Today, the school has been converted to a condominium complex.

My grammar school teachers laid the groundwork for my loving to learn. My teachers were: Miss Mildred Wing, Miss Claudia Young, Miss Louise Auger, Mrs. Dickinson, Mr. Kerrick and Mr. Robert Ierardi. In the fourth grade, we were introduced to French. I enjoyed studying French as Miss Auger was French and would often teach us French words and sing French songs. Since I took French every year thereafter as well, I ended up studying French for eight years by the time I had graduated high school.

Outside in the school yard at Shirley Street School, we played jump rope, red-rover, jacks, hop scotch and dodge ball. I always tried to get to school early so I could play with my friends in the school yard. We went home for lunch and returned within the hour as our school had no cafeteria, as most schools do today.

I clearly remember the day President John F. Kennedy was shot. I was in the fifth grade in Mr. Kerrick's class. Another teacher burst into our classroom crying. When she told Mr. Kerrick what had happened, he too cried. Mr. Kerrick was a very stern man so I knew something terrible had happened. He explained what happened and put the television on in our classroom for the rest of the day.

I also clearly remember being frightened for my life in the early 1960s as many women were being strangled and beaten in the Boston area. Thirteen of these women were later tied to the Boston Strangler (Al DeSalvo). Since they were women of all ages, I feared going anywhere alone after dark. Once Al DeSalvo was incarcerated, he escaped bringing back all my fears until he was caught again.

These were the days when bread was $.16 a loaf and a quart of milk was $.23. Postage stamps were $.03 each. Grocers gave my mother a piece of paper telling how much she owed. She paid them back when she got her next check.

ANN'S ADOLESCENCE

As a child, adolescent, and young adult, I faced an incredible number of challenges, that others may have considered insurmountable. How I coped with them shaped me into the person I am today and allowed me to succeed in life almost against all odds. My hope is that everyone who reads this memoir can take something away that allows them to believe in themselves, know they are not alone, and understand that they, too, can succeed. I give most of the credit to God for guiding me and holding my hand when others didn't or chose not to because of their own pain and circumstances. I give my teachers and mentors from my adult life credit for taking a genuine interest in helping me further my education. And, I thank myself for the fortitude and desire to become more than others thought possible for me.

I learned at an early age to get along at all costs. If it meant I needed to shift roles in order to be accepted, I did. If I was with the crowd, I would pretend I was interested in boys even though I thought they were immature and believed I was smarter than they were. If they talked about sex, I would act as if I knew it all, even though I didn't know anything, as they most likely didn't either. If I was in school, I played the perfect student, always doing my homework assignments on time, reading the most books, doing the most book reports, and singing the loudest. I didn't talk unless spoken to. I was considered an ideal student.

At home, I was quiet but challenging. I did just as many bad deeds as good deeds. I resented having to cook food, iron clothes, do laundry and wash dishes. I felt used by my mother and brothers. Despite my burning food and clothes, and breaking dishes as a form of rebellion, these tasks weren't taken away from me. I felt like a doormat for my mother who seemed to idolize my brothers, and probably felt like she was being similarly exploited by her mother!

Adolescence was a stressful time for me. It was even more complex because people who meant so little to me tried to change all I wanted for myself and my life. By this time, I had lost my Uncle Freddy too. He had remarried and moved to Budd Lake, New Jersey. Again, I found myself looking for a father figure. Since I was 14 years old, I thought I was looking for someone to love. I wanted someone to tell my innermost feelings to, someone who understood me as my uncle had.

I dated several older guys during my adolescence (e.g., Ronnie, Jimmy, Louie). None of these relationships ever worked out. I never dated boys my age as they were not looking for a relationship. They wanted someone with a big bust that would give them what they wanted. They dated older girls who were more developed and didn't have acne as girls my age did, including myself.

Paula and I hung around with girls in the neighborhood and played board games while babysitting her sister Cathy. We talked about everything and anything as best we knew it. We also had some fun making phony phone calls to people, telling them their refrigerators were running so they better go catch them, ordering pizza to be delivered to their homes, and similar childish pranks. We thought it was innocent then. With caller ID now established I can see it probably wasn't. I'm guessing a lot of other teenagers were doing similar things.

At this time in my life, I was extremely sensitive and withdrew somewhat into a shell. I was afraid to do things alone, afraid of the dark, afraid of what people would say and think. I didn't pass judgments quickly on people. I recognized everyone was living with something that didn't necessary please them. I learned to spend time getting to know people before I trusted them. I blushed easily in the presence of men as I suspected they were all out to play with me and hurt me. My uneasiness with people made me upset emotionally. I was always told this was a stage I was going through. I kept searching for answers but never found them. I didn't understand my own feelings. I had friends but I was still a lonely person. By then, I was moving onto high school.

I clearly remember the great northeast blackout in November 1965. I was afraid the world was ending at that time. I did my homework by candlelight and the house got extremely cold during the night. I believe the blackout lasted just 12 hours.

I also have vivid memories of going to see the Beatles play at Suffolk Downs in August 1966. I was just 13 years old and didn't have a ticket of my own but was able to sneak in and sit with my cousins. Since we spent most of the evening dancing and screaming, seats weren't really necessary.

WINTHROP HIGH SCHOOL

I entered Winthrop High School in September 1968. At the time, I was still living in my grandparents' house on Shirley Street in Winthrop.

Early in 1969, I met Eddie while sitting on the Winthrop Beach "Wall". Eddie was a Viet Nam veteran. I was still 15. He was 23. I knew of my mother's plans to marry Joe and move our family to East Boston and I was lonely and miserable about it. Eddie was more mature than I was. I found comfort in talking to him about everything. Eddie never suggested I do anything but what my mother wanted me to do. He was a decent, honest, respectable man, but a man he was and I was still a child in my mother's eyes.

During our first of two summers together, we became close. Eddie never inappropriately touched me. To both of us, it was a platonic relationship. We both dated others. While Eddie had been serving in Viet Nam, he had been ditched by a girl. I was still looking for a mature guy similar to uncle Freddy. I wanted someone to listen to me and my problems. Eddie served the purpose well. When I was 16 years old Eddie still hadn't kissed me, I began thinking something was wrong with him. I knew I loved talking to him and his wonderful family. His father, Phil, mother, Beatrice and brother, Mickey became family to me.

Since my mom had no money to pay for dental work for me, Eddie suggested he make me an appointment with the dentist where his mother worked. At Dr. Samuel Kane's office in East Boston, I met his young intern Dr. David Brodie. A year later, Dr. Brodie became my neighbor in East Boston. Dr. Brodie graduated college and wanted to start his own business. Since he needed some practice,

I was the perfect patient. By that time, I had already had 12 teeth pulled from my mouth as they rotted from lack of care.

First Dr. Brodie made me some partial plates so at least I could smile without a bunch of holes showing in my teeth. Three years later when I got a job with dental insurance, Dr. Brodie made me three sets of dentures. I promised Dr. Brodie I would continue to smile once my teeth were fixed and I haven't stopped yet. Later, to pay Dr. Brodie back for his kindness to me, I tutored his two sons Jeff and Jason in mathematics when they were in high school.

On March 22, 1969, my mother married Joe Sicuso, a man 18 years her senior. I could see it coming: someone old enough to be my grandfather was going to step in and be the father I never had. Joe had a home in East Boston so we moved there, to 206 Orient Avenue. East Boston was next to Winthrop and was a rival town. Initially, my brother Chucky drove me and my brother Dom to school. In the summer of 1969, after having a fight with Joe, my two brothers moved back to Winthrop to an apartment on Shore Drive. I got my license in September 1969 but couldn't afford a car until a few years later.

Since I didn't have a car, in order to continue going to WHS, I had to get myself there every day. Some days my mother drove me. On other days, I began my journey an hour before school started by walking down two flights of dangerously broken cement stairs. These stairs connected Orient Avenue to Gladstone Street. Another set of stairs connected Gladstone Street to Leyden Street. I then walked down Breed Street to Bennington Street where I crossed over the Orient Heights MBTA station to get the bus to take me to Winthrop.

If I timed it right, the bus was there. If it weren't I had to wait for a bus in whatever weather Boston offered or I could thumb a ride to Winthrop. Some days I was early for school so I could get off the bus near the school without being seen by anyone. If I missed the early bus, I would get off further away from the school so I wouldn't be seen, or so I thought.

On several occasions, I was noticed by Ms. Joann Ciampa, our class advisor. She asked me where I lived. My immediate reaction was to tell her I lived on Shirley Street. She confronted me again. She told me she saw me walking at Orient Heights and getting off the bus near the school, I confessed. She promised to keep my secret. At the time, she lived on the lower end of Orient Avenue and drove the same route to school I was using.

After school, two days a week, I worked in downtown Boston. Since I was alone and having to make my way to school in Winthrop, then to work in Boston and back home again late at night, I turned to Eddie for some help. Eddie and I continued seeing each other by sneaking around which naturally gave me guilt feelings as well as feelings of satisfaction for going against my mother and what I considered her elderly husband! Inevitably, they found out. I was labeled a whore, slut and tramp by many of my relatives although I still hadn't seen male private parts in my life at this point. When I came home late, my mother grabbed me by my long hair and banged my head against the wall. I remember one day physically fighting her back. I never did it again. I cried because I knew I had hurt her.

When my mother realized I was still seeing Eddie, even though she was now married to someone 18 years older than herself, she threatened to have Eddie arrested and put in jail! My mother and Joe also contacted my father and together they went to the high school and spoke to my guidance counselor, Mr. Gerald Battista. They requested his assistance in either getting me put in a boarding school in New Hampshire or being sure Eddie didn't come near me. They said I was a rebellious and disobedient child. Their attempts failed with the help of my teachers and Mr. Battista, who knew I was a model student getting good grades and playing sports in school.

My grades in school were dropping from all "A's" to all "B's" because I was a nervous wreck. I confided in my teachers for help and got plenty of comfort but no real answers as to how to deal with these people who meant so little to me. So, I searched for professional help. Finally a counselor called my mother and spoke to her. My mother claimed she didn't realize what she was doing to me. We discussed the situation and after a year and a half, I was allowed to bring Eddie into the house.

I still wasn't allowed to watch the television or use the phone or the radio in Joe's house. Joe had signs posted on index cards indicating which lights I was permitted to turn on and what time they had to be shut off. I was allowed one shower and one hair washing per week. I was 16 years old and a prisoner in Joe's house. My only escape was to join all the clubs I could at school.

I was on the yearbook staff, in the Italian Club and on the Math team. I was a member of the student council and was a teacher's aide. I played roving guard on the varsity basketball team and was the pitcher and captain of the varsity softball team. Sports served as an outlet to help release my pent up anxieties about my father, mother and step-father. Being a part of a sports team also gave me opportunities to take showers in the school gym and wash my hair.

During this time, other problems arose in my life. I was experiencing conflicts about my religion. I lost trust in God, as I had in my family, when, despite praying faithfully, I still got no help. I began thinking I had been brainwashed to believe all these man-made laws about which foods to eat and when, as well as church moral rules. Everything people enjoyed doing seemed to be a sin in the eyes of the church. I started thinking and living for myself, doing what I wanted to do, but still going to church on Sundays out of fear of death and hell.

Sexually, my adolescence was full of curiosity. Why had I gotten such good feelings when hugging and kissing Uncle Freddy? Was it because he was like the father I never had? Did I secretly wish he would take me away from this family and save me? I wondered if I would remain a virgin until I married. Everything I learned about sex was through reading paperback books I found when snooping through mom's drawers and talking to the girls who were labeled the "pigs" of the town.

Sex was a dirty thing in the old-fashioned Italian home. My grandmother called it, "doing the job". I was trying to learn about a subject that had no teacher. I had many sexual fantasies and I was terribly frightened I would escape from reality. I felt my dreams of having sexual intercourse would never come true, especially while I was dating Eddie. I never turned to masturbation for I had heard many stories about it causing blindness and an increase in acne and *that* I surely didn't need!

In high school, despite the limited time I had available after playing sports and working, I did manage to get into some mischief. I was sure not to bring shame to the family. Whenever I got myself in trouble, I learned how to get myself out. I turned to my girlfriends for help and they turned to me. We kept each other's secrets and will bring them to the grave with us, whether it was related to boys, or other activities we knew our families wouldn't approve of. Once I got a car, I had my share of getting stopped by the police for speeding and had my share of getting thrown off of the "wall" at Winthrop Beach. I was friends with quite a few boys from high school, as most of the popular ones were in my homeroom. But I never dated them or was sexually involved with anyone from my high school class.

Many of my friends' parents were members at the Cottage Park Yacht Club (CPYC). My girlfriend Leah and I would sneak out of her house when I was sleeping over. We would head over to the CPYC and drink on the boats with the boys. I usually secretly threw my drinks overboard as I was afraid to get drunk and lose control. I just wanted to look cool. I was afraid of alcohol and drugs because I saw their effects on others. I refused to smoke pot, although many people I knew were doing it and they had no qualms about smoking in front of me. One New Year's Eve, inside my brother Chucky's closet, my brothers were up to no good and they urged me to join them. I was too scared. They called me "Annie Straighty".

In March 1971, I went to Fort Lauderdale, FL for spring semester break. It just so happened, the trip occurred when my mother was in the hospital recovering from having a hysterectomy. When I booked the vacation, I had no way of knowing she was going to be having surgery that week. Since I paid for the vacation with my own money and I didn't want to throw the money away, I decided to go anyways. Some members of my family thought I was a horrible daughter for leaving as I did. None of them knew what I had been living with.

Also, since I took a week off from school that wasn't a sanctioned school vacation week, my chemistry teacher thought she would teach me a lesson and gave me a C grade for the term. To pay her back, the week before graduation, I gifted her with a dildo wrapped in a Kotex box with Christmas wrapping paper. Two of my other classmates and I left the gift on her chair, with a note indicating we hoped it gave her as many hours of pleasure as she had given us in her class. I was happy to be part of that little prank with Dick F. and Richard F. It gave me the feeling of finally getting back at someone who hadn't been nice to me.

When I graduated Winthrop High School in June 1971, I weighed 96 pounds from malnutrition. I wanted to attend Salem State College but didn't have the money to live there and didn't have the money to buy a car to get there. I was awarded a full-year scholarship to Northeastern University but I didn't attend there either for fear of my scholarship not being renewed in subsequent years. I accepted enrollment to Boston State College because, with or without a scholarship, I could earn enough money to put myself through college; I had been promised absolutely no financial support from either of my parents. My mother thought I was going to be wasting four years of my life going to college. My father was absent from my life at that time.

As it turned out, Boston State College offered me full tuition for four years along with other perks, (i.e., a work study job, money for books and transportation expenses). Going to Boston State College was probably the best decision I ever made in my life as it led me to the Transportation Systems Center (Volpe Center) where I worked from 1972 until my retirement in 2008.

June 1971 WHS Graduation

1972 Working at Kennedys

The week after my sixteenth birthday, my mother got me a job working at Kennedy's, a retail clothing store on Summer Street in Boston. Most people worked there for minimum wage. I worked on Monday and Wednesday evenings after school, from 3:00 PM until 9:00 PM, on Saturdays from 9:00 AM until 6:00 PM and full time in the summers. I found myself working with many mentally, physically, and emotionally challenged people as well as some normal and healthy people. I continued working at Kennedy's until the end of June 1972 even though I had also started another job working for the government as a work-study student from Boston State College. Working two jobs became second nature to me.

After work, I raced through the streets of Boston to get to the State Street subway station to catch the train to Orient Heights. I then walked up two flights of stairs on a pitch dark hill to the house at 206 Orient Avenue where I lived with my mother and Joe. I was scared out of my mind. Working allowed me to save money for my college expenses. I diligently saved one half of every pay check I earned.

At Kennedy's, I started as a File Clerk. I was responsible for filing patrons' credit card receipts into the appropriate account folders. I advanced to be an accounts biller. Beside my hourly wage, I earned one penny for each account I billed once I had billed over 500 accounts in a day. I went to work early and worked through breaks and lunch to maximize my earnings and I worked extra hours to make extra money. I also found myself working later at night because I was smitten with a man named David who worked at Kennedy's too.

I was attracted to David from the first day I met him. I wanted to date him but feared what might happen sexually. I kept using Eddie as my excuse for not dating him. In time, David stopped pursuing me and I became hurt. A year later, when I was 17 years old, I told David my mom and step-dad were going away for a week and my brothers didn't live with us. I would be home alone. I knew David would take it from there and he did. At about 12:30 AM he came to my house. By 5:30 that morning, I had lost my virginity and didn't have any guilt feelings about it. My only quilt feelings were that I had done this behind Eddie's back.

I had learned more from David than I ever dreamed possible. On subsequent dates with David, I never let him touch me for I knew he had the power and experience to really hurt me badly. Whenever I saw him, my heart would skip beats and I blushed. He knew the way I felt about him. I was separating love from sex. I didn't realize it then but I thought he loved me because he wanted to have sex with me. To me, giving sex was giving love. It took me years to learn my lesson when it came to separating love from sex. I knew the relationship between Eddie and I would end soon as I had crossed a line.

By now, my mother had found out that Eddies' family was financially comfortable so she started suggesting that Eddie and I get married right after I graduated high school. Financial stability meant more to her than love. I knew it was time for me to get away. A week after I turned 18 I took a trip to Fort Lauderdale. I left Eddie behind with a broken heart, my mother in the hospital, and David, who I wanted to be with. I still didn't allow myself to be with David because I knew it was for the wrong reason. I knew David didn't love me but instead loved the sex. I just kept telling myself, "A girl's got to do what a girl's got to do!"

At this point in my life, I was totally confused. I was trying to mature but couldn't understand why people wouldn't let me. Or was I really trying to stay a child and that's why I was refusing to have a relationship with David? I thought I was being serious about my feelings but nobody took me seriously. I wanted to be totally independent but my mother held me to ties and threats.

I looked forward to college with the hope I would be free from my mom and step-father's rules. I wanted to graduate from college more than anything so I would never end up as my mother did, being subservient to a man and begging for his support. I wanted to own my own house and have my own car. More than anything, I wanted to have children to love me unconditionally as I would love them. I wanted them to be proud of me as I wasn't proud of either of my parents. It wasn't until I matured more that I grew to admire my mother. I was hoping to meet a professional man in college who was a genuinely good person similar to Uncle Freddy. I wanted an intelligent, good-looking man to be my life partner and my cheerleader rooting me on as nobody had ever done before.

I now valued things I had never valued before and began voicing my opinion rather than trying to make everyone else happy. Yes, I was a classic people-pleaser. During my adolescence, I suffered from a tremendous lack of self-confidence. I almost always did what everyone else wanted me to do. I wanted to be a good girl since I saw what my brothers were putting my mother through. I saw the many tears she cried.

BOSTON STATE COLLEGE

*I*n September 1971, I started attending classes at Boston State College on Huntington Avenue in Boston's Roxbury district. Boston State specialized in educating prospective teachers. Ever since I had been a youngster, I wanted to be a teacher as I loved imparting knowledge to others and thought I could help children through life's struggles as Miss Auger had helped me. I admired Miss Auger and wanted to be like her.

Since I enjoyed mathematics and solving problems came easy to me, I decided to be a high school math teacher. I also took a lot of psychology classes so I could be a guidance counselor and perhaps help other teenagers through the many problems I had. I always believed if I had someone to confide in, adolescence would have been a fairly easy time for me. I had no problem communicating with my teachers because we shared a common interest to help and teach the uneducated.

In my first calculus class I met Patty MacInnis. Patty always had a smile on her face and soon became like a sister to me. Like my high school companions had, Patty, too, shared her family and her friends with me. I had found a new close friend and a new life away from East Boston. Patty was dating a man who went to Tufts University. There I met his fraternity brothers and went to many parties attended by eligible, smart, young men. We went to football games, took swimming lessons and studied together. I was overjoyed to have Patty in my life.

After two years at Boston State, Patty decided to transfer to Boston College. I understood she had a different career goal than I did, but I was devastated to see her go. By then, losing people I loved became second nature to me as I had already lost my grandmother Anne, Aunt Joann and Uncle Freddy. I vowed not to lose Patty so I kept in contact with her through phone calls and am happy to say we are still good friends today.

I put a lot of energy into my studies. I majored in mathematics with a minor in secondary education. I took many psychology courses so I could pursue guidance counseling in time. My psychology courses led me to start understanding my childhood and adolescence issues. They led me to study people and understand what made them tick. I learned I didn't have to say yes to everything anyone asked of me. They led me to realize that I, too, had rights and was a good person despite all the guilt I lived with. I learned not to trust everyone so easily.

I had my share of issues at Boston State too. In those days, inter-racial dating and marriage were out of the question from my family's point of view. I was expected to marry an Italian boy so our families could blend without religious or racial issues. At Boston State, I was asked out by many black classmates. I never accepted using the excuse that I was already dating someone and my boyfriend wouldn't appreciate it, even when I wasn't dating anyone at the time.

One day when I was walking across the area known as the Fens to attend classes at our satellite campus, I was attacked by a man. He grabbed at my chest as I tried running away from him. I wasn't sure if he wanted my book bag or planned to sexually assault me. Fortunately other people walked by and I started screaming. He released me. I ran to my car, drove myself to work, and called the Boston police. They wouldn't investigate the case unless I was willing to go back to the scene of the crime and re-enact it with them. I was in shock and scared, so I refused to go.

In January 1975, just prior to my attaining my Bachelor of Science Degree in Mathematics, I was required to do a semester of student teaching. I chose to return to Winthrop High School, as I knew the building, most of the teachers and what would be expected of me. During my student teaching, I learned how difficult a teaching career would be. I taught four classes: grade 12 calculus, grade 12 trigonometry, grade 10 algebra II and grade 10 geometry. The students, for the most part, were physically bigger than I was and were only four to six years younger than I was. The girls made fun of my prissy dresses. The boys flirted with me. What had happened in the four short years while I had been away at college? Children seemed to lose all respect!

Graduating from college and getting a good job were my most important goals at the time so I persisted. On June 7, 1975, at the Hynes Auditorium on Boylston Street in Boston, I got a Bachelor of Science Degree in mathematics cum laude. I had four invitations to the event, which I gave to my mother, father, husband and mother-in-law. My father didn't come, but then again, why would I have expected him to show?

THE VOLPE YEARS and NORTHEASTERN UNIVERSITY

At Boston State College, I participated in the work-study program as part of my financial aid package. The financial aid office let me select a job out of a book of potential positions. I chose the Transportation Systems Center (TSC) on 55 Broadway in Cambridge because it was on my way home from school. That choice changed the entire direction of my life.

Since I aspired to be a high school math teacher, I picked a position as a mathematician. I began work at TSC in May 1972, earning $1.10 per hour from the federal government and $1.65 per hour from Boston State College. I worked 15 hours per week during school time and 40 hours per week during school vacations and the summer.

The Volpe Center

TSC was established in 1970 as a research facility to provide analytical, scientific and engineering support to the U.S. Department of Transportation. Most of the professional staff had advanced degrees from the Massachusetts Institute of Technology (MIT) in various engineering disciplines. I met some amazing and brilliant people there, who believed Ann DiMare was more than just a pretty face! Four men -- Dr. Frank Tung, Bernie Blood, Donald Ward and Dr. James Hallock -- stand out in my mind as being the most intelligent men I had ever met. They all graduated from MIT and were all willing to mentor me to achieve higher goals than I myself thought I was capable of achieving and far more than any of my family members ever expected from me. I was fortunate that at one point in my career each of them was my direct supervisor.

At first I was assigned to a data collection position. One summer, I stood at the Auditorium Subway station with a clipboard and recorded bus arrival times, counted passengers getting on and off the buses and recorded the time for the buses to close their doors and get back into the flow of traffic. When I returned to the office, I entered the data into a PDP-10 machine for processing. At this time, energy efficiency was a major concern as the nation was experiencing an energy crisis. I remember waiting in long lines to refuel my 1972 Chevrolet Vega, which I bought myself to get to and from school and work. The data I collected assisted the MBTA in determining if they should reduce the bus fleet on major routes in order to conserve on fuel.

When I was nearing graduation, I started applying for permanent positions. I applied to Winthrop High School, Revere High School, and Saugus High School. I also applied to the TSC, just in case I didn't get the teaching position I wanted. At the time, teaching was paying $8,900 per year and the TSC was offering me $11,900 a year. I knew I couldn't make $3,000 over a summer so TSC was becoming more attractive to me. I was assured by my supervisor I would be hired in a short time.

In September 1975, I started substitute teaching while I waited for a permanent government position. I taught at Winthrop High School, Winthrop Junior High School, Saugus High School, Saugus Belmonte School, Revere High School, Revere's Garfield School and the Northeast Vocational School in Wakefield. I was working every day. The school principals called me the evening before to give me an assignment for the next day. Quite often I had to refuse work as I was booked for weeks at a time.

On November 3, 1975, I was sworn in and fingerprinted for my official government position as a mathematician. In my first professional job, I was responsible for developing algorithms to retrofit break and air conditioning systems on buses. Later I was assigned to do field data collection for speed limits in rural school zones in Mississippi, Alabama and Pittsfield, Maine. I couldn't believe I was actually handed an airline ticket and given money for hotel rooms and food to travel to these sights. As a child growing up in Winthrop, I watched airplanes fly overhead as they took off and landed at Logan Airport. I never in my wildest dreams imagined I would be able to fly in one of those planes and to do it for free!

I had always enjoyed working with numbers and with people so the direction my career was going in was a perfect match for me. A few months after returning to work after having my first daughter in January 1977, my supervisor Bernie Blood asked me what my intensions were to further my education. I said I had none at the time. I knew I wanted at least two children and couldn't imagine going to school while trying to work and raise my family. It wasn't the answer Bernie wanted to hear or was willing to settle for. He said, "Well, young lady, without an advanced degree, you won't be an asset to our team. I suggest you re-think your future and decide what it is you really want". Gosh, I trembled when he talked. He was a man of few words and only said what he really meant. When Bernie talked, I listened.

So, I came up with the brilliant idea to pursue an advanced degree in accounting as I enjoyed working with numbers and was interested in doing federal taxes. In 1977, I hadn't yet started my income tax business although I was doing income taxes for friends and family. Again, Bernie's voice echoed in my head as he said, "If you get a degree in accounting, we won't pay for it and we won't need you working here". Wow – I got the message. I asked what he suggested I do. He recommended I contact MIT or Northeastern University and pursue a degree in transportation engineering since I was working at the Transportation Systems Center. Now, why didn't I think of that? Oh, I know, because these were schools for rich and super intelligent people and I was a poor girl with average intelligence, or so I thought.

I contacted both MIT and Northeastern. I learned I needed to take the Graduate Record Exam to get into MIT. That settled it for me. I attended classes at Northeastern. I took one class per trimester. It took me four years to get a master's degree. A degree was something nobody could take away from me. I would have it and the government would pay for it. I started classes on January 4, 1978, my daughter Cara's first birthday. I was two months pregnant with my second daughter.

Since my classes were in the evenings on the peripheral of Roxbury, one of the toughest areas in Boston, I took my brother Chucky's dog, Arjuna with me to classes. At the time, Chucky lived in the basement apartment in my house. Arjuna was a mixed breed of black Labrador, German shepherd and cocker poodle. Arjuna knew her job was to protect me. I later learned I could take classes at Northeastern's Burlington campus and so I did.

One of my best professors at Northeastern was Dr. Geoffrey Berlin. He was my professor for three of my operations research analysis courses. After classes, Geoff invited the students to meet him for drinks at the Café Espadrille down the street from the campus. On a few occasions, I went. On one of those evenings, nobody showed except Geoff and me so we had a long conversation about his life and mine. We shared similar experiences and had a similar marital situation. We were both unhappy in our relationships.

As it turns out, Geoff not only taught at Northeastern, he also owned a computer software company, where he developed software to solve school district's transportation problems. His company was Modeling Systems, Inc. When I told Geoff about my work experience for the US DOT, he immediately saw a match in what I did and what his company needed. In 1979, Geoff offered me a job developing training materials for the various software packages he was developing for the school counties he serviced.

The software was used to re-route school buses based on where the largest populations of children lived in order to reduce the amount of buses and drivers needed. This served to save the school districts money. Geoff built me a "Heath-Kit" computer with specialized word processing software to do my work. I worked from home writing the training materials. I dropped my products off to Geoff on my way to and from work at TSC as he lived just across the river in Boston from where I worked in Kendall Square Cambridge.

Once the manuals were developed and proofread, Geoff offered me the opportunity to go to the application sites to deliver the training to the various superintendants of schools and data processing people. Through this work, I visited Cobb and DeKalb Counties in Atlanta, Georgia, Ann Arundel County in Baltimore, Maryland, Clark County in Las Vegas, Nevada and Orange County in Los Angeles, California. We also attended Operations Research Society of America (ORSA) meetings in San Diego, California.

Geoff paid me $10 an hour for every hour I worked on the training materials or for every hour I was away from my children as he knew I had to pay babysitters to watch them even though Joey and I were still living together at the time. Making $240 a day was incredible for me. Geoff made me promise him I would save the money for my daughter's education and I did. Thank goodness, my cousin Catherine was eager and willing to help. She stayed at my house babysitting my daughters and my husband. She was 12 years old at the time and loved being with my daughters.

I earned my Master of Science degree in civil engineering (transportation major) on June 20, 1982. Geoff came to the Boston Garden to congratulate me. I gave my four invitations to my mom, my mother-in-law, my husband and my father. My mother and mother-in-law had my daughters sit on their laps. My father didn't come!

I was amazed at how well I did in school, given I was the only girl in a class of 20 students. I was also the only person in the program with a bachelor degree in a discipline other than engineering. It wasn't easy going to classes in the evening after either working or caring for my daughters all day. Nonetheless, I endured and was rewarded in the end with an education that led me to prosperity and self-reliance. When I got my diploma, I made a copy of it and put it in a thank you card to Bernie Blood. He was touched by my gesture. He had me go to his office so he could thank me for the thank you card. He was chocked up and told me nobody had ever done anything so nice for him.

After I got my master's degree, I was promoted to a government pay scale GS-11 operations research analyst. I became eligible for further career advancement. The government pay scale was designed to either get a meager pay raise each year (called a step) or a hefty pay raise (called a grade). At the time (1982) I started noticing what was going on around me in the Center. The men were getting grade pay raises without having advanced degrees. I was getting yearly step increases. Men without bachelor's degrees were getting hired into positions because they knew someone. I had to earn the positions I wanted. Men were put in offices with two people. I was put in three-person offices. Men were sexually harassing women and all we could do was ignore them and walk away.

There were so few professional women then that there was little resistance to the many injustices being done. Out of 500 government employees, there were approximately 40 clerical people and 8 professional women. The others were professional and technical men who were running the Center as they saw fit. Some had higher political aspirations. There were also many on-sight contractors who had different rules than the government people.

This phenomenon was later referred to as the glass ceiling. Glass ceilings exist when two people do the same job and one gets paid more, when people are subjected to gender-based, ethnic, religious or racial discrimination, when people are excluded from networks, have stereotyping and preconceptions of their roles and abilities, failure of senior leadership to assume accountability for their (especially women's) advancement and lack of role models and mentoring. I didn't suffer from lack of role models or lack of mentoring but I certainly experienced all the other forms of the glass ceiling. I learned how to overcome it as well as the other obstacles in my life.

In 1984, I was assigned responsibility to lead multidisciplinary teams in the development and delivery of Federal Aviation Administration (FAA) training projects. That position was a perfect match for me and lasted for the next 20 years of my career. I worked with and led a technical teaching team of over 30 contractors. I traveled to 44 of the 50 states in the U. S. as well as to Germany to develop and deliver the training, all at the expense of Uncle Sam. First, I had to learn exactly what the Flight Standards Service (AFS) Division of the FAA did for work, learn how the new software packages being developed at the TSC (i.e., Flight Standards Automation Systems (FSAS) and Safety Performance Analysis System (SPAS)) would help the FAA, and then design and develop the training to train more than 3,500 FAA Operations, Maintenance and Avionics inspectors.

I was sent to Jamaica, New York to shadow a man named Joe McNeil. Joe and I had several telephone conversations planning my two-day visit. Jamaica had an FAA Regional Office (RO), a Flight Standards District Office (FSDO) and an International Field Office (IFO). Joe planned to take me to each of these offices and have the office managers explain their work. He planned to introduce me to field inspectors so I could ask questions. He then planned to take me onto the airport tarmac to see exactly how the inspectors did their work. So, I boarded a Pan American plane in Boston headed for John Fitzgerald Kennedy Airport in NY. I was the only Caucasian person on the plane, so I thought I would know who Joe was when I get there, fully expecting Joe McNeil to be white and Irish. When I arrived at JFK, I was still the only Caucasian person. There stood an African American man about 5'8" tall, thin and handsome wearing an FAA badge, holding a sign with my name on it and asking, *"Sister Ann, is that you?"* I recognized the voice so I knew it was Joe McNeil!

Joe was a humble man, soft spoken, intelligent and ever so friendly. I was immediately impressed by him. Our first stop was to a delicatessen for bagels and cream cheese! Over the following years, I invited Joe to my home for numerous parties and gatherings of FAA people after meetings held in Boston. He met my daughters and we became like family. Joe knew I had a tax business and was also interested in doing taxes so we teased about one day merging and having me do taxes in the North (Boston) and Joe do taxes in the South (New York). It wasn't until years later I learned more about General Joe (as he became affectionately known to me). Joe was a retired U.S. Air Force Major General and an original member of the Greensboro Four, a group of four college students who on February 1, 1960, sat down at the lunch counter inside the Woolworth's store in Greensboro, North Carolina, and ordered coffee. The waiter refused to serve them at the "whites only" counter and the store manager asked them to leave. They stayed until the store closed using non-violent protests for civil rights. The stools they sat on are now in the Smithsonian Museum and a statue of the Greensboro Four stands on the campus of North Carolina Agricultural and Technical State University in Greensboro, North Carolina. Today, Joe and I are friends on Facebook.

The education I got from Joe McNeil started me in my "real" career with the government. I was introduced to people in the Headquarters Office, located in Washington, D.C. They liked me. I liked them. When they gave me assignments, I got them done on time and within budget. In the government if you and your contractors produce quality products and keep to your budgets and schedules, you will succeed. I was a master at getting people to work for me and delivering top notch products the field inspectors could relate to and learn from. After all, I used the field inspectors as my subject matter experts so how could I lose? I also contracted with one of the best training companies in the USA at the time, using the competitive contracting process. I met the folks at Brattle Systems, Inc. from Arlington, Massachusetts and knew immediately we would be a good fit for working together. It was convenient and saved the government thousands of dollars to have Brattle Systems located closely to the Volpe Center. For the next 20 years, we worked side by side to produce the best training the Flight Standards Service will have ever known.

In 1990, the TSC was renamed to the John A. Volpe Transportation Systems Center in honor of former Governor John Volpe. On January 20, 1969, John Volpe became the second U.S. Secretary of Transportation and in 1973, President Nixon appointed Secretary Volpe to the post of United States Ambassador to Italy, in which position he served, with distinction, until 1976.

One aspect of training development is to show the importance of a particular training program to the people who will receive the training. For that reason, we usually started our training programs with a short video tape highlighting the current Director, Administrator, Secretary or other person who suggested the legislation that put the training in the hands of the inspectors and network administrators in the first place.

The pictures that follow show me with Thomas Accardi, Jane Garvey, Senator John McCain and Anousheh Ansari. Tom was the Director AFS from 1991-1997. Tom is an intelligent man who had a passion for his work. When Value Jet Flight #592 landed in the Everglades on May 11, 1996, Tom was one of the men who took the fall for the rest of the agency. He was transferred to the FAA's Federal Executive Institute as a senior faculty member in Charlottesville, North Carolina. The FAA was cited for not properly supervising ValuJet and not requiring active fire suppression equipment in the cargo compartment.

The picture with Jane Garvey includes John Hughes, Brattle Systems, Inc. Jane was the FAA Administrator from 1997 – 2002. The picture was taken at the Center for Management Development in Palm Coast, FL. The Safety Performance Analysis System (SPAS) development team went to the Center as a team building exercise. Jane was the first administrator appointed to a five-year term, the first female administrator, and the first administrator who was not a licensed pilot. She had previously worked as a teacher, highway safety administrator, and the director of Logan International Airport in Boston, MA.

In 2001, I was assigned to develop training for another AFS program. The Air Tours Management Program (ATMP) was going to be implemented to govern the airspace over national parks so helicopters could transport handicapped people and others to see the parks without disturbing the ecosystem or wildlife in the parks. Senator John McCain proposed the legislation since he was concerned about the airspace over the Grand Canyon National Park in his state of Arizona. He was also concerned about the preservation of the other National Parks. When I suggested the Program Manager get me access to interview Senator McCain, he asked me if I was serious. Yes, I was. I was anxious to meet a great American and thought this would be the closest I came to one, although by this time, I had attended lectures given at Salem State College by former Presidents George Bush and Bill Clinton.

*Ann with Mr. Thomas Accardi
1997*

*Ann with Ms. Jane Garvey and John Hughes
November 1998*

*Ann with Senator John McCain
September 5, 2001*

*Ann with Anousheh Ansari
February 2007*

Ann R. DiMare

On September 5, 2001, six days prior to the historical Terrorist Attacks of September 11, 2001, I walked up Capitol Hill and into Senator McCain's office for a one-hour interview. Had the interview not happened that week, chances are it never would have happened. In Senator McCain's office, I met his wife, Cindy, and sat knee-to-knee with the Senator while a camera man videotaped my interviewing him. I have the raw footage of the video where you can hear my voice asking questions. On camera, you only see the Senator. At the end of our interview, I asked him to take a picture with me. He was accommodating, not only in taking a picture with me but also in signing pictures for me and my fiancées father, Angelo a staunch Republican. Since Senator McCain ran for President in 2008, I still proudly display our picture in my home office.

After 9-11, FAA training funds were diverted to cover Homeland Security initiatives. I was reassigned to manage technical research for commercial space transportation projects as well as FAA and Federal Motor Carrier Safety Administration (FMCSA) rulemaking efforts. I directed and coordinated the work of the project teams and served as the Contracting Officer's Technical Representative for three contracts simultaneously. Shortly after the space shuttle *Columbia* accident occurred on February 1, 2003, I competed for my supervisor's position and was reassigned to be Chief, Aviation Safety Division. My supervisor, Dr. James Hallock was summoned to the National Aeronautics and Space Administration (NASA) in Houston, Texas to join the *Columbia* Accident Investigation Board (CAIB) to investigate the destruction and determine the cause of the accident. The CAIB released its final report on August 26, 2003. For Jim's efforts on the CAIB, I nominated him for a government award. We were both invited to a gala event in Washington D.C in October 2003. There I met Mr. Sean O'Keefe, the NASA Administrator at that time.

Through my work with the Commercial Space Transportation project, I met some amazing space pioneers and attended many conferences. Of particular interest were the astronauts I met at the conferences I attended. I was most impressed by Anousheh Ansari. On September 18, 2006, she captured headlines around the world as the first female private space explorer. Ansari was the fourth self-funded space tourist and the first self-funded woman to fly to the International Space Station. At the conference I attended in February 2007, she told her story and was happy to take a picture with me when I asked.

Through my work at the Volpe Center, I also made many lifetime friends for which I will forever be grateful. My friends include people from the Volpe Center, the FAA and Contractor personnel. They became my extended family and in many cases have adopted me into their own families. They opened their homes and their hearts to me and my daughters. They attended my family parties and I attended theirs. They watched my daughters grow up. They taught me how to invest money. They taught me how to work within the government system to get ahead in my career. Most of all, through their actions, they showed me there are good, honest and loving people that would care more for me than my own family did. My first life-long friends were Sue Mayo and Joyce Lovetere.

I always credit Sue with teaching me how to drink beer. It was Sue who took me to the Falmouth hospital to get stitches in my finger the night I cracked a coconut open with an axe. Joyce was the life-long sister I never had. We had our first daughters two days apart and spent time together in the hospital. We raised our children together. Joyce babysat my daughter Cara when I returned to work after Cara was born. Joyce is my daughter Deana's Godmother. We fondly refer to Joyce as "Auntie Joyce".

I have so many other friends from my Volpe years. There are too many to mention them all. They know who they are and how much I love them dearly. My "sisters" I am still close to today include: Joyce, Sue, Carol, Carrie, Rita, Roberta, Pat, Donna,

Deborah and Elia. My "brothers" I am also still close to today include Andy, John and David. Helen Papulis "adopted" me when my mom died. We kept in constant communication after her retirement in 1997. Helen passed away on April 18, 2011. Dr. Frank Tung was like a father to me, always watching out for my best interests. Dr. Tung passed away on November 15, 2006.

When first hired at the TSC, I made a salary of $11,900 per year. When I left the Volpe Center in June 2008, I was making over $127,000 a year. Every time I got a pay raise, I thought I had gone to heaven! Who would have thought a "poor girl" brought up on welfare in Winthrop would succeed in such a remarkable way?

The people I met and my career at Volpe was the most amazing experience that ever happened to me. On the day of my retirement party, 75 of my colleagues and contractors attended a party in my honor at the Marriott Hotel in Cambridge, MA. I played the music to "I Had the Time of My Life". I retired at age 55 and was able to put both my daughters through college so they could have good lives too.

Throughout my career with the federal government, I received numerous awards including the distinguished Administrator's Award for Superior Achievement (Bronze Medal) in 1991 and again in 1998. It was an amazing ride and I enjoyed the incredible journey.

Don Ward & Ann

Ann & Jim Hallock

Ann & Helen Papulis

Joyce, Sue, Carol & Ann

Ann, Donna, Pat & John

Sue & Dr. Tung

Jim H., Roberta, Rita, Tony, Katy, Olive, Barbara, Jim C.

*I*n my late teens, I spent a few years looking for love, going to nightclubs dancing with my girlfriends, getting picked up by smelly, drunk men, and spending time with insincere men who used me as much as I used them. I wanted to settle down and have a family of my own.

In January 1973, while attending a party at my friend Terry's house in Winthrop, I met the man I eventually married. Joseph "Joey" Fulchino had dark curly hair and an outgoing personality. He had a secure job as a shoe sales man for Thom McAn Shoe, making decent money for those days. He was a personable guy who would give anyone the shirt off his back.

Joey came from a large Italian family who enjoyed getting together regularly. He was a local guy who valued people and friendships as I did, or so I thought. I was desperate to have a family of my own to love and a house of my own to live in. Joey's parents, Joe and Anna accepted me immediately. His sister Robin was eight years his junior and like the sister I never had. In turn, I was the sister she never had. We attended family dinners on Sundays, played cards with his aunts, uncles and cousins, and enjoyed our time with friends and family.

When Joey proposed to me just a year later, I accepted. I was ready to become a wife and mother and get on with an adult life. I was a responsible person and knew I could handle the demands of marriage. On October 13, 1974, Joey and I married at St. Anthony's Church in Revere. Robin was our maid of honor. Joey's cousin Phil was our best man. We had our reception at the Tremont Villa in Everett. The reception was attended by about 250 friends and family members. I paid for my own wedding with money I had saved over the years. My in-laws paid for an open bar!

Prior to my marrying Joey, after approximately three years of having no contact with my father, I tried to make amends with him and Shirley yet again. I visited their home with my future in-laws and told them Joey and I would be married. I asked my father to walk me down the aisle as I thought it would please him and bring us close again. He accepted. He asked me how I thought Joey would support me on a shoe salesman's salary. I wasn't concerned as I knew Joey would support me better than my own father ever had.

When my father agreed to walk me down the aisle, I didn't realize the price I would have to pay. On the day of my wedding, as we walked side by side, Shirley gave me the *malocchio*. The *malocchio*, or evil eye is an intentional hand signal given as a witchcraft-type curse meant to harm and cause misfortune to the recipient. I had stayed out of her life but she still hated me. Several people told me she did this from the back of the church. Later at the reception, she caused another scene unbecoming a lady!

The other reason having my father walk me down the aisle was a mistake was because it genuinely hurt my mother. She felt dad didn't deserve the honor as he had been absent from my life for so long. My mother thought my grandfather Domenic or my brother Chucky deserved the honor. At the time, I didn't feel close to either of them so it didn't make any sense to me.

After the wedding reception, Joey and I returned to my mother's home to open our gifts. Since I had paid for my own wedding, my mother handed me her wedding gift. It was a savings passbook with $600 in it. She told me it represented all the child support my father had ever sent for me over the eight years they were divorced. She also told me I had hurt her more than anyone ever could by my letting my father walk me down the aisle. For my wedding gift, my father and Shirley gave me a silver-plated cake knife!

Joey and I had an apartment at 137 School Street in Revere, MA. I continued going to college and working at the TSC. Soon after our marriage, it became apparent to me that something was drastically wrong. Joey continued partying as a teenager would, smoking marijuana and popping pills, while I was getting more serious about having a house and a family. I saw myself mothering Joey trying to get him to become a man. He married me hoping I would never change but I did. I married him hoping he would change but he didn't. He continued with his partying ways only now he was spending my money in addition to his own on his pot, cigarettes and alcohol. I married an Italian which was what my mother wanted. But I married a baby, not a man. Joey had a pot room in our first apartment, fully equipped with dark lamps, and Joey's pipe collection.

How did I get myself in this mess? The answer was simple. I was still trying to please my mother so I did what I thought would please her. My mother was thrilled that Joey and his family included her in all their family gatherings. She too had found a family since by now, her second husband was deceased and my brothers were still out of her life.

I vowed never to divorce Joey as I knew I was strong enough to survive anything. I would just show him what a good wife I would be to gain his affection until he grew up. I vowed to love him more and prayed to God for help. I worked harder and saved more money. A year later, in 1975, we were able to buy our first house at 15 Greenwood Avenue in Saugus. The house was a bungalow. It had an in-law apartment in the rear to help us with the mortgage payments.

Because we were still going out partying with our friends on weekends, I stopped going to church on Sundays. What a mistake that was! When I needed God the most, I turned away from Him. He had been there for me through the years and I let someone else's pleasure influence me into making a bad decision.

Back row: Tony, Chris, Phil, Robin, Ann, Joe, Tom, Peter Front row: Patty, Joyce Carol, Joan

137 School Street Revere, MA

15 Greenwood Avenue Saugus, MA

136 Fairmount Avenue Saugus, MA

I did continue praying, this time for a baby; I thought a child would help settle Joey down. On May 20, 1976, I learned I was pregnant with my first born child. I was elated. To accommodate our growing family, Joey's parents gave us $2,000 to add to the money we had saved to have a house built. Having an apartment in our house didn't bother either of us so we decided to have one built in our new home to allow us to collect rent. In April 1977 the builder broke ground. We moved into our new house at 136 Fairmount Avenue on July 22, 1977, just six months after our first daughter was born.

Having a child didn't help the situation with Joey. Instead, he became more and more child-like himself. He started experimenting with all kinds of drugs. He was snorting cocaine, smoking pot and using various pills, (e.g., THC, Christmas Trees). He was hiding guns in our attic for his cousin, who used the guns in South America to steal marijuana from the farmers there. I was scared for my life and scared for my child. I had a government job providing us far more income than Joey's job provided us. I didn't want to lose my house or my job.

So, what did I do? I became pregnant again when Cara was just 9 months old! Joey was thrilled, thinking he would have the son he wanted. For a short time, he stopped using drugs. I thought he was fixed and we would go on to wedded bliss. When Deana was born in August 1978, Joey got worse. He wanted a third child because he wanted a son. I thought, "I already have three children: Cara and Deana -- and you". Secretly I had prayed for another daughter as I wanted Cara to have a sister since I never had one. Yes, God answered my prayers again.

Money started disappearing from my wallet. Joey started disappearing. Whenever a friend called and wanted anything, Joey went running. Even if we were eating dinner, Joey would leave. I knew he was selling drugs but pretended I didn't as I was anxious for him to have more income since he was spending more than he and I were making together.

The bills piled up as Joey continued snorting and spending. We didn't fight a lot because, similar to my mother, I kept quiet about how miserable I was. My friends and family thought I had it all. They thought Joey was wonderful and was providing nicely for me and the girls. NOT! When I did complain to Joey's mom, she suggested I work more hours. At the time, I was working two days per week so I could be the person who most influenced my daughters. I was also going to Northeastern University at night for my master's degree, figuring that, when I got the degree, I could make more money by being promoted.

In late 1981, (Cara was 4, Deana was 3), when I came home from school one night, Cara asked me why daddy smokes pot and I didn't. She wanted to know why daddy did drugs and I didn't. She wanted to know why daddy smoked cigarettes and I didn't. What an eye opener that was for me! Deana was in her crib, soaking wet and with a loaded diaper. I asked myself what I was doing to these kids leaving them with Joey. So, I started having babysitters watch the kids even though Joey would be home while I went to classes. So, now I was paying for someone to safeguard my children as I knew their father wouldn't.

In June 1982, when I graduated Northeastern, Joey became extremely angry. It was Father's Day and he wanted to be honored. Instead, his family and mine were honoring me at a dinner at Jimmy's Pier 4 in Boston! From then on, his drug use got worse. He told me repeatedly I was boring and didn't understand how drugs were good for people as they made them relax when they were anxious and made them energetic when they were tired. I simply thought drugs made people insane and lethargic. I always had more energy than Joey.

On Thanksgiving Day, 1982, Joey announced at the dinner table that this would be our last Thanksgiving together as he was going to be leaving me shortly. I was shocked. We had never discussed separating or divorcing. How would I continue to work and raise the girls on a part time salary? I was Catholic and Catholics weren't supposed to get divorced, at least not me!

I wanted my marriage to end differently than my parent's had. I thought if I just kept my mouth shut, he would forget what he said. Surely he must have been on some kind of drug. But, on January 5, 1983, one day after Cara's sixth birthday, Joey came home from work and told me he was leaving me because I deserved better. Was he serious? He told me it was obvious to him I would never accept his drug use and he didn't want to be married to someone that didn't accept him for who he was. I was shocked but felt a total sense of relief; a massive burden had been lifted from my shoulders. I asked him if he was seriously choosing drugs over his family. He emphatically said, "YES just to show you how stupid you are." Since I knew I wasn't "stupid", I said, "No problem" and Joey left, but only for the moment.

A week later, he realized how stupid his decision had been and started begging to come back. By then, I had changed the locks on the house and settled into my new reality that I was going to do whatever it took to raise the girls alone and responsibly in a drug-free, smoke-free environment. On February 15, 1983 (Joey's birthday) we went before a judge in Essex Probate Court and were declared legally separated. Joey was supposed to give me $75 per week for the support of the two children. Since he didn't make much more at the time, he moved in with his parents. I thought his doing that would mean I would get the money, but 18 months later when he still hadn't sent me any money, I contacted my attorney to have a wage assignment put on his check from his job. At least I would be assured of getting some financial support for the children as Joey continued doing his drugs and spending his money on dating other women.

Joey's family and my family were livid. My mother loved the life she had with us. Joey's mother insisted her son wasn't addicted to drugs. My friends were shocked. I was physically ill but mentally adjusting. Joey threatened to burn the house down with me in it. He ripped our storm door right off the hinges. He threatened to kill himself if I didn't take him back. He called me at all hours of the night and breathed heavily on the phone just to scare me and disturb my sleep.

Within a year of our separating, Joey checked himself into a psychiatric ward for drug addiction at the Winthrop Hospital. I participated in a couple of therapy sessions with his counselors and him. The counselors determined since Joey treated me as if I were his mother and I treated him as if he were my son, our marriage was doomed from the beginning.

At the hospital, Joey met Joanne Nania. Once their relationship blossomed, he filed for a divorce from me. Our divorce was final in June 1985. Joey married Joanne one week later on June 21, 1985, but not before begging me one last time to take him back! Joey went on to have two daughters with Joanne. Leah and Jessica are my daughter's half-sisters.

Years later, their marriage also had trouble. Joanne called me crying about the things Joey was doing to her. I wasn't surprised as many of the things he did to her he had also done to me. The difference was that both Joey and Joanne were doing drugs at that time. I never did drugs. Joanne told me she intended to divorce Joey and take his house away from him. Since I had put the down payment on the house they were living in and I felt the house not only belonged to their children but also my daughters, I had a friend of mine call Joey's mom, Anna and anonymously fill her in on what was going on.

Anna got an attorney and Joey filed for divorce before Joanne did. As their marriage was dissolving, the Massachusetts Child Enforcement Division interviewed me and asked me to accept custody of Leah and Jessica. They didn't feel comfortable placing the children with either Joey or Joanne. I refused custody as I wasn't in a position to have Joey or Joanne coming to my house for visitation. I believed it would create a hostile environment in my house since they were both volatile at that time.

Ultimately in order to support her habit, Joanne turned to unhealthy ways to get money, eventually ending up in jail. When she was in jail, she called me several times to beg me to watch over her daughters. When their divorce became final, Joey got custody of their daughters. Soon after, Joanne was diagnosed with breast cancer. On January 11, 2005, Joanne died at 47 years of age.

Joey's child support to my daughters ended when they reached 18 years of age. I was left paying for both their college educations and both their weddings. Fortunately for me, I was a saver. Through the years, I only bought what I needed, not what I wanted. I lived a modest life and always looked for bargains. To my credit, Joey still publically compliments me on how I raised our daughters. He has warned me that the good die young! He has said, "I don't know how you did it." Truth is, sometimes I don't know how I did it either, but for the grace of God. The years of their childhood are like a blur to me now.

MY DAUGHTERS

Cara

On May 20, 1976, I learned I was pregnant with my first daughter Cara. I was elated. My pregnancy was an easy one with no nausea or other side effects. I gained over 30 pounds as I was incredibly happy and ate anything. After all, I was eating for two!

I wanted a child to love more than anything in life so finding out I was pregnant nearly sent me over the moon. I worked throughout my pregnancy. I was due on Christmas Eve, so I stopped working on December 22 and patiently waited for Cara to arrive. I didn't know I was having a girl but I definitely was praying for one. Joey wanted a boy. Having grown up with two brothers and always feeling inferior to them, I knew I would be happier with a baby girl.

When Cara hadn't arrived by December 29 (my mother's birthday), I asked the doctor to induce labor that day as I thought it would be an honor for my mother to have my daughter born on her birthday. Also, I was still trying to make up for the disappointment I gave her from having my dad walk me down on the aisle on my wedding day. The doctor refused to induce labor but said he would on January 6 if the baby wasn't born by then. I knew I didn't want to have a baby on January 6. That was the day my aunt Joann (mom's sister) died during childbirth. I didn't want to suffer the same fate, so I prayed again.

On January 4, right after Joey left for work, my water broke. I spent the next half hour on the toilet waiting for him to come home to take me to the hospital. I had taken Lamaze Classes so I knew the breathing techniques to use to keep relaxed and make the labor go more quickly. I arrived at the Malden Hospital at 11:40 A.M. and by 1:14 P.M., Cara Ann Fulchino popped out of me into Dr. Frank DiMasi's hands. I was amazed as I held my baby girl in my arms. Joey instantly said, "We need to try again so I can get my son". Cara was born with dry skin as she was 11 days late. She weighed 6 pounds 9 ounces and was 20 ½ inches long.

Cara was an angel from the start. I had decided not to breastfeed her, which upon reflection, was a mistake. Most people didn't breast feed then so I was afraid to try it. Cara drank her formula, threw it up and drank again. I will never know if she would have had the same problem with breast milk. Cara was an active baby, always wanting to be swinging or moving. She walked at 10 months old.

Cara was a wonderful child from infancy up through adulthood. She never gave me a hard time, was always cooperative, and is a kind, gentle, and loving soul. Her smile is incredible and her laugh makes you laugh with her. As a youngster, Cara was an introvert and did whatever pleased me and others. She was an easy child to rear. She glowed when I walked in the room and she loved being with me. She would sing, "I'm your buddy" which thrilled me. I often felt guilty I hadn't given Cara enough alone time before I became pregnant with Deana but since Cara didn't seem to mind, I relieved myself of the guilt and just simply enjoyed being her mother. She was a best friend to me. I talked to her as if she were an adult even when she was a child. Perhaps I made her grow up too fast. Cara never did anything before it was legally permissible. It was a promise she had made to herself.

Cara did well academically. She played sports and had many friends. Her teachers loved her. She enjoyed playing with her sister and our neighbors, Jennifer and Jillian. Cara graduated

Saugus High School in 1995. During her high school years, she worked part time jobs at T.J. Maxx, the Hilltop Butcher Shop, and Camerlengo and Associates, an accounting firm. Phil Camerlengo is Cara's Godfather. He needed an office manager. Cara was perfect for the position and loved being with Phil.

When Cara graduated from high school, she enrolled in Salem State College in their accounting program. I was thrilled since Salem State was the college I wanted to go to. While at Salem State, Cara continued working for Phil. She was due to graduate in May 1999; however in the fall 1998, Phil offered her a full time position which she accepted. She continued her studies at Salem State but instead of graduating in May 1999, Cara graduated in May 2000, despite having completed her coursework by December 1999. Cara graduated with a Bachelor of Science Degree on May 20, 2000. We had a graduation party for Cara at the Knights of Columbus in Saugus.

When Cara was 16 years old, she worked at TJ Maxx. There she met David Silipigni. David came from a well-known family in Saugus. Initially Cara was shy around David but soon learned his love for her was genuine and he would never ever hurt her. How could anyone hurt her? She was an angel! Cara and David started dating in November 1993. They did everything together and loved being with each other, their friends and their family. Cara was glowing. I was happy for her. She found a best friend for life.

In September 2000, Cara and David got engaged. I hosted an engagement party at our house. In March 2001, her mother-in-law Jeanette hosted a beautiful bridal shower for her at Spinnelli's in Lynnfield.

On May 5, 2001, Cara and David were married at Blessed Sacrament Parish in Saugus. I hosted their reception at Jimmy's Allenhurst in Danvers. What an incredible wedding they had!

121

Since it was a springtime wedding and we had been pent up for the winter, we celebrated late into the night. We sang and danced and waved our napkins in the air. David and Cara sang a duet to each other from the movie "Grease". After their wedding, I got telephone calls, cards and letters from my aunts and friends telling me how wonderful the wedding was and how happy they were for me and Cara. Cara and David live in Saugus on Orcutt Avenue, in a home they had built in August 2001.

CARA FULCHINO

Salem State College Graduation
May 20, 2000

Cara and David Wedding
May 5, 2001

Deana

My pregnancy with Deana was a bit of a challenge. Since Cara was still in diapers, I gagged and got nauseous whenever I changed her diaper. I got pregnant with Deana when Cara was only 9 months old. I also was working two days a week and still attending classes in the evenings at Northeastern. On July 30, 1978, Joey and I attended his cousin Sandra's wedding. We danced a lot and I ate like a piggy. I worked on Monday, July 31 and intended to go to work the next day. However, on August 1, 1978 at about 8:30 A.M., I went into labor and started my Lamaze breathing. Joey was home so he took me to the hospital. We left Cara with my brother Chucky.

By 9:42 A.M. Deana Marie Fulchino came into the world, all covered in a white creamy substance. She weighed 8 pounds 2 ounces, my same birth weight when I had been born. She was 19 ½ inches long, also the same length I was when I had been born. Joey cried in the delivery room because we had another girl. Dr. DiMasi told him to "Grow up!" Since Deana was bigger than Cara, I needed an episiotomy for her delivery. I didn't, however, require any medication for either of the births. Truly passing my many kidney stones over the years was far more difficult than delivering my babies.

While pregnant I decided to breast feed Deana so I wouldn't have to go through the work of preparing and sterilizing bottles as I did for Cara. Breast feeding came easy to me and Deana. However, when she was on amoxicillin for an ear infection, because she had some of the medication in her mouth, I broke out in a terrible rash all over my breasts. I knew I was allergic to penicillin and now I learned I was also allergic to amoxicillin.

Deana, too, was an incredible child. She slept in her crib for many hours. Even when she wasn't sleeping, she was content just to lie in her crib. As Deana grew, she required more attention. She was an extrovert and was always getting into something. One time, I found Deana chomping on our dog Rosco's food. Deana walked at 8 months old. She was amazing for a baby her size.

From infancy up through adolescence, Deana was more of a challenge than her sister. At a young age, she learned how to climb out of her crib and her car seat. At 15 months, on Christmas Eve, Deana fell out of my car as my mom opened the door to get in. Instead of rushing to my in-laws for dinner, we rushed to the hospital. When we arrived at the in-laws, Deana was wrapped in white mummy-like bandages with her head stitched up.

Another time at home, Deana ran down the hall and smacked her head on the corner of a doorway: more stitches! In the fourth grade, while attending an "outward bound" school event, Deana fell. When the bus arrived back at the Lynnhurst School in Saugus, a teacher carried her off the bus. Her leg was bandaged from her accident. I immediately took her to her pediatrician's office. I nearly threw up watching Dr. Glazier dig gravel out of her knee.

Deana didn't give me a hard time, she was just extremely active! In high school, Deana sprained her ankle. She drank alcohol at 14 years old and drove her friend's car at 15 years old (unlicensed). She was into everything and always wanting to be the best at what she did. Deana's friends were older so quite often she was influenced by what they did. She skipped school from time to time to be with her friends.

Unlike her sister, Deana didn't wait for anything to be legally permissible before she did it. Deana did whatever she thought she could get away with. While I was on a three-week business trip to Europe, I thought I had secured the house so Deana could not get in. I made arrangements for her and her sister to stay with their father. Prior to my securing the house, Deana unlocked a window so she could gain entry to the house while I was away. When I returned, one of her friend's mothers told me about the incredible party at my house and how the police broke it up. Why wasn't I surprised? Joey obviously didn't watch the girls as I hoped he would. Deana took advantage of a good situation.

Deana did well academically always making the honor roll. She, too, played sports and had many friends. Deana graduated from Saugus High School in 1996. During her high school days, she worked part time jobs at Star Market and Camerlengo and Associates. After Deana graduated from high school, she enrolled in Bentley College in Waltham despite getting a full academic scholarship to Merrimack College in North Andover. Deana enrolled in Bentley's accounting program. Deana wanted to live at Bentley College and so she did, despite the cost of tuition, fees, room and board being prohibitively expensive.

When the girls were babies, I had started saving for their education. By the time they graduated high school, I had about $75,000 for each put away. My plan was to use it for their college, their weddings and perhaps a car or a down payment on a house for them. Deana's money all went to her education. She got $5,000 a year as an academic scholarship and several student loans from the government. After her graduation, she had to pay back the student loans and an outstanding loan with me for her last year at Bentley College. To me, it was an expensive price to pay given I always believed it is how you apply yourself that counts and not the name of the school one attends especially for their undergraduate degree.

Deana thrived at Bentley. She joined a sorority. In her senior year she was the sorority president. In her freshman year, Deana didn't work but when she realized I wasn't going to support her inactivity, she got a part time job at College Pro Painters. Deana graduated college on May 20, 2000 with a Bachelor of Science degree in accounting. I attended her graduation ceremony where Senator Edward M. Kennedy gave the commencement address.

Deana got her first professional job (which she still holds), as an accountant at Feeley and Driscoll, an outstanding accounting firm in Boston. Deana attained her masters' degree in finance at Bentley College (renamed to Bentley University in 2009) and is a certified public accountant (CPA). Over the years, Deana paid back her student loan to me without ever missing a payment. I am anxious to see what she pays for when her children go to college or if she set limits for them as I did for her.

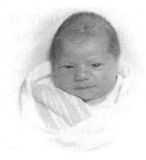

DEANA FULCHINO

Bentley College Graduation
May 20, 2000

Deana and Sean's Wedding
May 31, 2008

Since Cara graduated the same day at the same time, 26 miles away, David and Cara's in-laws to-be attended her graduation and video-taped the event for me to see. We had a joint graduation party for Cara and Deana at the Knights of Columbus in Saugus. They both invited whomever they wanted and we had a tremendous celebration. I always considered their college graduation *my* achievement as well. I thought once they had graduated college, my job was done. I was fooled again!

In May 2006, Deana ran into an old "flame" at a friend's wedding. By the end of that summer, Deana and Sean McGovern were inseparable. In 1994 they had dated for a short time and kept their friendship alive through the years so they were able to quickly pick up where they had left off. In October 2007, they got engaged and on May 31, 2008, they were married at Blessed Sacrament Parish in Saugus, MA.

Deana wanted an elegant reception with fewer people than Cara had at her wedding and so, typical of Deana throughout the years, she did it her way. Deana and Sean's reception was at the Hyatt Regency at Logan Airport. They invited only their closest family and friends. As you can see, they were both elated to have found each other again. They danced to "Bless the Broken Road". I have included the lyrics here. The song was most appropriate given how they got back together after 12 years.

Bless the Broken Road lyrics
Songwriters: Boyd, Bobby C; Hannah, Jeff; Hummon, Marcus;
I set out on a narrow way, many years ago
Hoping I would find true love along the broken road
But I got lost a time or two
Wiped my brow and kept pushing through
I couldn't see how every sign pointed straight to you
Every long lost dream led me to where you are
Others who broke my heart, they were like northern stars
Pointing me on my way into your loving arms
This much I know is true
That God blessed the broken road
That led me straight to you
Yes He did
I think about the years I spent, just passing through
I'd like to have the time I lost, and give it back to you
But you just smile and take my hand
You've been there, you understand
It's all part of a grander plan that is coming true
Every long lost dream led me to where you are
Others who broke my heart, they were like northern stars
Pointing me on my way into your loving arms
This much I know is true
That God blessed the broken road
That led me straight to you
But now I'm just rolling home into my lover's arms
This much I know is true
That God blessed the broken road
That led me straight to you
That God blessed the broken road
That led me straight to you

Ten months later, Deana and Sean blessed me with my first grandchild. Logan Anthony was born on March 30, 2009 at the MGH in Boston, MA. He was 7 pounds 9 ounces and 20 inches long. My whole world changed the day my "little man" was born.

My second grandson, Mason Kevin was born on June 3, 2011at the MGH in Boston, MA. He weighed 8 pounds 12 ounces and was 20 inches long.

Deana, Sean, Logan and Mason are my neighbors. They live next door to me in Saugus on Kayla Drive.

Having Cara and Deana for daughters was the greatest blessing in my life. *Nobody* had better daughters than I. I have always been proud of them. Over the years, my daughter's brought me endless joy and steadfast unconditional love! Logan and Mason are now my little angels.

PHOTOS OF MY DAUGHTERS WITH ME

1981

August 1, 1982

1983

1985

1987

May 20, 2000

April 2008

May 31, 2008

130

PHOTOS OF MY GRANDSONS

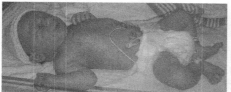

Logan Anthony March 30, 2009

May 30, 2009

December 24, 2009

March 30, 2010

April 4, 2010

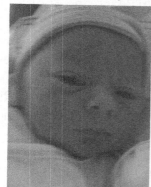

Mason Kevin June 3, 2011

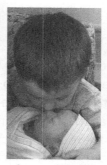

Logan kissing Mason

June 4, 2011

Logan & Mason

*A*s a child, the only vacation I remember taking as a family was to Niagara Falls in Canada. I vowed that, when I had children, I would take them on vacations once a year. I started this tradition in 1984 after I was divorced. At first we took vacations by car to places close to home (i.e., Story Land, skiing in NH, Cape Cod and Canobie Lake Park). When finances were more plentiful, we traveled by bus, air or boat. As often as possible, in the summers, I took the girls on business trips with me to Fort Lauderdale, Florida. I enjoyed watching them interact with my colleagues and friends at dinners.

On multiple occasions, we visited Disney World and relatives and friends in south Florida (Miami, Royal Palm Beach and Bonita Springs).

Deana, her girlfriend Christina and I went on a cruise to Key West and Cancun during her senior year in college. In September 2001, Deana and I also went to London together to visit our friends Rita and Tony, who served as our private tour guides to all the main attractions.

Cara, David and I went to San Francisco in June 1998 for Liz Abbott's high school graduation and to Washington D.C. in 2006. On a few occasions, we took a babysitter and on many occasions, we took friends with us as there were times when each child could travel for free providing there was an adult paying full fare. We still enjoy family vacations together. The pictures on the next page are from some of our vacations.

Disney World 1986   *New York City 1987*   *Washington D.C.*
with Jake & mom   *Twin Towers in back*   *June 1988*

    Bermuda August 1989   *Atlantic City August 1995*

Disney World July 1996   *New York City for*
with Richard, Matt, Liz,   *New Years Eve 1997-1998*
David & Ryan   *with Liz, David & Kristy*

Bahamas Cruise November 2002   *Disney World December 2010*
  with Sean, David & Logan

As a youngster, I learned about religion from my grandmother Anne. She taught me to trust God. She said He would always be with me and guide me as long as I prayed to Him. I was baptized, received my First Communion and Confirmation at St. John's the Evangelist Church in Winthrop. As a Confirmation gift, my father gave me a set of cyrstal rosary beads. I still have them today and will take them to my final resting place with me.

I got married in St. Anthony's Church in Revere and vowed to bring my children up Roman Catholic. The photographs below show some of the religious sacraments we celebrated. I would have included pictures here of my First Communion and Confirmation however, unfortunately my brother misplaced the family photo albums so that is not possible.

Instead of looking for a Christening outfit for Cara, I had my mother's cousin Angelina Noe make a gown and coat for her out of my wedding gown. My wedding gown was a size 4. Cara was baptized at St. Anthony's Church in Revere on February 20, 1977. Cara's christening reception was at the Sons of Italy Hall in Winthrop. Her Godparents are Phil Camerlengo and Robin Fulchino Driscoll.

Deana was baptized at St. Anthony's Church in Revere on September 17, 1978. She, too, wore the gown made from my wedding dress. Deana's party was at our house after the christening.

Cara and Deana made their First Communion on April 26, 1986. They wore matching dresses and looked absolutely angelic. I still have their dresses and am hoping some day I will have a granddaughter who can wear it to her First Communion.

In May, 1993, Cara asked her Godmother Robin to be her confirmation sponsor. After the church ceremony, we had a party at the house. A year later, Deana asked me to be her confirmation sponsor. The day was bittersweet as my mom had died two months prior to the event. As we listened to the Bishop talk, Deana cried because my mom wasn't there. We had a party for Deana at the house too.

Cara April 1986

Deana April 1986

**Cara & Deana with
Father Larry Novello**

Cara May 1993

Deana May 1994

Cara married David Leo Silipigni on May 5, 2001 at Blessed Sacrament Parish. Their reception was at Jimmy's Allenhurst in Danvers. They invited more than 300 people and 265 attended. Joey and I walked Cara down the aisle.

Deana married Sean Frederick McGovern on May 31, 2008 at Blessed Sacrament Parish. Their reception was at the Hyatt Regency at Logan Airport in Boston. They invited a little over 200 people. Joey and I also walked Deana down the aisle.

Logan's Christening

On July 12, 2009, Logan was christened at St. Mary of the Annunciation Parish in Melrose. Sean and Deana invited 100 people including nine members of the DiMare family. Only my father came for five minutes. He hastily departed saying he was "too busy" to stay. Five members of the Faro family came. Chucky didn't come and has yet to meet Logan. Logan's christening day was the last time my father saw his great-grandson. Cara is Logan's Godmother. Sean's brother, Tim, is Logan's Godfather.

Mason's Christening

On July 10, 2011, Mason was christened at Blessed Sacrament Parish in Saugus. Mason's reception was at Spinnelli's in Lynnfield. Sean's sister Kathy is Mason's Godmother. My son-in-law, David, is Mason's Godfather. My nephew Jacob and his fiancé, Jackie celebrated with us along with my dear friend Joyce and her husband John.

This day I will marry my best friend,
the one I laugh with, live for, love
Ms. Ann DiMare
requests the honour of your presence
at the marriage of her daughter
Cara Ann Fulchino
to
David Leo Silipigni
son of Mr. and Mrs. Lawrence Silipigni
Hope that you will join in this celebration
on Saturday, the fifth of May
two thousand and one
at five-thirty in the afternoon
Blessed Sacrament Church
14 Summer Street
Saugus, Massachusetts

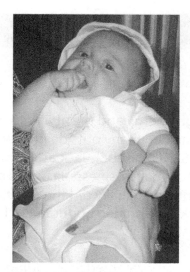

Tim, Sean, Logan, Deana & Cara

Logan July 12, 2009

David, Kathy, Deana, Mason, Sean & Logan

Mason July 10, 2011

*S*ince I was gifted with high energy and the ability to be extremely organized, I pursued many outside interests through the years. In 1982, a neighbor, Jack asked me to do his taxes and suggested I start a small business. Jack was a Revere police officer. The accountant who usually did the taxes for the officers took ill that year. Jack encouraged about ten of his colleagues to have me do their taxes.

To prevent any mathematical errors, I programmed my Leading Edge Computer using VisiCalc and created data entry sheets, which emulated the various tax forms. When the clients arrived, I interviewed them, gathered their information, and entered it into the computer program. At that time, few tax preparers used computers to do taxes. I wouldn't have done them without a computer.

When the clients left my home, I printed their information and give it to one of my daughters to enter into the federal and state income tax forms. I got the forms from the local library and post office. From 1982 to the present, my tax business grew from doing a dozen returns each year to now doing between 250 and 300 returns each year. Jack was instrumental in getting me more Revere police officers' business. They, in turn, told their state trooper friends about me. Through them, I met Matt McGovern. He encouraged many people from the District Court probation departments and sheriff's department to come to me as well. Cara and Deana were happy to help. They were rewarded for their efforts and are now both accountants.

By 1982, I was raising the girls as a single mom. I had "rules" for us to live by. It gave both the girls and me stability as we knew what to expect from each other. I told them my *"job"* was to go to work and make money so I could provide them with a nice home, food, clothing and an education. It was their *"job"* to get the best grades they could and participate in school sports so they could get scholarships to help reduce the cost of their college education.

To show I meant what I said, I tutored children in high school mathematics for $25 per hour and later worked at Saugus High School as the official score keeper for the Girl's basketball team. I earned $50 for each game I scored. From my earnings, I gave the girls an allowance for helping around the house. For each year of their age they were given $1 per week allowance so when they were 6 years old, their allowance was $6 per week. For that money, they had to make their bed. When they turned 7 years old, their allowance went up to $7 per week and they had to empty the dishwasher. For each successive year, they got a $1 allowance raise with the promise I would continue to give it to them as long as they did their chores. Once they turned 16, there would be no more allowance but instead they had to get a wage earning job themselves.

After age 16, I promised to continue to feed them, provide a roof over their heads and give them an education but refused to buy their clothes or give them spending money, unless it was what they wanted for their birthday or Christmas. Everything was clear and we never had any problems. They are amazing ladies and I am extremely proud to be their mother. I also take pride in having both my daughters attain accounting degrees (what I really wanted for myself) and both now have professional careers as accountants.

I also did volunteer work for Blessed Sacrament Parish in Saugus, publishing the weekly bulletin, teaching Christian Doctrine classes and selling donuts at the Sunday night bingo games. The girls were members of the church choir and did other volunteer work in the town and at the school. I am a notary public and a certified secondary education teacher in the Commonwealth of Massachusetts, although based on the new certification requirements my certification is probably no longer valid.

When I look back at those years, what I find most amazing is that during the school year, I was working four jobs to survive. I had my day job with the U.S. Government and at night was either tutoring high school children in mathematics, scorekeeping for basketball games or doing income tax returns. There were many days when I did all four jobs in one day. Whew, I wish I had that energy now!

Since my retirement, I have been a member of a committee organizing our 40th Winthrop High School reunion and have volunteered at professional sports alumni golf events. Through this work, I have met many retired sports professionals.

Babe Parilli (Patriots)

Gino Cappelletti (Patriots) & Karen Mustone

Rico Petrocelli (Red Sox)

Joe Morgan (Red Sox)

Milt Schmidt (Bruins)

Bob Sweeney (Bruins)

Rico Petrocelli (Red Sox) Ken Hodge (Bruins)

Derek Sanderson (Bruins)

Reggie Lemelin (Bruins)

Joe Andruzzi (Patriots)

Steve Grogan (Patriots)

Mike Lynch - WCVB

SINGLE and OUT

*I*n January 1982, when I became single, initially I was severely depressed and my immune system was weak. I spent the first six months painting my house and using all my nervous energy to get my affairs in order. At night when the girls went to bed, I cried myself to sleep as I was lonely and thought I was doomed to a life of being alone. I was afraid to let my guard down again, to trust again, to lose control, and to get hurt again. After all, I had seen what had happened to my mother. She was still single after many years of never having met another man she could trust.

When I finally was able to, I put a smile on my face and noticed a change in my life. When I first met a man and start dating him, he was in awe of my energy and ability to multitask so effectively. Men were in awe of my education and my position with the federal government. They were in awe of how clean I kept my house and how I cooked for my kids. They were in awe of the dinner parties I threw as I showed special attention to detail by having fresh flowers, nice linen tablecloths and place cards on the table. They were in awe of the whole Ann DiMare package.

Initially, each man would want to see me several nights a week and on both Friday and Saturday evenings. They wanted to occupy all my time, meet my family, do everything and anything that was part of my life. Then, once they knew they had secured their relationship with me, things changed. They found me too caught up in my job, too close to my kids and too concerned about keeping a clean house.

They found other things to do such as golfing…taking their dog for a walk…taking their mom out to dinner…meeting with their friends to play tennis…having drinks…go skiing….taking courses…traveling, etc. I was amazed at how their "love" changed especially when they learned I wasn't going to sit around waiting for them to notice me again and stop treating me as if I were a second-hand rose or a second-class citizen. I let them know, they couldn't control me; I wasn't going to play second fiddle to their sport, their mother or their dog. I understood if their job was demanding; mine was too. I understood if they had children issues; I did too. But, I never understood their wanting me in their lives for when they had nothing better to do and thus my relationships with Michael, Bob, and others were short-lived.

I'm not saying I didn't meet some nice men along the way because I did. But when a man had more issues to deal with than I did, I knew nothing good could come of that. My mother used to warn me that all men were no good and that, in time they would all "show their true colors". She wasn't 100 percent right about that but gosh she was close! When they showed their true colors or when my daughters expressed unhappiness about my relationship with someone, I knew it was time to say goodbye.

Throughout the years, I had only three one-night stands. These were all with police officers Jack introduced me to. I didn't care for any of them. What I really wanted to do at this point in my life was to concentrate on raising my daughters and not having any commitment to men.

In March 1999, I met Jeff B. Jeff told me he was single as his wife had been killed in a brutal car crash in South Florida. Jeff told me her body parts were placed in two body bags from the accident on Route 95. I was so gullible, I believed his story! My heart went out to him and since he was charming, I fell for his whole pack of lies.

Jeff was available most weeknights but on weekends Jeff was always away or busy. That should have been a clue to me. I bought a book entitled *100 Lies Men Tell and Why Women Believe Them*. While reading the book, I counted 86 lies Jeff told me. I confirmed Jeff was married by help from my dentist and various internet websites. I found out his real name, his wife's name and their address.

The last time I saw Jeff was in February 2000. As payback for his lies, I decided to play a trick on him. When I met him, he had been working a construction job in Boston. By September 1999, he had been transferred to a job in Dallas, Texas. When I checked the internet dating sites in Dallas, I found his ad so I figured he was playing some other woman as he had done to me. Sure enough, Jeff was up to his usual shenanigans, only now in Dallas.

I created a fake screen name for myself (Denton Doll) and contacted Jeff telling him that my name was Debbie Denton and that I looked like Michelle Pfieffer. Jeff fell for it hook, line and sinker! We emailed each other several times daily. Once I had said enough to get him interested in meeting me, we set up a date at a restaurant in Dallas. Naturally, I didn't show. However, I called the restaurant and asked them to tell him I got a flat tire and was sorry I couldn't make it. Jeff understood and via email set up another date with me. This time, I told him I would be in Fort Lauderdale, Florida over Thanksgiving vacation. I knew he lived in a suburb of Fort Lauderdale so he would most likely be home for the holiday. He was overjoyed he would get to meet me on his own turf.

I was in Fort Lauderdale at the time but had no intention of meeting him so I asked my girlfriend Rita, who looks like Michelle Pfieffer, to meet him and tell him I was in a terrible car crash and in the hospital in Boca Raton. Rita met Jeff. At first he thought Rita was Debbie Denton. They chatted for a half hour. Jeff showed great concern and wanted to see Debbie in the hospital. Naturally,

Rita said it wouldn't be a good idea. He told Rita he thought an old flame might be playing a game on him.

So much of Debbie Denton's life coincidentally matched up with things his old girlfriend knew about him (i.e., her birthday was the same as his, her father's birthday was the same as his son's, her favorite restaurant was the same as his, etc.). Throughout the time I did this (February through November 2000), my friends and people in my office laughed hysterically at what a fool he was making of himself. It was great therapy for me. Before parting from Rita, he asked her if he should continue emailing me. She told him of course, he could but she didn't know how long it was going to take for Debby to get well.

A week after Thanksgiving, once I was safely back in Boston, I opened Jeff's emails to Debby. I emailed him to tell him my girlfriend who he met was a therapist and she insisted he showed signs of being a married man cheating on his wife. I told him never to contact me again. That was the end of Jeff B. I still have the many letters, cards and emails he sent me. Although many of my friends suggested I send them to his wife, I did not. She clearly is living with enough pain just having him for a husband.

While being single, I experienced other challenges. The house I had built on Fairmount Avenue had several floods. I was forced to pump knee-high water out of my finished basement on several occasions. I had tenants living in the basement apartment that either didn't pay rent or made demands on me for new carpeting or new appliances when none were needed. Three of the tenants reported me to the Town of Saugus for renting an "illegal" in-law apartment.

Another incident occurred when I was having my back deck rebuilt. The contractor increased the price by more than $1,000 after the contract was signed. I sued him in small claims court to defend myself from having to pay the increased cost. I

147

represented myself and won the case. The contractor was ordered to cease and desist and leave all the wood he purchased at my house and to stay away from me.

In 1990, I moved to another house just three doors away and rented my unit. The tenant stopped paying rent for six months and had my basement tenant removed from the apartment. My basement tenant was deaf and kept his television too loud. The upstairs tenant was annoyed. That incident, together with a picture of my house, was reported in the local newspaper. It brought to light the illegal use of in-law apartments to generate income in Saugus. Yes, I rented the apartment to non- relatives as I wanted to provide for my daughters without having to get on welfare and without losing my house.

Finally, the last set of tenants, Jim and Dena, moved into my house when they had one child and over the years had three more children. They asked to have Jim's mother rent the in-law apartment. I agreed she could. Once Jim's mother moved out and my nephew moved in, they complained to the town and stopped paying rent. They wanted the whole house (ten rooms) for the same rent. I was forced to file eviction papers and have them removed by the courts. It cost me over $11,000 in attorney fees and lost rent. I have a judgment against them which I will never collect on as I fear retaliation.

So, over the 31 years I owned the house, I had one robbery, six floods, was in litigation with the town twice and had four tenants who didn't pay rent for extended periods of time. I found myself in court for evictions and small claims. In 2008, I sold the house and moved to another part of town as I didn't want to be fighting those battles for the rest of my life. Sometimes it's best to just say "goodbye"!

Charlie

J met Charles W. Greenan, Jr. on February 23, 1984 at the Beachmont Veterans of Foreign Wars (VFW) Post in Revere. I was with my neighbor, Elaine. Her husband Jack, a Revere police officer, was on duty at a function there. Soon after our arrival, a master of ceremonies announced everyone should rise as the State Commander of the VFW, Commander Charles W. Greenan, Jr. was about to enter the room. Next thing I know, this handsome charming man sauntered by surrounded by his security team. I was naïve, I had no idea what it meant to be the State Commander of the VFW but I soon learned.

As the night went on, Elaine approached Commander Greenan and asked him if he wouldn't mind dancing with her friend Annie. I quickly found myself dancing with this man, who, later that evening followed me home! It was pleasant to have someone show interest in me after three years of being divorced and hearing from various would-be suitors comments along the lines of "You are nice but I don't want rug rats (referring to my children) in my life", or "I want to date you…but my dog and my mother come first".

Charlie was a charming, charismatic, friendly, warm, loving and humorous man --when sober. He told me that his former wife, Gilda, broke his heart when they divorced because she took his son Charles W. Greenan, III and moved to live in England. Charlie rarely got to see Charles III. It devastated him. Charlie had two children with a young woman named Cheri: James, age 3 and Meagan, age 1.

Charlie questioned James's paternity. He told me that Cheri had agreed to have a paternity test done to prove James was Charlie's child but he hadn't received the results yet. He knew Meagan was his daughter and loved her with all his heart. Charlie supported James and Meagan as best he could but didn't provide support for Charles III as Gilda was from a wealthy family and had plenty of resources from her parents.

Charlie likened himself to Irish poets who had lives of misery, ultimately dying in jail as alcoholics or by committing suicide. Charlie had a B.A. in English from Suffolk University and loved to read Shakespeare books aloud. Sometimes he changed his voice and acted out some of the parts. He was also a drinker and a gambler but entertaining and sweet.

We were guests of honor at several VFW functions almost every weekend. We always sat at the head table and I was gifted bouquets of flowers as I entered the function halls on Charlie's arm. We were introduced as State Commander Charles W. Greenan, Jr. and Miss Annie. We traveled all over the state of Massachusetts to VFW functions. We also attended the annual National VFW Convention in Dallas. I was the official driver of Charlie's Lincoln Town car as I was a non-drinker. His license plate was VFW 1. I enjoyed my weekends eating fabulous food and dancing.

I enjoyed the limelight while being the escort of the State Commander. I will never forget when Charlie was asked to throw the opening pitch at a Red Sox game at Fenway Park. I went and proudly sat next to him. They showed us on the large park screen. Jim Rice handed Charlie the ball and took pictures with us. Charlie threw the pitch and actually got it over the plate!

I was also excited to meet then Governor of Massachusetts Michael Dukakis and the Speaker of the House George Keverian. Charlie served as the Grand Marshall in many Veterans Day and Memorial Day parades. He insisted on walking the route. I followed in his Lincoln Town Car. We then were on the reviewing stands and were invited to the banquets that followed. How could a poor girl from Winthrop be having this much fun? I actually bought new outfits for each weekend. I felt uncomfortable buying myself anything as I needed all the money I had to save for my daughters' education and to keep us in our home!

My cousin Carla, who was attending law school in Boston, lived with me at the time. She was happy to babysit my daughters and enjoyed our bustling happy home. It was a fabulous arrangement for me. My daughters and I loved having my cousin living with us.

Soon thereafter, it was time to pay the piper! Good times don't last forever. When Carla moved into her own condominium, I was happy for her but sad for me. Around the same time, Charlie told me he was going to kill himself. Why on earth would someone who had so much going for him want to commit suicide? I thought perhaps it was the alcohol getting to him. He clearly was alcoholic drinking more than a dozen beers daily! Charlie had six siblings and he told me five of them were alcoholic as were his parents.

But, no, that wasn't it. Charlie confessed to me he had done something terribly wrong. He had committed a felony; he had embezzled money from the credit union where he worked as a loan officer. Cheri was putting pressure on him for more child support. He had spent all his money on alcohol and gambling. He said he knew it was just a matter of time before he would be arrested, have to stand trial and be sent to jail. I was shocked and didn't believe it would really happen. He knew he could not continue paying rent on his apartment while in jail so in July 1985, he asked if he could move his furniture into my basement and live with me. Then while he was "away", he wanted me to sell his stuff and send him money. I agreed.

Once Charlie moved in, the wait began. We didn't know when the long arm of the law would come knocking. Charlie quit his job hoping it might satisfy the credit union and perhaps avoid his arrest. He became my wife. When I was at work and my daughters were at school, Charlie did the laundry, cleaned the house, did yard work and gardening, and cooked our dinners. It was nice to come home to a set table with dinner served. Charlie refused to eat with us and would only eat anything we had leftover. He didn't want to take food out of the kids' mouths. Once I caught on to what he was doing, I just bought extra food as I sincerely appreciated all he was doing for me. He was there for my daughters if they had a day off from school. He was there for me to talk to at night. My family loved him. He was personable, came to all family functions and fit right in.

Then on January 24, 1986, Ms. Anne Toye, a probation officer, came knocking. She interviewed me for a couple of hours, asking about my relationship with Charlie and what kind of support he gave me to live with me. The answer was nothing as he had nothing to give. At the time, he was selling some of his possessions to get money. The social worker was concerned as to how I would get along should Charlie go to jail. The answer was simple: I would get by just as I had before he moved in! I didn't need Charlie for his money; I had more than he did.

On February 5, 1986, Charlie was sentenced to 6 months in jail and 3 years probation for embezzling funds from the Stone and Webster Credit Union. Charlie was temporarily sent to the Essex County Jail in Salem, MA. My brother Domenic was incarcerated in Salem at the same time so my mother and I visited the two of them together. That didn't last long.

Within a couple of weeks, Charlie was moved to the federal prison in Allenwood, Pennsylvania. In Allenwood, Charlie said he met men from the now famous Watergate Hotel break-in during the Nixon Administration. He specifically talked about John Dean but I have never been able to validate he was there at the same time.

In March 1986, Charlie was moved to the Federal Medical Center prison in Rochester, Minnesota. This prison specialized in the treatment of alcoholic federal offenders. I thought it was a perfect place to help Charlie get sober. Charlie only served four months. He was released on June 20, 1986 for good behavior. I wasn't surprised. Charlie had a knack for changing his personality and being a nice person when he wasn't under the influence of alcohol. While he was in prison, I sent Charlie money for cigarettes and soft drinks. What surprised me was Charlie's behavior once he was out of prison. Not knowing he was now a dry drunk, I welcomed Charlie back to the house.

Behind my back, Charlie started drinking again. Since I was at work and the kids were in school, Charlie had time to drink privately and destroy the evidence. When I was at home with him, in the evenings, he would use his silver tongue to be cutting and nasty to me. What had I done to deserve this treatment? Why was he acting out so badly? Why was he telling me how boring I was and negatively criticizing everything I said and did?

Initially, I just went to bed and tried to ignore him but when my neighbor told me he saw Charlie bringing cases of beer into my house, when I was at work, and Cheri coming to visit on multiple occasions, I asked Charlie to leave. By January 1987, he moved out. Charlie admitted he started drinking at 12:00 PM as if a bell went off in his head. He stopped drinking when I came home and continued drinking when I went to bed. He treated me nastily so I would go to bed!

Ann R. DiMare

**Charlie & Ann with Jim Rice
Fenway Park June 1985**

**Speaker of the House George Keverian, Ann
& Charle in Dallas, Texas August 1985**

May 22, 1985 in Governor Dukakis' Office at the State House in Boston

Saugus embezzler depicted as having dual personalities

BOSTON — A Saugus man, described by a U.S. District Court judge as having a dual personality, was sentenced to six months' imprisonment and three years' probation for embezzling credit union funds.

Charles W. Greenan Jr., 37, 136 Fairmount Ave., admitted Jan. 3 to embezzling $27,950 from the Stone & Webster Credit Union in Boston. At the time, Greenan was employed by the credit union as a loan officer.

According to court documents, Greenan created false loan accounts at the credit union which he converted to his own use. When confronted, Greenan confessed to embezzling the money in order to pay debts including some incurred because of gambling losses.

Some $10,000 of the stolen funds was also used to help purchase a luxury car from the Massachusetts Veterans of Foreign Wars. Greenan, who had been the state commander of the VFW, purchased the automobile at the time he left the post in June 1985.

"I don't feel I'm a true criminal," Greenan told federal Judge Mark Wolf. "I always had the intention of paying the money back," he said. He explained that he felt he was borrowing the money with full intention of paying the loan. However, gambling and alcohol dependency led to the crime, he said.

Judge Wolf told the defendant that he is a person with "two distinctly different dimensions." The positive dimension is the person who cares much for family and children and is active in community activities like the VFW. The other dimension is a man with debilitating drinking problems, a person who had financial responsibilities and abused them."

In handing down the sentence, Judge Wold also ordered Greenan to perform eight hours per week of community service during the remainder of a two-year suspended prison term and to enter an alcohol rehabilitation program.

154

A few years later when Charlie became sober, he rented my in-law apartment. He introduced me to his girlfriend Marie, her two daughters Amy and Amanda and her son James. Charlie, Marie, her daughters, my daughters and I enjoyed each other, often eating, partying and playing scrabble together in the back yard. In June 1993 Charlie and Marie got married. I was happy for them and attended their wedding. Charlie and Marie were later divorced. Marie and I are still good friends. Charlie passed away on October 14, 2010 after a brief battle with lung cancer. Charlie's daughter, Meagan, visited in December 2010. I gave her many pictures and mementos of my time with Charlie. We are keeping in contact with each other via Facebook.

Richard

I met Richard in August 1989 at a meeting in Washington D.C. He had expressed interest in my girlfriend Sandy and told me he had pursued her in the past but to no avail. I confirmed it with Sandy. She said they had had some dinners together but she just wasn't interested in him. He didn't wear a wedding ring so I assumed he was single. He certainly acted as if he were. We spent a lot of time talking mostly about the development of the training program we were developing for the FAA Flight Standards Service inspectors but also about our personal lives. I told Richard about my ex-husband's drug use and asked if he did drugs. He assured me he did not.

Richard was a bright, energetic, and engaged man when it came to his work. He had a passion for it. So, I requested him as a subject matter expert to help with a training development effort. He was all for it. He told me he was interested in getting away from his unhappy family life and was therefore willing to attend meetings in Boston and elsewhere. It turned out that Richard was married and had two young children living in Danville, California. He told me he had spent a lot of time working in Nevada. He had a female friend there who he had a relationship with despite his being married. I should have hesitated getting closer to him at that point but I didn't.

Over the next six months my girlfriend Sandy and I got repeated late night telephone calls. A whispering voice would threaten us and call us cruel names, swearing and cursing. Even when I was on travel for my work, the calls persisted. They scared my mother so much she suggested I get a tracer put on my telephone. My friend Jack suggested I have Richard check his home phone bills to see if the calls were coming from his home phone. I had no enemies and didn't know anyone who would make such disturbing calls.

Sandy and I also got calls at work, threatening to tell our supervisors what whores we were. Since we were getting the same calls, we knew the caller had seen our telephone numbers somewhere and was looking for information to find answers she didn't have. Jack assured me it was a woman since a man wouldn't have said the things she said. Jack said a man would have been soliciting for sex. I later learned the caller got my work phone number by calling my house and telling my daughter she was a friend of mine from high school and needed to talk to me. My daughter gave her my work phone number! When Richard got divorced, the calls ceased!

A year after we met, Richard asked to move east and be with me and my kids. Initially, I not only said no but *hell* no! He was still legally married and I wasn't going to be a home wrecker like Shirley. I told Richard that, if he was serious, he had to separate, file for divorce and live alone in California for a year. In October 1990 he moved out of his home. We had many opportunities to see each other because we worked on many of the same teams.

While living alone in California, Richard looked for positions in the New England area. He found one at the Regional Office and another at the Flight Standards District Office, but they wanted him to start in August 1991. So, on June 13, 1991 even though a year hadn't passed, I flew to San Francisco and after making a brief visit to his mom's grave, we started driving from San Francisco to Boston. Richard had lived apart from his family for only eight months but he had filed for divorce so I knew the marriage was over and I knew it wasn't because of me. Richard had been unfaithful before. I never thought he would be again.

On June 20, 1991, we arrived in Saugus to begin our life together. Richard missed his kids so we made arrangements for them to spend time in the summers with us. Cara and Deana were 14 and 12 at the time. Matthew and Liz were 11 and 10 at the time. I was confident the kids would get along. When Matt and Liz came to visit later that summer, Richard introduced them to me and my children but then took them to Washington D.C. to visit his brother. I was devastated as I was trying to form a "family". Richard was avoiding it. He wanted alone time with his children. I understood but was hurt nonetheless.

In November 1991, Richard expressed dissatisfaction with living in the house I had lived in with my ex-husband and Charlie. He pressured me to look for another house for us to move into. He said he would be helping with the expenses so we should be able to afford it. My daughters had no interest in leaving the neighborhood they had grown up in so I ended up buying a house at 2 Stonecrest Drive in Saugus, just three doors away from our house. This kept my daughters in the neighborhood and allowed me to oversee the former property as I intended to rent it rather than to sell it. I knew that my daughters were getting older and would someday marry. I thought it would have been nice to have one of them live in the old house and be close by, while still living in separate houses.

Deana, Liz, Cara
Matthew, RIchard
Ann

2 Stonecrest Drive Saugus, MA

When Matt and Liz were in California, Richard called them at least once a week. He found it tedious to call since he had to go through their mother to talk to them. When the kids came to visit in the summer of 1991 we were one happy family or so I thought.

In October 1992, Richard had a three week long business trip to San Francisco. I asked if I could go out to California over the Columbus Day weekend to see him, Matt and Liz. He said he wanted to spend time with his kids alone. I understood how much he missed them so I was okay with his decision. Over the two weekends Richard spent in San Francisco, he hardly called. I assumed he was off with his kids having fun so I didn't want to bother him.

When Richard returned home three weeks later, he was different. He started negatively criticizing many things I did. He put another phone line in my house for his personal use. He didn't want to spend time with me and my kids. He rudely walked away when people came to visit us. He went to bed without saying goodnight. I didn't know what was going on with him.

The day after Thanksgiving 1992, Richard asked me to go Christmas shopping with him early in the morning. He wanted to go to downtown Boston. When we got there at 7:00 AM, he told me to go my way and he would go his way and we could catch up with each other later in the afternoon. I was shocked. What was that all about? I swallowed my pride, got on the subway and went to my office. While there, I cried for hours and then called my daughter to ask for a ride home. She came to get me. Richard came home at 9:00 P.M. He showed me all the things he bought for his kids for Christmas. I was livid with his behavior earlier that day so I wasn't impressed with the gifts he bought. I kept asking him what was going on. He kept replying, "Nothing". I told him I thought we needed to sleep apart until he could treat me with more love.

That night he slept in the guest room. In the morning, I went downstairs to find him on the couch crying. I asked what the problem was. He blew me away with a revelation about how he cheated on me during his stay in San Francisco. He had spent the entire three weeks with a girl named Karen. He said he didn't know if he loved her. He had also seen her in Chicago earlier in November when they both attended a meeting at United Airlines to discuss the findings of their San Francisco inspection. When I asked about the details of his affair, he confessed to everything.

As I look back on it now, I kept asking the questions. He kept answering so perhaps my having too much information was my own fault. I learned that he had done everything sexually possible with this girl, so there was nothing sacred left about our relationship. His dilemma was that Karen was going to be in New York City for a week of training the following week. He wanted to go see her. What was I to do, but let him go? I was always told if you love something, set it free and if it comes back to you it is yours. If it doesn't, it never was yours so you are better off without it.

I told Richard he could go but I asked specifically when he would be leaving and when he would be returning. He said he would leave on Saturday and return the following Friday. I said, "That works for me. It will give me plenty of time to change the locks and put your stuff on the front lawn so when you return, you can find someplace else to live". Richard was shocked at my strength to say what I said. I even surprised myself. I then woke my daughter Cara and took her to church with me where I prayed to God for help. Cara rubbed my back and cried with me. She was disturbed yet another man I had given so much to treated me so badly. This was the third time my daughters saw me support a man only to be betrayed by him (their father, Charlie and now Richard).

When we got back to the house, Cara yelled at Richard, called him names and told him to get out of her mothers' house. Richard insisted this was between me and him. He had called Karen to tell her their relationship was off. He wanted to work it out with me. I had lived with my father's cheating and his lying. I wasn't about to live with Richard's. I told him we could go on living as roommates but I didn't know for how long as I wasn't sure I could ever get over what he did to our relationship. I should have put myself in therapy at the time but I didn't.

Instead, I encouraged Richard to go to college to get a degree. I thought his having to attend classes in the evenings would keep him from traveling and keep him out of trouble and away from Karen. Perhaps that is what really ended their relationship. I will never know.

Because of Richard's actions, I couldn't resume a loving sexual relationship with him.

We agreed to live together as friends. Richard went to school at Salem State College and I continued my work at Volpe, doing taxes, tutoring and teaching Christian doctrine classes. A year after he told me that he had cheated on me, Richard presented me with a beautiful pear shaped diamond ring. I told him I didn't plan to marry him but he wanted me to wear the ring anyways. Since I had been burnt three times, I believed I would never remarry. I accepted the ring and the new relationship with Richard as being my life's lot. I also increased Richard's room and board charges so I wouldn't feel used by him for a cheap place to live.

For the next six years, Richard and I ate dinners together and present ourselves publically as a couple. Our intimate relationship became nonexistent but our friendship stayed intact. Richard was there for me when my mother died in 1994. He treated my children well and was there for them when I traveled for business. In 1994, Richard came to Heidelberg, Germany with me for a week. We visited a lot of Germany, Paris and Switzerland during the weekend. In March 1995, Richard and I traveled to Greece and Italy. We visited Athens, Delphi, Patras, Brindisi, Ostuni, Rome, Florence and Tuscany. In March 1998, Richard came with me, my Uncle Joe, Aunt Mary and my DiMare cousins to Sicily.

As a child, Richard lived for about four years in Venezuela. He spoke fluent Spanish and could understand most of the French and Italian we heard spoken on our travels. Richard was a pleasure to travel with as we had similar interests in seeing how people in foreign countries lived. We also traveled to Grand Cayman, Kansas City, Washington, D.C., the baseball Hall of Fame in Cooperstown, Niagara Falls, Cleveland, Des Moines, Cheyenne, Salt lake City, Lake Tahoe and all over the state of Florida, including a trip to Disney World and New York City for New Year's Eve with his children and mine.

In July 1998, I was on a business trip to the West Coast. Over the telephone, Richard and I talked about my disappointments in our relationship. With everything said, within three days, he bought a home of his own in Newburyport, MA. When I came home, he told me he would be moving. We spent many hours crying together but it was probably for the best. Neither of us was prepared to or could give the other what they needed in a relationship.

Today, Richard is married to a woman he met at a support group meeting. He lives in the north shore area. His daughter Liz is married and lives in Washington. She is the proud mom of a beautiful baby girl. Liz and I still communicate via email. Richard's son, Matthew lives in the San Francisco area and his ex-wife Patsy and I are friends on Facebook, a social networking sight.

HALF BROTHERS

For almost 35 years, my mom suspected dad had more than one other child. Mom said Frances, dad's girlfriend, called more than once and told her she was pregnant with Dad's child. When we moved to California in 1958, dad appeared with a child and asked mom to adopt the child. He said it was Frances's baby so mom knew it was the child Frances had referred to in one of her phone calls. My half-brother Sal was born in July 1958 so we now know he was the baby presented to mom that year.

In 1992, my brother Chucky pursued finding out if there were indeed other siblings. He said he did it because he was annoyed by something Shirley told his wife Joan. According to Chucky, Shirley told Joan that two boys had shown up at her house claiming to be Sal's sons and that our dad had thrown them out. Knowing our dad would not have thrown them out, Chucky decided to seek the truth.

Using his legal expertise and an ability to act coyly (such a lawyer), he went to the Registry of Deeds/Archives in Boston and looked through the vital records of births there. Through further investigation and phone calls, he was able to find our half-brother Phil. Later, he had a conversation with our dad revealing the truth about our other two half-brothers. Our father insisted Chucky never tell me about the half brothers. He was determined to take the secret to his grave.

On December 29, 1992, (my mother's 63rd birthday), Dad and Chucky took me to lunch at Anthony's By the Sea in Swampscott. Slowly, through the course of the luncheon, they revealed the story of how Chucky found our three half-brothers. I was amazed at the double life dad had lived. Phil had been put up for adoption as an infant. Sal and Tony were raised in the Beachmont section of Revere, a few miles away from where we lived in Winthrop! Since they were in a different town we never crossed paths.

Chuck and dad told me the story then because my brother Tony planned to call me that evening. Tony had looked up my name and telephone number. He wanted to talk to his half-sister. By then Chucky had also planned a reunion with our brothers in Roseburg, Oregon. Phil was going to fly to Boston the next week to meet our dad. After a short visit, Phil and Chucky were going to fly to Oregon. Phil wanted to meet his mother Frances and Chucky wanted to meet our two half-brothers Sal and Tony.

It all makes sense to me now why on Christmas Eve 1992 at our mother's house, Chucky asked me if I would go on a vacation with him. He suggested we go for three days to the West Coast. I told him I had no interest in going to the West Coast but agreed to go with him to a warm and sunny destination. Little did I know, four days later, Chucky would reveal his findings and the purpose of the trip. Even if I had known the purpose of the trip I would not have gone. I didn't want to hurt my mother any more than she had already been hurt.

On January 5, 1993, Dad, Chucky and I went to the airport to meet Phil. When Phil deplaned and approached us, we knew immediately he was our sibling. Many of us walk like ducks. We keep our toes pointed outward. Phil walked like a duck too! Phil had a camcorder with him. When Dad and Phil first embraced, Phil said to dad, "I've waited my entire life to meet you. Thank you for coming". I cried as it was touching to see these two men showing emotion to each other. Emotion is something I hardly ever saw in my father. We spent the entire day visiting places Dad went with Frances, me taking snapshots, Phil taking movies of everything.

That night, we had dinner with my daughters and their boyfriends. On January 6, 1993, we went to Dom's restaurant in Worcester where Phil met Dom, Jacob and Max. On January 7, 1993, Chucky and Phil left for the west coast. They stopped in Chicago to meet Karen Boisvert. Karen was Frances's daughter from a previous relationship. Karen was born Kathy but was also put up for adoption. Her adoptive parents renamed her Karen. This was also Karen's first time meeting her mother Frances.

I considered Chucky's finding Phil and Karen an extraordinary gift to Frances. Chucky took a letter dad wrote and asked him to deliver to Frances. In the letter, he apologized to her for the mess he made of her life. He had given her three sons promising after each one to marry her some day but never kept his word to her. I was told Frances read the letter aloud at dinner that evening and declared our father was "full of shit". Phil videotaped many segments of their meeting and gave me a copy of the video. From time to time, I watch the video. I also consider Chucky's finding our half brothers a gift to me.

Unfortunately, dad met Shirley and married her. Had he not met Shirley, he might have married Frances after divorcing my mom. Most likely we would have met our half-brothers much sooner than we did and all of our lives might have been very different.

Ann R. DiMare

Sal, Tony, Phil, Chucky - January 1993

Phil, Chucky, Dad - January 5, 1993

*Chucky, Frances, Karen, Teresa, Phil, Mary (Frances'
Sister, Tony In front are Michael & Zachary
Photo taken in January 1993 in Roseburg, OR*

Robert Charles DiMare was born in Boston, MA on May 4, 1955 to dad and Frances. His adoptive parents renamed him Philip Charles Vaden. Phil lives in the Virginia area. He married Katherine Dickey and has two daughters Stefanie and Courtney. Phil and Kathy divorced. This photo of Phil and his daughters was taken in 1992.

Stefanie married Kenneth Milling on July 7, 2010. They have two sons: Devin and Jordan Milling. This picture shows Stefanie holding Jordan, Devin and Kenneth

Salvatore Robert DiMare, Jr. was born on July 5, 1958 in Los Angeles, CA to dad and Frances. Sal was named after our father. Sal married Rhonda Ledbetter. They have three sons: Andrew, Alex and Abraham. When I met Sal, he was the Pastor of a Four Square Gospel Church in Ellensburg, WA. Sal and Rhonda are now the Pastors of the Wenatchee Valley Praise Center in East Wenatchee, WA, where they still live.

Andrew married Sarah Vander Waal in August 2008. On July 15, 2010, they had a son August Robert DiMare.

Anthony "Tony" Francis DiMare was born on December 28, 1961 to dad and Frances. Tony married Teresa Lynn Fugate. They had two sons: Michael and Zachary. Tony is the Fire Marshall of his home town, Roseburg, Oregon. Teresa works as a travel agent.

Chucky told me Frances was a loving and kind lady. She was religious and brought the boys up as best she could. She put Karen and Phil up for adoption because our father promised to marry her if she did. She was in love with him and did as he asked. Similar to my mom, Frances would have done anything to keep our dad. He had charisma and good looks but little else to keep a woman happy.

In February 1993, while on a business trip to Washington D.C., I had dinner with Phil. I was excited to have a brother who wanted to spend time with me so we repeated visits on subsequent business trips in April, June and September that year.

In July 1993, Phil, Kathy, Stephanie and Courtney came to Boston. They stayed at my house in Saugus. Chucky, Joan, Jenna and Carina came to visit. Each day during their stay, dad came to visit as well. One day dad, Chucky and Phil went fishing. When they returned, dad cut and cleaned the fish, then made dinner for all of us. It was special for me as I don't have any other memories of my dad cooking for me.

In November 1993, Dad, Chucky and I went to Virginia. Tony and Teresa came from Oregon. Tony, Teresa and I stayed at Phil's house. Dad and Chucky stayed in a hotel. Dad told us that he told Shirley he was going to a refrigeration and air conditioning conference. He claimed he did that so he could spend two days with his children without any hassle from her. We helped cover for him by going to the conference and gathering free pens! We visited Mt. Vernon (in the rain) and many of the Washington monuments. We went to lunch at Tony-Joes and to a local library to do some family research. One night we went out to dinner and then went dancing. The second night, we played Monopoly at Phil's house and went in his outdoor Jacuzzi in the snow.

In July 1994, Tony, Teresa, Michael and Zachary came to Boston. We visited the Constitution and Faneuil Hall in Boston. Since they came during the 4th of July festivities, we also participated in relay races at the local park and went to Auntie Margie and Uncle Jim's for their annual July 4th BBQ. At the BBQ, Tony met many of his DiMare cousins, aunts and uncles.

In April 1996, I visited Phil again while on a business trip to Washington, D.C. Phil and I had dinner and discussed possibilities for uniting the whole family. I had not yet met our brother Sal and his family.

From July 23 to August 2, 1997, I had a business trip to Seattle. I was working on a project that required a dry-run and the Seattle office volunteered to help. Since I would be there over a weekend, Tony and Teresa came to Seattle and drove me to Ellensburg, Washington to meet Sal, Rhonda, Andrew, Alex and Abraham.

Kathy, Deana, Dad, Cara, Ann Jenna, Courtney, Stefanie, Joan & Carina - July 1993

Chucky, Stefanie, Dad, Courtney, Teresa, Ann, Kathy, Tony & Phil - November 1993 in Washington, D.C.

Zachary, Michael, Alex, Abraham & Andrew - July 1997

Tony, Ann & Sal - July 1997 in Ellensburg, WA

Phil, Sal, Ann & Tony - June 1998 Roseburg, OR

It was customary for Tony and Sal to loudly proclaim, "Let the festivities begin!" when they got together so I acted in kind and shouted it when we arrived. We had an amazing weekend filled with caring, sharing and love for each other. I learned my brothers enjoy playing cards as much as I do. We had a Hearts tournament. In order to show them I could hold my own, I beat them in many of the games.

We also went for a ride to the top of a local mountain. The views were incredible. I was thrilled to meet Sal and his family as I was willing to go anywhere with them despite my fear of high places. My nephews let me shoot their guns. I got the tin can down in the first shot. They were impressed! I noticed the mountains still had snow in July!

In order to spend even more time together, Sal brought his family to Seattle for a night. The boys enjoyed the pool and we went out to dinner. Tony and his family stayed in Seattle for a few more days. In the late afternoon (after work of course), we went boating on Puget Sound with my colleagues. I had an amazing time and truly felt loved as I had never felt before! I was sad we couldn't stay together forever!

In June 1998, I went to Roseburg, Oregon for the first time. Phil, Sal and Sal's family met me there. We celebrated Tony's college graduation. We visited Bandon and Coos Bay on the Pacific Coast. We traveled through a forest that was on fire. I was petrified. Tony knew the route to take to keep us out of harm's way. While there, Tony showed me his family photos from his childhood. I was amazed to see our dad in the exact same poses with Tony and his mom as the pictures my mom had from my childhood. Tony had pictures with dad at the beach and in front of their Christmas tree just as I did.

Over the next few years I traveled to Seattle several times as I was assigned a project working with the Boeing Company. I was developing training materials to teach the FAA inspectors how to identify suspected unapproved parts (SUPs). Whenever feasible, Tony and Sal would bring their families to the Seattle area to see me. I was always thrilled to see them and be able to watch my nephews grow.

I enjoyed having the boys call me Aunt Annie. I was close to Jacob and Max when they were youngsters. When my mother died (in 1994) I lost touch with Jacob and Max as well as with my nieces, Jenna and Carina. In June 1998, while I was in Seattle, Sal and Rhonda brought the boys to visit with me. Sal had a friend Dave who lived in the area so he was able to combine his visit with me to see Dave as well.

On one trip, I worked in Long Beach, California the week after I worked in Seattle so I drove from Seattle to Long Beach with some friends over the weekend. I was able to visit Tony and Teresa as I passed through their area. We met at the Seven Feather's Casino in Canyonville, Oregon, not too far from their house.

In July 1998, dad asked me to invite Karen (Frances's daughter) to lunch. He wanted to meet her and apologize for his part in her not growing up with her mom. Karen met us at the Hilltop Restaurant. Chucky joined us for the lunch. Dad commented on how much Karen looked like Frances when Frances was younger. He said she was beautiful.

In November 1998, Tony, Teresa, Michael and Zachary visited for Thanksgiving. I brought them to DiMare Lobster Company in Revere to get lobsters and meet some more of their cousins. There they met Ricky and Paul. During their visit, we went to the Saugus Iron Works and Salem. Phil, Stefanie and Courtney, Karen and her son Brian joined us for Thanksgiving dinner. Uncle Joe, Auntie Mary, Cousins Joey, Donna, Rick, Jonathan and Christopher stopped by as well.

In April 1999, I once again traveled to Seattle. Sal, Tony and their families came to my hotel to visit. The picture shows Sal wearing his Praise Center shirt, Ann wearing her FAA shirt and Tony wearing his fire department shirt. This was not planned! We are incredibly similar but then, we are siblings! Each of us is proud of our profession and is happy to display it!

In September 1999, I was diagnosed with a parotid gland tumor that required six hours of major surgery. I promised myself if I lived through the procedure, I was going to buy a condo in Fort Lauderdale, Florida as I had worked hard and deserved to have a piece of paradise to call my own. I had my surgery in October 1999 and from November 18-28, 1999, Teresa and I went to Florida to search for the perfect condo for me to live in when I retired.

Karen, Dad, Chucky & Ann July 1998 Hilltop Restaurant

Sal, Ann & Tony April 1999 Seattle, WA

Sal & Dom February 2000

Cara, Abraham, Andrew, Max, Deana, Jacob, & Alex February 2000

First, we visited Dad as Shirley was in Boston. Dad took us out on his boat and seemed to genuinely enjoy our visit. Teresa and I also visited South Beach and other area attractions. During our stay, Deana and Kristy came to Florida and for the first time since I was toddler, I had Thanksgiving dinner with my dad.

In February 2000, Sal brought his family to Boston. Dom, Laura, Jacob and Max joined us for a family dinner. This was Dom's first opportunity to meet Sal, Rhonda, Andrew, Alex and Abraham and for the cousins to meet each other.

On May 20, 2000, Cara and Deana graduated college. Tony and Teresa came to Boston for the graduation. The day before the party, Dad and Tony baked biscotti cookies together. Dad, Tony and Teresa came with me to Deana's ceremony at Bentley College. Cara's future in-laws went to her ceremony at Salem State College. We had a joint graduation party at the Saugus Knights of Columbus Hall. The day after the party, Michael and Lisa DiMare, people I met on the internet, came to meet everyone. Dad said we are not related to Michael and Lisa despite Michael and Tony looking exactly alike!

A year later, in May 2001, Phil, Sal, Tony and Teresa came to Cara and Dave's wedding. Phil brought Stefanie and Courtney with him. Sal, Tony and Teresa came without their children. We attended the rehearsal dinner at La Finestra Restaurant in Wakefield and Cara and Dave's wedding the night after.

On May 29, 2001, I went to Seattle to receive an FAA Good Friend Award. I was invited to bring a guest to the ceremony and the dinner. The FAA paid for me to stay in Seattle for the week as part of the award. I chose my brother Sal to accompany me. He was happy to oblige. When giving my acceptance speech after receiving my award, I mentioned how excited I was to be able to spend three days with my family. Sal brought his family to his friend Dave's house and we enjoyed loving family time together. What a blessing!

In June 2002, my boyfriend, Dick and I traveled to Washington D.C. to attend my niece Stefanie's High School graduation party. At the party, Kathy taught me how to eat crabs. I always knew how to get all the meat out of a lobster having come from two fishing families. This was my first time dissecting a crab.

In the fall of 2001, we decided to have a family reunion cruise in November 2002. Having a year's notice allowed everyone to plan and save money. Dad agreed to come with us. He and Shirley were divorced and living apart at that time. In the summer of 2002, when Shirley resumed living in Florida with dad, he backed out of his commitment to come. He told us it was because he couldn't afford the trip so we offered to pay for him. He still didn't come. We knew why!

Teresa, Deana, Dad, Cara, Tony
May 20, 2000

Chucky, Dad, Sal, Phil, Ann & Tony
La Finestra Restaurant May 4, 2001

The DiMare Family at Cara & David's Wedding May 5, 2001
Kneeling: Jenna, Carina, Stefanie, Courtney
1st Row: Cara, Ann, Sal, Joe, Jimmy, Charlie, Sherrie, Karen, Teresa
2nd Row: Deana, Joan, Chucky, Phil, Sal, Tony, Mary, Donna, Carla,
David, Margie, Bella, Dom Russo, Jay, Christopher

Sal, Phil, Ann, Chucky, Dom, Tony
Dad
May 5, 2001

We were disappointed but decided to do the cruise without him. From November 8-11, 2002, 24 of us sailed out of the Port of Miami on Carnival Cruise's Fascination boat. We made wonderful memories relaxing in the sun, swimming in the pools, eating, shopping, and visiting Atlantis in the Bahamas. When we returned, Sal and his family came to my condo. They helped clean a flood which occurred as a result of my air conditioner malfunctioning. The children fished off the dock in front of my condo.

Since we always enjoy being together, we look for opportunities to see each other. On September 24-26, 2004, we met in New Orleans. Tony and Teresa had booked a cruise sailing from New Orleans. Phil brought his girlfriend Diane and her parents. I brought Dick and Chucky had a friend meet us there. It was my first visit to New Orleans and most likely my last since a year later in September 2005, Hurricane Rita, a category 3 hurricane devastated the area causing more than $11 billion in damage.

On May 4, 2005 we reunited for a weekend in Washington D.C. to celebrate Phil's 50th birthday. Teresa's friend Tina joined us for the celebration.

On July 30, 2006 Teresa visited. Dick made a wonderful dinner for us. Dad came over to see Teresa. The following day, we picked Teresa's girlfriend Sharon up in Boston and toured the North End.

Our last big gathering was from July 3-6, 2008 in Wenatchee, WA followed by a visit to Roseburg, OR from July 6-10, 2008. We celebrated Sal's 50th birthday. We went to a candy factory and a dam on the Columbia River. We did a lot of eating. I bought Massachusetts T-shirts for everyone to wear so we could show we were a family.

On Sunday, July 6, we went to Sal's Church, the Wenatchee Valley Praise Center and observed our brother, Pastor Sal, celebrate Mass. Sal introduced each of us to the congregation and told everyone we were there to celebrate his 50th birthday. Rhonda and my three nephews played instruments and sang praises to God. What an incredibly talented family they have. We also met Andrew's fiancée Sarah. They were married in August 2008. In July 2010, they had their first child and named him August Robert DiMare.

From Wenatchee, I went to Tony and Teresa's house in Roseburg, Oregon. I spent three days relaxing and hanging out with my nephew Michael. We talked a lot and went swimming at the Country Club where Tony plays golf. I caddied for Tony one morning. I met Teresa's dad and step-mom, her horses, chickens and wiener dogs, picked cherries off their cherry trees, drove Tony's tractor and went blueberry picking. I knew Dick would be thrilled if I came home with some fresh fruit. I was amazed that every morning before the sun rose, Teresa bravely took her flashlight and fed her animals. I could hear the crickets and the rooster hadn't crowed yet!

In November 2010, Michael, Tony and Teresa visited with me in Fort Lauderdale. Michael and I spent 5 days together. Tony, Teresa, Dick and I went to the DiMare Tomato plant in Florida City.

We are hoping to get together every couple of years and look for opportunities to gather. We have already planned our next visit for January 2012 to celebrate Tony's 50th birthday. Every visit with my half-brothers and their families has meant more to me than they can possibly imagine. They are the family I never had with my full brothers. There are no hidden agendas when we are together. We genuinely enjoy each other's company. They are honest, real and loving people with loving spouses and children.

I understand our dad has limited his communication with my half-brothers and their families to an occasional email, card or phone call.

September 24-26, 2004 New Orleans, LA

Bahama Cruise November 2002

July 3, 2008 Wenatchee, WA

July 3, 2008 Wenatchee, WA
Visiting a candy factory

July 5, 2008 (Sal's Birthda)
Watching Fireworks Wenatchee, WA

Michael & Auntie Ann
July 9, 2008 Roseburg, OR

Ann & Tony
November 2010 in
Florida City, FL

On January 28, 1994, Dr. Milton Henderson performed laparoscopic gallbladder surgery on Mom (this procedure was new) at the Melrose-Wakefield Hospital in Melrose. After performing the surgery, he left for vacation. The covering physician was Dr. Louis Alfano Jr.

On January 29, after mom had a violent reaction to the pain medication, Dr. Alfano tried to discharge her from the hospital. Mom told me she was put on Percocet and she had been hallucinating through the night. She said she was scared and nervous. When I arrived at the hospital to get her, she was all dressed and ready to go. When I saw the condition she was in, I spoke to a nurse about keeping mom one more day. Actually, I refused to take her out as Mom lived alone and was under heavy pain medication. On January 30, a nurse called and told me I had to get mom as they were discharging her. The nurse said she was physically fine and the hospital was not a convalescent home. I went to the hospital and took mom home.

On January 31, I visited her. She had still not moved her bowels and was extremely bloated. Over the next three days, Mom made repeated calls to Dr. Alfano for help. He told her to drink water and take Tylenol for pain or discomfort. He told her to stop the pain medication as it may have been causing her constipation. On Friday, February 4, 1994, Mom had a follow up visit with Dr. Alfano in his office. He told her to take milk of magnesia or Maalox to help move her bowels.

Later that evening mom called Dr. Alfano in severe pain as the pain was moving to her stomach. He told her to drink Gatorade. Mom was 64 years old but she appeared to be 84 (her mother's age at the time). She had lost a tremendous amount of weight and was extremely weak. Dr. Alfano told my mother there was nothing more they could do for her. He scheduled her for a follow up visit on February 15 with Dr. Henderson as Dr. Henderson would be back from vacation by then. Dr. Alfano then went on vacation himself, leaving my mother in the care of a third physician, Dr. Thomas.

Each day at home, mom ate a light diet of soup and crackers. Each time I saw her, she looked sicker and sicker. I asked if I could take her back to the hospital but she said, "No, they called me a baby and I don't want to go back there".

At this time in my life, I was taking swimming lessons on Monday nights (still trying to overcome my fear of the water), working full time at the Volpe Center, bringing Deana to Saugus High School basketball practices, games and physical therapy (for a sprained ankle), doing income tax returns and tutoring high school children in math two to three days a week. During the week, I called my mother each day. She told me about her visitors (her sister Winnie, Connie Monaco, her girlfriends). Feeling a bit guilty at not spending quality time with mom, I dedicated my entire weekend of February 4-6 to helping her.

During that weekend, we had some pretty heavy discussions about her life, her mother, our relationship, my life, my brothers, my father and people in general. She showed me where all her paperwork was in the event of her untimely death. She told me to check through pockets and hems for rainy day money. She told me she wanted me to administer her estate. She said she didn't want any of her jewelry to go to my sisters-in-law as they had their mothers to give them their stuff. I was her only daughter. She wanted me to have it all. I later learned that only a couple pieces of my mom's jewelry was real gold or silver although I am sure she thought it all was.

Mom told me that when she died, I would see what my father and brothers were really all about. She warned me that I viewed the world through rose-colored glasses and I thought everyone was nice. She told me my father and brothers were selfish and cold blooded, as she said most men were and they would transfer the hatred they had for her to me as they simply hated and had no respect for women. I kept trying to relax her by telling her she wasn't going anywhere and that she would get better with each day. As a child I always thought my mom favored Chuck because he was the oldest and Dom because he was the baby. I learned differently over that weekend.

On Sunday, February 6, my aunt Lillian and I were visiting with my mom. She was in extreme pain. She still had not had a bowel movement (9 days post-op). Auntie Lillian and I begged her to let us take her to the hospital. She still refused. I told her I wouldn't be able to see her on Monday or Tuesday but if she were still in pain on Wednesday, February 9, I was taking her back to the hospital whether she liked it or not. She agreed.

On February 7, I went to work at my contractor's office in Arlington. On my way home to get Deana for physical therapy, I got a telephone call from my officemate, Donna. Donna told me my mom had called screaming on my answering machine. She was not feeling well and had thrown up. She wanted me to change her bed sheets. I immediately called her back. By then, her girlfriend Gloria had arrived to help. Gloria told me she had changed mom's sheets and was getting mom back into bed. Mom had taken a shower and told Gloria she felt better to get all the stuff out of her. She still hadn't had a bowel movement (10 days post op) and she wasn't urinating. Gloria stayed with her until 4:00 P.M. Mary, her tenant saw her at 5:00 P.M. and she said she felt better.

That afternoon, I got Deana and took her to a physical therapy session for her sprained ankle from playing basketball. I then went home, fed my daughters and did a tax return before going to my swimming lesson. I got home from swimming at 9:00 P.M. and called my mom before going to bed. I apologized for not being able to go over but told her what I had done that afternoon. She replied, "That's okay, you would have been no good to me anyways".

On February 8, 1994 and every year since then, I have relived the horror of that day. It was a freezing cold winter day. I called my mom's house at about 7:00 A.M. There was no answer. I figured she was in the bathroom or may have taken the phone off the hook so she could get some sleep. I waited a short time and called her back. When there was no answer at 8:00 A.M., I thought perhaps she felt better and had gone out with her girlfriend or one of my aunts (Winnie or Lillian) for breakfast. When there was still no answer at 11:00 A.M., I called my aunt Winnie then called my aunt Lillian. There was no answer at either of their houses.

I then thought maybe her doctor's appointment was today and not on Friday so I called the doctor's offices (Dr. Henderson and Dr. Alfano). She wasn't at either place and didn't have scheduled appointments with them. I then called Melrose Wakefield Hospital to see if they had admitted her in the emergency room there. They said no they had not.

I then called my cousin Joan to see where her parents were. She said they were at the senior citizens center in East Boston and my mom was not with them. I called my aunt Winnie back but still there was no answer. By this time, I was frantic so I called my daughters. They were home from school due to a snow storm. I told them I couldn't get a hold of my mom and I was coming home from work to get her key so we could go to her house and make sure everything was okay.

Deana told me Mary, my mother's tenant called and was also concerned as my mom wasn't answering the phone when she tried to call her. Deana gave Mary my car phone number and she called me. Mary told me she hadn't been able to reach mom but her television volume was up and perhaps she just didn't hear the phone ring. I thought my mother was angry with me and trying to punish me by not answering the phone. I told Mary I was going to get my daughters and the key to my mother's house and I would meet her there.

By 12:00 P.M., I had picked Cara and Deana up and we went to my mother's house with her key in hand. As I put the key in the keyhole, the door popped open. I immediately smelled a stench as I had never smelled before. I had Deana in front of me and Cara behind me. We walked like a train from room to room. As we entered Mom's bedroom, Deana let out a scream. "Ma, she's on the floor!" We looked in the room to find my mother with her head against her bathroom door, with a beautiful smile on her face. I knew she had seen Jesus and he had guided her safely to heaven.

I immediately called 911. The Saugus fire department responded within minutes but it seemed like forever. The girls and I sat in the kitchen as they tried to revive my mother. I called Chucky. He stayed on the line and talked to Deana and Lt. Cataldo. Police Officer McGrath came and stayed with us as well. Then one of the Firemen approached me asking, "How old was your mother?" I knew he meant she was deceased. I started to vomit. I had never and have still never felt as sick as I did that day.

Officer McGrath told me to call a funeral home since the medical examiner was not going to come over because of the terrible weather conditions. He asked me about my mom's medical history and relayed the information to the medical examiner on the phone. The medical examiner was Dr. Schub. He asked to talk to me. He told me my mother appeared to die of natural causes. I told him I didn't believe him as my mom was a fairly healthy woman. I told him my brother wanted an autopsy performed. He said he wasn't going to order an autopsy since all indications were she died of a heart attack.

I called Chucky back and asked him to come help me with the arrangements. He said he couldn't. I then called Dom and asked him to come. He too said he couldn't. Both agreed to come the next day after I had made all the arrangements for the wake and funeral. Neither had been in contact with our mother since Christmas Eve 1993. Neither had come to her birthday party on December 29, 1993. Neither had come to the hospital when she had her surgery and neither was willing to come now that she died. So, I called my aunt Winnie and my aunt Lillian. They both arrived at my mom's house within the hour and we waited for Caggiano's Funeral home to come get mom's body.

When Mr. Caggiano, the funeral director, arrived, he asked if we wanted an autopsy done to determine my mother's cause of death, I called my brother Chucky back. He said, "Of course we do". Chucky told me he intended to sue the doctor for mom's death. He wanted to be sure he had the proof he needed to go forward against the doctor and the hospital. He believed the autopsy would provide him the proof.

My aunts, uncles, daughters and I went in mom's dining room and waited for them to take my mother's body out to the hearse. We then all went to the funeral parlor to pick out her casket and make arrangements for her wake and funeral. My mom's will stated she wanted to be buried with her sister, Joann. She had told me that on the Sunday as well. I knew I needed to get in touch with my Uncle Freddy. I called him from the funeral parlor. He agreed to sign paperwork to grant mom her wish.

When I arrived home that evening, I called my father to tell him my mom had passed away. I will never forget the painful words he said; they have echoed in my mind over the years, **"This is the happiest day of my life"**. Not knowing how to respond, I just hung up the phone. I later learned my brother Chucky had already called our father to tell him the news.

The next day, my brothers went to my mother's house prior to showing up at the funeral home for her wake. Chucky brought undelivered Christmas gifts from our mother's house with him to the funeral parlor to deliver to people who hadn't yet seen our mother for Christmas. After the wake, Chucky and Dom came to my house for a short while. I read them Mom's will. It was a page and a half long with three paragraphs. It was written in February 1975, when Chucky lived in Vermont and Dom was addicted to drugs.

I, CARMELA C. SICUSO, of Winthrop, Massachusetts declare this to be my last will, hereby revoking all prior wills and codicils.

After the payment of my debts and expenses, I give, devise and bequeath as follows:

FIRST: All my estate, real or personal, wherever situated, in equal shares to such of my children as are living at my death, to Charles J. DiMare, of South Royalton, Vermont; Ann R. Fulchino, of Revere, Massachusetts; and Domenic J. DiMare, of Winthrop, Massachusetts and the issue then living of any who shall have predeceased me, such issue taking the share which their parent would have taken if he or she had survived me.

SECOND: I request that my body be buried in the lot in Winthrop Cemetery where my sister, JoAnn Battista, is buried and my name and date of death be inscribed upon a marker in said lot.

THIRD: I nominate and appoint my daughter, Ann R. Fulchino, to be the executrix of this will and if she fails or ceases to serve, her brother, Charles J. DiMare to be the executor in her place; and request that they or whoever is appointed to complete the settlement of my estate be exempt from giving bond or sureties on their bonds. I confer upon my executor or upon any person who may be appointed to complete the settlement of my estate full power to sell any and all real or personal property at public or private sale, without order or license from any court, and to execute and deliver all deeds and instruments necessary therefore.

IN TESTIMONY WHEREOF I hereto set my hand and in the presence of three witnesses declare this to be my last will this 26th day of February 1975.

Carmela C. Sicuso

On this 26th day of February 1975, CARMELA C. SICUSO, of Winthrop, Massachusetts signed the foregoing instrument in our presence, declaring it to be her last will; and as witnesses thereto we three do now at her request, in her presence, and in the presence of each other, hereto subscribe our names.

Joseph Indresano	of	3. Locust st Winthrop
	of	
Robert	of	63 Pine St, Winthrop, Mass.

-2-

Chucky's immediate reaction was to tell me I wasn't an attorney and I had no knowledge of how to administer an estate. He said since he was an attorney, I should allow him to administer the estate. When I refused, he said, "then let my wife Joan do it since she is an attorney". I again refused. Later Chucky said some harsh words to me regarding suing me if I were to take any fees for administering the estate. I told him Ma wanted me to administer the estate and I intended to do it. He stated, "Mom is dead. It doesn't matter if you let me do it. She will never know". I told Chucky I would know and I needed to do what her will requested. I saw a different side of Chucky that day and frankly, I was disappointed.

After the first evening's wake, my brothers returned to my mom's house. Dom spent the evening there as we had yet another day for the wake. The funeral would be on the Friday, February 11. When Dom returned in the morning, he told me Chucky and Joan had ransacked my mom's house, packed boxes of her possessions and put them in their car. When I asked Chucky about this, he said he only took gifts he had given mom through the years.

At the time of our mom's death, Chucky owed my mom about $23,000 as she had paid for some of his law school. He was paying her back at about $20 a month. His initial loan was for $25,000. Dom owed our mom about $6,000. Mom had spent $9,000 to make an apartment in the basement of her house for Dom as he had no place to live. In lieu of rent, Dom was paying back the loan. Dom was sending approximately $100 a month to mom even though he wasn't living in the apartment any more.

After my reading mom's will, Chucky and Dom asked about their loans. I immediately excused them from having to pay back as mom was now deceased. Had I known that later my brother Chucky would maliciously accuse me of stealing from my mom's estate despite my having done everything totally above board and under the direction on two pro-bono attorneys (my cousin Carla and an attorney at my office), I may have done something differently.

187

Mom was buried on February 11, 1994. It was a frigid cold snowy day. My life changed that day and has never been the same. I no longer see the world through rose-colored glasses. I see the cruel reality of how my mother's complaints through the years regarding my brothers and my father were totally justified. In retrospect, I wish she could have sought therapy to not allow them to hurt her as they did.

Following my mother's death, I cleaned her house and got her affairs in order. My daughter's Deana and Cara came with me every Saturday for over a year to do this. The town of Saugus only allows ten bags be put curbside for pickup each week so every Saturday morning, we would go to my mom's house and put ten bags out, then return the following week. I asked Chucky and Dom to come help me with this overwhelming chore but neither would.

Once I had donated mom's clothes, I asked my brothers what they wanted from her estate. Chucky asked for her hope chest, a gift from my dad to mom during their courtship, all the family photo albums, mom's jewelry, mom's car and guns that were in the hope chest. The guns belonged to our step-dad, Joe who was deceased in 1973.

Dom asked for her living room furniture, dining room furniture, and box spring and mattress, along with some dishes and other culinary utensils. I took her bedroom set and her ten-year-old Ford Escort (which she had paid $2,000 for in 1984), as a gift to my daughter Deana for all her help in cleaning out the house. I made a listing of what I had given each of my brothers as part of the settlement of the estate. Chucky was extremely angry about my gifting the car to Deana, his niece and Godchild. He said he wanted to keep the car for his daughter, Jenna. Deana was 16 years old when my mom died. Jenna was 7 years old. Chucky said he would put the car on cinder blocks in his driveway and give it to Jenna when she was old enough to drive.

When Chucky insisted on having mom's jewelry and all the photo albums, I relented by giving him a shoebox full of her costume jewelry and 12 photo albums. These albums included pictures from 1947-1974, my mom's wedding albums (to my dad and Joe Sicuso), my grandparents wedding picture and 50th anniversary album, my mom's vacation pictures from her trips to Italy and all her written calendars from 1975 to 1994.

Chucky told me he would preserve the albums and scan pictures for me whenever I wanted them. Over the years I asked for various pictures from time to time but never got any. In January 2009, when I asked for my childhood album, Chucky couldn't find the album with all my childhood pictures. Fortunately for me, I kept a few pictures to show my children and grandchildren prior to giving Chucky the albums.

Chucky wanted to sue the doctor and the hospital after my mother's death. Since I was the Administrator of the estate, he had me running around gathering mom's medical records and sending them to his friend, Attorney Clyde Bergstresser, a medical malpractice attorney in Boston. Chucky was confident we could sue for $3,000,000 and we would win the case or at least plea bargain for a lesser but substantial amount. I was amazed he was trying to exploit our mother's death to get rich but I went along for fear of his wrath if I hadn't.

I met him in Boston at Clyde's office and signed the necessary paperwork to initiate the suit. After researching the case, Attorney Bergstresser decided not to move forward with the suit because he couldn't find any physicians willing to testify against Dr. Alfano. He claimed it was because in their reading of the autopsy report, there was no concluding remark that stated emphatically the cause of death. Even though the death certificate said "peritonitis", the autopsy report didn't concur with that finding. The law suit was dropped and I was left with an attorney bill to pay. By the time the suit was dropped, I had already distributed the estate monies and Chucky refused to pay any of the legal bills so I paid a portion of the bill from my own money.

Ann R. DiMare

As the months went on following mom's death, I gathered documents needed to administer her estate. I got help from attorneys and accountants. I took every step required by the Essex Probate Court to properly administer the estate. This all took time. By May 1995, I was ready to close out mom's estate. I was later told I had done a remarkable job as if it were being done by an attorney it would have taken a few years to settle and cost approximately ten percent of the value of the estate.

My father told me that Chucky said some nasty things about me during the administration process. He said Chuck insisted I had conned our mother into naming me as Administrator. Chucky wasn't acknowledging he had left our mother behind in 1969 when she married Joe and in 1975, when mom made her will, he was not in her life, with the exception of a few visits each year. Chucky also didn't know that when mom needed money, she borrowed it from me.

Chucky continued to show his true colors when he wrote a letter to our dad and Shirley telling them what an evil person I allegedly was. Because Shirley thrived on making other people fight, she called me and read me the letter. Dad took pleasure in telling me Chucky thought I was a thief and I had stolen money from my mother's estate. Dad said, "Chucky told me he didn't know how you did it but he knew you did."

Through the years, Dad and Shirley kept encouraging a bad relationship between me and Chucky. Or perhaps Chucky really said and did what they claim he did. Clearly, Chucky forgot about the $23,000 I pardoned him from paying to mom's estate. As Shakespeare said, he "doth protest too much". Chucky needed to look himself in the mirror, but similar to dad, to my knowledge, he never did.

When mom died, perhaps in her honor, I literally started seeing her in the mirror every time I looked. Up until her death, I always thought my looks emulated my father. When mom died, I started having weight problems as she did. I started being weak and doing more for others than I did for myself, as she did. I started taking the abuse from my father and brothers that she predicted they would bestow on me. No matter how badly they treated me, I accepted them in my life and treated them with respect.

Later in 1994, Chucky hosted an open house at his new house in Amherst and invited everyone in the family except me and my daughters to attend. My female cousins didn't go as they were annoyed with Chucky's hateful ways and attitude. My male cousins, aunts and uncles went. Unfortunately Chuck's choices led my family and his family to be estranged from each other for many years. This resulted in my daughters not knowing their cousins and my not knowing my nieces. Both my nieces were special to me. Jenna was born on my birthday. Carina was my Godchild.

In January 2009, 15 years after our mother's death, Chucky invited me to his house. Prayer helped me through those years. When I heard Chucky's name mentioned, I would instantly say the Serenity Prayer: "Lord grant me the serenity to accept the things I cannot change, the courage to change the things I can and the wisdom to know the difference". To this day, that prayer comes to mind when I think of Chucky's behavior following my mother's death. It is still a prayer I say on a daily basis.

When mom passed away, my brothers and I each took some of her furniture. Everything mom owned is now considered an antique as most of her possessions were purchased in the early 1950s. I have my mother's bedroom set, her wedding gown and her mother's ring along with a ceramic nativity set mom made in ceramic classes. Dom has her living room and dining room sets, which belonged to Joe Sicuso. They were probably purchased in the 1940s or earlier. Chucky has the hope chest and most of the family photo albums. Unfortunately, he has misplaced some of them.

This picture was taken in September 1993 at the Eastpointe nursing home in Chelsea, where my grandmother was living. It is the last picture taken with my mother and grandmother. It includes 4 generations: Mom, Cara, Nana Josephine Faro, Deana and me. During my visits to my grandmother after my mom's death, I told my grandmother that my mom (her daughter) was working as my aunts and uncles didn't want me to tell her mom was deceased.

This is my aunt Joann and mom's gravestone at Winthrop
Cemetery. From time to time, I visit the cemetery and decorate
their grave with flowers. Mom would be pleased to know I carried
out the wishes in her will. She is buried with her sister. Her name,
birth year and death year are inscribed on the stone, as she asked.
To the left of her their gravestone is my aunt Lillian and my uncle,
Angelo's grave stone, although they are not yet deceased. To
the right of their gravestone, my grandfather Domenic and my
grandmother Josephine are buried. A short distance away in the
cemetery is my aunt Winnie, my uncle Sam and cousin Sammy's
grave. Many of my mom's cousins are also in the area, as is my
cousin Domenic's son, who died at birth.

PAROTID GLAND TUMOR SURGERY

*I*n September 1999, I was scheduled for my annual exam with my gynecologist and my primary care physician on the same day. I visited my gynecologist first and asked him about a little lump on my face. It was the size of a pea and located to the left of my nose. He suggested I show it to my primary care physician. He thought it was a tumor or a cyst. After leaving his office, I went to see my primary care physician, Dr. Alla Feygina. She measured the lump and told me to return in two weeks. When I returned, she called the Mass Eye and Ear clinic in Stoneham and asked for an immediate appointment. The tumor had doubled in size and was now the size of a grape. Dr. Richard Bowling saw me that afternoon and scheduled me for a parotidectomy at the Melrose-Wakefield Hospital. He assured me the surgery would be successful but indicated he wouldn't know if the tumor was benign or malignant until after it was removed and a pathology study done.

Prior to my surgery, I made arrangements for friends to help my daughters in case of my untimely death. Neither my father nor either of my brothers came to see me nor called me. I wasn't surprised based on what had transpired since my mother's death. The words she said before she died kept resonating in my head.

I had the surgery on October 12, 1999 and remained in the hospital for seven days. The surgery lasted six hours while the doctors "peeled" open my face to snip the tumor and its tentacles out of it. The surgery was successful. I was left with slight paralysis on the left side of my face. The tumor was benign. I stayed at home recovering for six weeks. During that time I had many visitors including aunts, uncles and some cousins along with my friends, my daughters and my daughters' friends. I got plenty of phone calls, flowers and cards. I learned who really cared about me and who would be there for me when the chips were down. I also learned my mom was a lot smarter than people gave her credit for being. She saw things clearly even though she acted as if she didn't.

Shortly after the Parotid gland surgery, in January 2000, I needed surgery to remove my left ovary. These surgeries made me rethink my life. I was fiscally responsible, always saving for a rainy day. I decided it was time to start living some of my dreams.

In 1971, I went on my first vacation with friends to Fort Lauderdale, FL. We went for spring semester break even though we were still in high school. From then on, I dreamed of the day I would buy a place there to retreat to. I considered Fort Lauderdale to be heaven on earth. After my surgeries, I knew it was time to get serious about buying my piece of Paradise!

On March 14, 2000 (my 47th birthday), I put a deposit on a condo at 2700 Yacht Club Boulevard on the Inter-coastal Waterway in Fort Lauderdale. I invited all my colleagues to dinner at Shooters and announced what I had done. We had a tremendous celebration. The condo has two bedrooms and two bathrooms, a galley kitchen, living room and dining room. My unit is called the "Fish Bowl" as it has water on three sides of it. The Inter-coastal is on the east and the south sides. The pool is on the west side. I am on the first floor. The condo was perfect for me!

My intention was to retire there someday so I looked for a community where I would be comfortable. My condo is located close to the beach, restaurants and shopping centers. I expected to take swimming lessons again, perhaps at the Swimming Hall of Fame. I also expected to go to a local college (down the street from the condo) and pursue more education in taxation.

When I purchased the condo, I started counting the days until my retirement. When I am in Fort Lauderdale, I have my close friends, peace, tranquility, sunshine and a lot of shopping! In June 2008, I retired and have found myself using the condo less than I had thought I would because my priorities shifted when I met Dick and when my grandson Logan was born.

**2700 Yacht Club Blvd.
Fort Lauderdale, FL**

view from my condo

Surgery scar

On October 24, 2005, Hurricane Wilma devastated the entire Fort Lauderdale area, including my condo. The windows on the west side were pushed into the condo by the force of the wind. My hurricane shutters were blown right off the building and into the adjacent inter-coastal waters of Coral Cove. When I arrived at my condo one week later, there was still no electricity in the area and the condo was flooded with water, plantation debris, bugs and glass. The furniture in my living room was a total loss as were my living room windows and shutters. For the next year, my condo was boarded up on the west side while I waited for my windows and shutters to be replaced. By the grace of God, nobody in our development was injured. We all learned that objects can be replaced.

t the turn of the century, I could see my life was about to change. Cara and Deana had both graduated college and were both professionally employed. Cara was about to get married and move out of the house. Deana had already moved to an apartment in Medford. I became more interested in having another relationship than I had in a long time. I turned to God and prayed for a man who would value the same things I did (family, friends, religion, work and sports). I wanted a man who would go to church with me and put God in our lives. I wanted someone who would connect with me psychologically, physically and spiritually.

I chatted with Dick via love@aol on February 18, 2001. Our first meeting was on February 24, 2001. Dick suggested we have dinner at La Finestra restaurant in Wakefield. Since I knew Ro McLeod, the hostess there, and my daughter Cara's rehearsal dinner was scheduled there in May 2001, I figured it was a perfect location for a first date. I thought I could taste the food and decide what to order at the rehearsal dinner!

We met at 7:00 P.M. and at 11:00 P.M., we were the only two people left in the restaurant. We were still sitting there with plenty to say. When Dick excused himself to the restroom, Ro told me what happened prior to my arrival. Dick arrived at the restaurant at 6:00 PM and had a glass of wine at the bar. He was excited to be meeting me so he showed Ro my picture. He told her he was meeting an internet date. Ro didn't let on she knew me so Dick kept her entertained by telling her what he knew about me for the whole hour. When I arrived, Dick rushed to the door and led me back to the bar where he introduced me to Ro and said, "Isn't she pretty?" Ro agreed and brought us to our table.

In our early conversations, Dick and I shared much about our lives and our values, although Dick remained a bit reserved on some topics (where he worked, where he lived, what he did for work). We both valued family, friends, good food, an education and hard work. We were both middle children in our families. We both had fathers who left our moms and remarried. Both our fathers had other children. Both our moms raised three children. We both graduated from Northeastern University, and both had a daughter who attended Bentley College in Waltham.

In the beginning, Dick asked me out once during the week and on Saturday evenings. Dick reserved Thursday nights for dinner with his daughter Julie at a restaurant in North Andover (Orzo's) and Friday nights for his male friends to go to the North End of Boston for dinner and drinks. Saturday night was date night so he usually asked me out on Saturday nights. He presented himself as being a class above me so I suspected our relationship would never work as I was probably from the wrong side of the tracks!

Since I was proficient on the computer, I checked out "Richard Orlando" and learned a lot about him. On our second date, I asked leading questions to see if he was an honest man. For the most part, Dick answered honestly. He insisted he was a troubleshooter at Saztec International. I knew he was the Chief Executive Officer (CEO) and I knew his salary since Saztec was a public company. He insisted he lived on the North Shore of Boston. I knew he lived in North Andover. Dick prided himself on being a great communicator and mentioned Bob Davis, then CEO of Lycos, had authored a book where he gave Dick credit for teaching him how to communicate. Dick showed me the book to prove it. I was impressed.

Within a month of our meeting, I introduced Dick to my daughters. We were going to my nephew Jacob's wedding on March 17, 2001 and Dick was going to escort me to my daughter Cara's wedding on May 5, 2001, so I thought the time was right. My daughters immediately liked Dick. He had an outgoing personality, was entertaining and showed interest in them as people. Everyone was getting along extremely well, I was thrilled. In the past, if my daughters didn't like someone I was dating, I stopped liking them too. Since I was 48 years old, I was hoping to find someone I could settle down with for the rest of my life.

Dick wasn't ready to introduce me to his children until late May. On Memorial Day 2001, Dick brought me to his house in North Andover. I met his son Marc and Marc's wife Tina, Dick's daughters Lynn and Julie, and his granddaughter Hayley. Hayley was almost a year old at the time. Since then, Dick has had three other granddaughters. Sophia was born on June 1, 2001. Jenna was born on February 20, 2004 and Alexa was born on August 8, 2005.

I was immediately drawn to Tina. Tina was pregnant with her first child, who was born five days later. Tina reminded me of myself. She had an outgoing personality, was friendly, and made me feel instantly comfortable. She showed respect by including me in the conversation, asking my opinion of things and generally taking interest in me. Marc was friendly but reserved. He talked to me, although not to the extent that Tina did. He included me and took interest asking questions about my job, education and daughters. Lynn and Julie didn't have anything to say making me feel very uncomfortable.

On our way home from that visit, Dick made an odd comment. He said he needed to "protect his daughters at all costs". I didn't know what he meant. Over the next few years I learned. Dick chooses to avoid confrontation at all costs so he says very little. He says he knows he can't change people so he doesn't try. Dick has asked me not to take it personal and to forgive. I do forgive but I don't forget. Dick has never seen his four granddaughters together despite the oldest being 11 years old and the youngest being 6 years old. He told me it breaks his heart but he doesn't know what to do. He believes in time, relationships will work themselves out. Dick takes the high road. I put myself in psychotherapy in 2002 to learn how to deal with the situation. Thank goodness for Dr. Tedford.

Dick and I receive continuous unconditional love from Marc and Tina. They call at least once a week and always show respect to Dick and me. For our birthdays, they call and send gifts and cards. For all other holidays they do the same unless they are in Saugus to celebrate with us. They invite us to their home in Syracuse. Dick and I make three visits each year to Syracuse to see Marc, Tina, Sophia and Jenna. Tina's family treats us as if we are their family too, so we enjoy our visits. Marc brings his family to Saugus two to three times a year. My daughters come over when they are here as they have become friends too. Logan calls them Uncle Marc and Auntie Tina.

In February 2002, after both my daughters have moved out, I relocated back to Fairmount Avenue as the house on Stonecrest Drive was too big for me alone. In April 2002, Dick moved to a condo on Chatham Circle in North Andover. His new home was six miles further away than his old home. At first I thought he was giving me a hint that he wanted more single life but when he asked me to decorate the condo and included me in many decisions about the condo, I knew that wasn't the case.

I found myself spending weekends in North Andover and weekdays in my house in Saugus. If circumstances were different, I may have continued my visits to his condo for a long time but I was giving up precious time with my daughters to be there. In February 2004, I took my possessions, left the condo and refused to spend any more time there. Dick came to Saugus to see me and in June 2004, he sold the condo and moved to Saugus.

Dick and I enjoyed each other's company from the onset. We both enjoyed dinners with our friends and traveling. Our first trip was to Bar Harbor, Maine. We had a wonderful time. I was "hooked"! We loved it so much, we went back again. We travel to Fort Lauderdale and try to spend our New Year's Eve's there. We spent a few New Year's Eves in Boston and were asleep by 9:00 PM. In Fort Lauderdale, we ring in the New Year at the local Capital Grill after having a dinner at either Angelo's or Café Vico's. We have traveled together to Bermuda, the Bahamas, Turks and Caicos, Washington D.C., East Wenatchee, Las Vegas, Saratoga, Syracuse and New York City. We enjoy getting away with friends and family. Dick and I enjoy attending Patriots games, Red Sox games, Celtics games and Broadway in Boston plays together.

Dick enjoys cooking for his elderly dad and step-mom and for my daughters and their families. Dick shows love through his cooking. He is an amazing cook and enjoys cooking for me and my family. Dick and I cooked for Marc's 30th birthday and Sophia and Jenna's 1st birthday parties. We invited friends to the condo in North Andover. We planned the menu over two months in advance and had Marc and Tina test the recipes weeks ahead of the party. We made a great timpano! A timpano is an Italian baked pasta dish. It was featured in the movie *Big Night*.

On Mother's Day in 2006, the northeast area of the country was hit with a storm that caused tremendous flooding. Saugus was harder hit than most areas. When I awoke that day, I found my basement in about six inches of water that increased to about 18 inches during the course of the day. Deana was living in my basement at the time. All her possessions were destroyed as well. Dick, Cara, Deana and I spent the entire day trying to get rid of the water and safeguarding whatever possessions we could. This was the sixth flood I had experienced at this house and I knew it would be my last. I made up my mind that day I was going to move as soon as financially possible. If it had not been for my son-in-law, David's dad bringing over an industrial pump, we would have been there for weeks.

Two years later, the housing market was falling. I knew it was the right time to move. In June 2008, I put a deposit on 12 Kayla Drive in Saugus and sold Fairmount Avenue a couple of months later in August 2008. Dick and I still live at 12 Kayla Drive. Two years later, in August 2010, Deana and Sean bought the house next door to us. I love having my grandsons as neighbors!

On Christmas, 2008, Dick proposed to me and gave me a beautiful diamond ring. I accepted his proposal providing he protect me. I asked him to make out a will. It doesn't matter to me who he leaves his possessions to so long as I read his will and he signs a pre-nuptial agreement. I intend to leave him something of equal value to whatever he leaves me. I had been burnt too many times to have it any other way. We have been engaged for over two years. Dick told me it is special when I call him my fiancé. We are both very happy with our relationship and living arrangement.

Throughout my battle with cancer (see next section), Dick was my caretaker. I couldn't have asked for a better caretaker and life partner. We haven't married yet perhaps because we both have been hurt by love relationships in the past. I believe some day we will take the plunge but not until our life preservers are in place!

12 Kayla Drive Saugus, MA   *July 18, 2009 Dick's 60th Birthday*

Dick, Senator Scott Brown, Ann
April 3, 2011

ENDOMETRIAL CANCER

*I*n early October 2009, I experienced bleeding that caused me concern. I contacted my gynecologist, Dr. Steven Dakoyannis. He asked to see me immediately. He did a biopsy and ordered a Dilation and Curettage (D&C) procedure. The procedure was done on October 27, 2009. The next day, he called and asked to see me on October 30, 2009. I also had an appointment with Dr. Feygina that day. Since I suspected he was going to tell me the results of the D&C and I felt fine, I went alone.

As I left the development where I live, I couldn't help but to think I had it all. I live in a beautiful home with a wonderful man. I have two loving daughters and two loving sons-in-law. I have an adorable grandson and fabulous friends. The sun was shining. I have a condo in Florida, am retired and had my good health, or so I thought.

When Dr. Dakoyannis walked in the office, I immediately knew something was wrong since he didn't look me straight in the eye. He quietly said, "I don't know how to tell you this so I will just say it. You have cancer". I said, "I have what?" He said, "Ann, you have a high grade (3 of 3) endometrial cancer papillary serous carcinoma and clear cell carcinoma. These types usually develop in postmenopausal women and are more likely to metastasize and recur".

I went into shock and asked, "What does that mean?"
Dr. Dakoyannis said it meant I would need a radical hysterectomy, followed by radiation and chemotherapy. I started shaking and

tears started flowing from my eyes. I didn't hear anything else he said, except that he would schedule the surgery for when I returned from Florida. I had already told him I was going to Florida from November 1st to November 21st.

When I got in my car to drive to my next doctor's appointment, I cried uncontrollably and was nearly vomiting. I called Dick and Rita as I knew they would provide me the comfort and reassurance I needed. I begged God to let me live. Once again, I was too young to die. Dick left work immediately. Rita offered what help she could from Miami.

Later that day Dr. Dakoyannis's nurse called to tell me my surgery was scheduled for December 8th at Melrose Wakefield Hospital. Dr. Adel Hamid, Dr. Dakoyannis's college professor would perform the operation. They expected me to be in the hospital for a week. My recovery would take an additional four months. That just didn't fit well with my schedule but I accepted what he offered.

When Dick got home he insisted I move the surgery to be done as soon as possible and suggested I see another doctor for a second opinion. All I knew was I had an aggressive tumor and I trusted Dr. Dakoyannis with my life as he had assured me he wouldn't let me die. Also, Dr. Dakoyannis had performed my ovary surgery in January 2000. I also trusted Dr. Hamid, who I hadn't met yet, as he was the head of Gynecological Oncology at the Boston Medical Center and a professor at Boston University. He had to be good right?

I called Dr. Dakoyannis back and asked if we could reschedule the surgery for an earlier date. He gave me a date of November 24th providing I met Dr. Hamid on November 10th. Again I asked for a sooner date. If I met Dr. Hamid on November 10th, why couldn't I have the surgery right after the meeting? Since there was an operating room available on Friday November 13th at 10:00 AM, Dr. Dakoyannis scheduled my surgery for that day.

I then called my brother Tony to cancel our plans to get together for Thanksgiving as I would be recovering from surgery at that time. I know Tony called my father and told him about my condition because later that day, Chucky called me to ask if what dad told him was true. He asked, "Do you really have cancer? How did this happen?" That was in October 2009. I haven't seen my brother Chucky since then and haven't seen or heard from my father since July 2009.

The night before my surgery, my brother, Pastor Sal called me. We prayed together. I believe my faith in God and the prayers of my friends carried me through yet another obstacle in my life.

Dr. Dakoyannis assisted Dr. Hamid in performing a total abdominal hysterectomy, bilateral sappingo-oophorectomy, pelvic and peri-aortic node dissection and omentectomy. I was moved to room 501A by 4:30 PM and visitors started arriving. Dick stayed at the hospital throughout the day. I was in and out of consciousness. I know my daughters, their husbands and my girlfriends Joyce and Liz came but the visitor I remember the most was my grandson Logan. It was that evening he first uttered "NANA, NANA, NANA". At first I thought I was dreaming but later Deana confirmed he was indeed calling for me.

I was released from the hospital on November 17th with a walker, brace, portable potty and pain killers. I could barely walk and it hurt to laugh, cough turn over, talk, sneeze and sit up. My biggest fear, however, was infection. Since I was supposed to change my own bandages but couldn't bear the thought of looking at the 12-inch scar on my abdomen, I asked one of my tax clients (a registered nurse) to help me. She did. What an angel! I was home recuperating for over six weeks. I started reading the Bible.

Reading the Bible cover to cover was on my bucket list of things to do before I die so I figured there was no time like the present to get started. I was humbled by the outpouring of love from my friends, cousins, aunts, uncles, daughters and half-brothers.

After a couple of post-operative visits to Dr. Hamid, I met Dr. Anthony Russell at the Massachusetts General Hospital for my radiation therapy and Dr. Khatoon at the Hematology and Oncology Center in Stoneham, MA for my chemotherapy. On December 23, 2009, I had my first short hair cut in over 30 years. Dr. Khatoon told me I would lose my hair after my second chemo treatment but I refused to believe it. Instead of having it shaved off, I had it cut short just in case it didn't fall out.

On January 4, 2010, my daughter Cara's 33rd birthday, I had my first of three radiation treatments. My other treatments were on January 11 and January 20. On January 5, 2010, I had my first of three chemotherapy treatments. My other chemotherapy treatments were on January 26 and February 16. The day after each chemotherapy treatment, I returned to the chemo center for an injection of Neulasta to help rebuild the white blood cells destroyed by the chemotherapy.

By the middle of January, I started losing my hair in bunches. At first I laughed. By the end of the month I had patches of bald spots so I went to a hairdresser and had my head shaved. I cried for days. I couldn't help but to notice my perfectly shaped egg head appeared just in time for Easter! Neither of my daughters had any interest in seeing my bald head. Were they in denial their mom could be vulnerable? They were used to seeing me handle everything. Did I really hide the tears through the years so well?

December 23, 2009
Short Haircut

March 30, 2010
Wearing wig

July 9, 2010
Hair growing back!

I resorted to wearing a wig, and called myself Erika when I wore it, since that was the wig's given name at the wig shop.

In March 2010, a CT scan revealed blood clots in my stomach. I was put on Coumadin for the next five months along with six Levynox shots to break up the clots.

In May 2010, my hair started growing back. By July I had enough hair that I didn't have to wear the wig any longer. I am told I have a 90 percent chance of survival as I had both radiation and chemotherapy. If the cancer recurs, my survival chances drop to 30 percent.

In June 2010, I passed a kidney stone after two trips to the emergency room. In July 2010, I had a cystoscopy to determine the cause of my bleeding and on August 9, 2010, I had a stent put in my left kidney. While performing that surgery, my Urologist, Dr. Sidney Rubenstein, found yet another kidney stone. Each illness required more medicine and more doctor visits.

My next three CT scans showed no visible sign of cancer, no blood clots and no kidney stones or blockages. My oncologist has given me a clean bill of health and will order CT scans periodically over the next five years. For now, we are treating my neuropathy with over-the-counter creams and Metanx. Ladies and gentlemen: we need to do everything we can to help ourselves and educate others about the silent killer known as cancer.

Appendix B contains excerpts from my CaringBridge.com journal entries and guestbook messages. Rather than repeat the day-by-day details of my journey to wellness, you are welcome to read the Appendix. My blog has had over 8600 hits. People have left over 900 messages of love encouraging me to stay strong.

My life has changed forever. I pray daily. I keep stress out of my life as much as possible and am living each day to the fullest. I have joined a cancer support group in Winthrop called Survivors by the Sea and will continue to participate in American Cancer Society support and survival fund raisers. God bless you all for caring enough to read my book.

OBSTACLES I OVERCAME

A list of the obstacles I overcame to become the person I am today includes:

Having a broken leg as an infant
Being brought up by a single mom
Being from a divorced family and a minimal relationship with my father
Having a father who had no respect for women
Being brought up by Sicilian grandparents
Being brought up on welfare
Being raised in an environment where education wasn't important (being told not to go to college)
Having a father, mother, and brothers who all smoked (I never did)
Discrimination against Italian Americans
Discrimination against women
Moving our family at age 16 to a rival town
Losing my brothers at age 16
Working at age 16 in downtown Boston without safe transportation
Untimely death of my grandmother Anne, my aunt Joann and my mother
Being emotionally abused
Being physically battered
Finding 3 half brothers at 39 years of age
Having both parents remarry giving me 3 step-sisters
Jealousy of my step-mother
Lying father, husband and boyfriends
Being attacked on the way to classes at Boston State College

Alcohol and/or drug abuse by husband, boyfriends, father and brother
Cheating father, husband and boyfriends,
Boyfriends who expected me to support them financially
Boyfriends who gambled
Raising two daughters as a single mom
Litigation with tenants and contractors
Tenants who didn't pay rent
Floods in my house and condo
Hurricane hitting my condo
Sexual harassment at work
Glass ceiling at work
Medical issues throughout my life (multiple kidney stones, tumors and ovary surgeries, battle with cancer, rotted teeth as a child)
Cancer surgery, radiation and chemotherapy

One might think that, faced with this many obstacles, it would be nearly impossible to succeed. I took it as a challenge. Some have called me a maverick. I call myself persistent.

Despite almost any obstacles, *everyone* can succeed. I looked at people without an education who grew businesses. I looked at people with an education and asked how they invested. I asked my supervisors what I needed to do to get to the next level and I worked many hours at home for which I received no pay. I did this because I was a perfectionist and expected nothing but the best from myself. Some say, I was too detail-oriented and was too hard on myself. Perhaps I was at times but it's the end result that matters and in the end (I pray this isn't my end) I achieved and succeeded. I could have spent my life trying to heal from the hurt and pain of my family situation but instead I was adopted by other's families who gave me more love than I got from my own.

I still have not learned how to swim so I haven't overcome all the obstacles in my life. Perhaps I will overcome my fear of the water in time too. Right now, I am not up to the challenge, but as my grandsons learn how to swim, I may choose to learn with them.

Some say I have shown amazing strengths in bearing hardships and carrying burdens others wouldn't have carried. There were many times I cried but I had amazing friends, both male and female, that gave me a shoulder to cry on. They believed in me and taught me to believe in myself. I tried not to be selfish. I gave back. I was an ear to many. I learned to be an attentive listener. I gave my love unconditionally. There were many times I was frightened but I put a smile on my face and took the next step forward. I cried when I was happy and I cried when I was sad. My heart broke many times over when my friends and loved ones died. There were times I thought I had no strength left but something always brought me joy and hope. My daughters gave me unconditional love and God was always by my side.

LESSONS I LEARNED

Here is a list of many of the lessons I learned through the years. Some of them are well known clichés.

Acknowledge all that you have and be thankful.
Acknowledge each day as a blessing.
Advocate for yourself.
As a single parent, ask for help and help people who help you.
As a single parent, be prepared to do everything yourself.
Aspire to be more than you think you will ever achieve.
Be frugal.
Be generous with people who appreciate.
Be patient.
Be persistent.
Be the best person you can be.
Be true to yourself.
Be your own biggest supporter
Believe in miracles.
Changing your thoughts can change your reality.
Create and maintain your own happiness.
Cry with someone, it's more healing than crying alone.
Don't be lazy.
Don't carry guilt.
Don't do anything for the wrong reason.
Don't dwell on what "isn't".
Don't give anyone permission to treat you badly.
Don't go where you are not wanted.
Don't let anyone who doesn't love you get you to do something you don't want to do.
Don't let selfish people use you.

Don't listen to people who say "If I were you". They *aren't* you.
Don't listen to people who say, "You should" especially when they haven't!
Don't live to please others.
Don't tell people what's good for them. They won't believe you anyways.
Don't waste money.
Don't waste time.
Don't worry. Be happy.
Embrace each experience.
Envy is a waste of time.
Everything can change in the blink of an eye.
Expect others to treat you with respect. If they don't, walk away.
External beauty fades without internal beauty.
Forgive everyone everything.
Go after what you love in life, don't take no for an answer.
God *does* help those who help themselves.
God is a *fair* and *loving* God.
God loves you, not because of what you did or didn't do.
Help people who appreciate it.
Help people who want to help themselves.
However good or bad it is, a situation will change.
If a relationship has to be a secret, you shouldn't be in it.
Ignore what others say about you.
In the end, all that truly matters is that you loved.
It's ok to let your children see you cry.
Know that you are touched by grace. Everything happens for a reason.
Laugh out loud even at yourself.
Life is a give and take. Don't take unless you plan to give back some day.
Life is too short to waste your time hating anyone.
Life isn't fair but it is still good. Show up and make the most of it.

Life isn't tied with a bow but it is still a gift.
Love is meaningless when it is forced.
Make one change at a time.
Make peace with your past so it doesn't mess up your present.
No one is in charge of your happiness but you.
Open your mind, your heart and your wallet.
Pay it forward; do something nice for someone if someone has done something nice for you.
People show their true colors and others see through them too.
Protect yourself.
Relationships take effort. If the relationships are good ones, the effort is worth it. If the relationships are not, you are better off without those people in your life.
Relax and enjoy good friends.
Run your own life.
Surround yourself with people who genuinely love you.
You can tell by their actions, not their words.
Surround yourself with people who have a good heart and good intentions.
Surround yourself with people who want the best for themselves and care about themselves as they have a better chance of caring about you too.
Surround yourself with supportive, caring people.
Take responsibility for your actions and your life.
The best is yet to come.
Time heals most everything. Give time time.
Whatever doesn't kill you does make you stronger.
When in doubt, just take the next small step.
When in doubt, take the high road.
Work hard. It pays in a lot of ways.
Yield.
You can do anything you put your mind to doing.
You can learn something from everyone.
You can't make someone love you.

**You don't have to win every argument. Agree to disagree.
You don't need to tell everyone your opinion of everything.
You don't owe anyone who hasn't helped you or walked in
your shoes.
You never stop learning until you die.
Your only limits are self imposed.
Your thoughts become your experience.**

I have learned that it's not what one achieves in life that really matters, it's what they overcome. Achievements are only a part of setting an example for others. Character and decency are what really count.

I learned that history does repeat itself when people let it by not breaking the mold or pattern. My dad was not there when I was born; he was not there when my daughters were born and has chosen not to be there for his great-grandsons.

I have learned that relations that deteriorate or are too much of a struggle to keep are sometimes not worth fighting for. True love comes easily and should be enjoyed by both parties. When someone no longer wants you in their life or no longer wants to be in your life, it's best to let them go. This raises the question, "Does one ever really get over a parent not loving them?"

I have forgiven those who have abused me or have been unkind to me in any way so that I am free to continue to grow and love. Thank you to all the good people that have been in and out of my life over the years. It has been from you and your prayers for me that I have gathered my strength to continue on.

And, thank you God for my life. It is a precious gift.

*A*ppendix A includes a sampling of the letters written to my mom by Father Domenic Silvestro (my father's cousin) and Anne DiMare (my father's mother). They speak for themselves.

CAPUCHIN FATHERS,
MARY IMMACULATE FRIARY,
Glenclyffe,
GARRISON, N. Y.

Dear Carmela,   April 3,1958

The Lord give you His peace...

Perhaps you remember me. It has been a very long time
since we've met. When I was very young I used to go to
Winthrop often with my mother and father. I remember your
grandfather and grandmother very well.

My reason for writing to you is your husband. He has
been writing to me about once a week for the past six weeks.
Today I got a letter from him asking me to write to you. He
wants me to tell you of his honest intention to be a good
husband. For myself, I can say that certainly God has given
him the grace to see the evil that he has done. Moreover,
God has given him the grace to confess his sins and to fight
to regain his dignity as a man. He is trying very very hard.
But, as in every effort to rise from evil to good, he needs
help and encouragement. Your help and your encouragement
would do him more than anyone else's. He is unworthy. But,
he is your husband and the father of your children. I think
(I don't know all the facts and it is hard to judge such a
case) it would be a good thing for you to take him back.

I know that he must have made you suffer a great deal.
A man who shows contempt for his marriage vows, for his wife
and for his children is a hard man to forgive. But to forgive
is God's will. Hard as it may be at times we must try harder
to forgive. You are both young. You can start over in the
love you had when you first married. Other women have had
a lot to forgive too. Because of your children, if for no
other reason, try to forgive him.

This is a hard letter for me to write because I know so
little of the circumstances. But I do know he is trying
to amend his life and I also know that in the long run a
wife does best in taking a man like this back. Make him
know how much he has hurt you but hold out hope for him to

begin again.

He has some problems which he must meet. They are big
problems. If he gets discouraged, if you offer him no
encouragement, he will fall back into the evil he is trying
to escape. He tells me he has a good job and that he is
reluctant to leave it. I feel that he must leave that part
of the country and return to you. I'm afraid that for the
sake of money he is risking his soul again. It would be
far better for him to be poor and out of work than to have
a good job but to be in danger of sin.

Write to him often. It will help him. I too shall write
as often as I can. Above all else pray for him. He is going
to mass every morning. If you can go, go yourself to mass.
Pray the rosary in your spare moments. God's grace will
make hard things easy. Our Blessed Mother will help you do
what's right.

Be sure of my prayers for you and the children. May
Jesus and Mary bless you and comfort you and give you holy
peace.

Sincerely in Christ,
fr. Dominic Silvestro

219

MARY IMMACULATE SEMINARY

GLENCLYFFE
GARRISON, NEW YORK

Dear Carmela,   June 8,1958

The peace of Christ be with you.

I would have answered your letter sooner, but the past few weeks have
been pretty busy. We had exams and there was other work that had to be
done.

I can imagine what you have been through. Really, I think I know. It's
natural to become bitter when our trust is abused and we are humiliated.
Nothing hurts more than to the best in us despised as nothing. Love is a
terrible thing. The more we love, the more we are likely to be hurt. God
knows. For love of us Christ became a man, yet men despised him, they insulted him, they hounded him like a criminal and then murdered him.

Yet God still loves us, he still forgives us. We are supposed to be like
God because we are going to be children of his. We're supposed to forgive
too. He asks us to forgive others as he forgives us. It's not easy to do
this. God did not say it was easy. In fact, it's probably the hardest
thing we can do. But if we are like God and forgive, you know we will have
the reward for being like God. We will have the peace of God in our hearts.
A bitter heart comes from not forgiving.

It's easy to tell some one else to forgive. But the man who tells others
to be saints should be a saint himself. Carmela, I'm not a saint, that's
why giving you advice is so hard for me. But forget that it's me telling you
these things and realize that it's really God's command.

It seems that Salvi is really sincere. I am very much impressed by the
good will and the efforts he is making. He has received a great deal of
grace, a tremendous gift. I am amazed at it. He will gradually begin to
realize the malice of his sins and the pain and shame and humiliation he has
inflicted on you. As he does grow in his realization of these things he will
equally grow in his love and devotion to you. It may take time, but in the
end it will be worth waiting and praying for.

Yes, I think you should go to him. He may hurt you again but it is worth
the chance. When we love it is always a chance that we will be hurt. But
there is also the chance that our love will be returned. For the children's
sake I think it's necessary as I know you do. Your place is with him--for better
or for worse. God will help as long as you are faithful to your duty. He needs
you.

Be certain of my prayers for all of you. May Jesus and Mary give you
peace in your home, love and kindness and patience with each other. Pray
to Mary for help.

                                    Sincerely,
                                    fro. Dominic

MARY IMMACULATE SEMINARY

GLENCLYFFE

GARRISON, NEW YORK

Dear Carmela,   Oct. 9,1958

The Good Lord give you His peace...

Your letter arrived this morning. It was bad news for me—yet, in a
way I fearfully expected it. Dear Carmela, know that more than anything
in this world I want to help you and encourage you, but I feel as if I
have failed you. May God help me to help you.

You are a very good and brave girl. I admire you. If you continue to
be as courageous and unselfish as you are and don't get tired of doing
good, then you will reap your reward. Don't ever start to feel sorry for
yourself. Realize that not the slightest act of self sacrifice you do is
unnoticed by God. God often afflicts those he loves more than others.

Your husband is a very weak man. Weak in the sense that whatever flatters
his ego wins his support and affection immediately. The woman whom he has
is clever enough to realize that Salvi is an easy catch. It seems that she
has no intention yet of leaving him alone. Because he loves to be made to
feel like a movie star he will probably continue to see her until she gets
tired of him and finds some one else. Salvi is just one of a long string
of "friends" she has had. He told me about her and I can assure you, Carmela,
she's just a tramp, an ordinary street walker. Of course Salvi doesn't think
so. He likes to think that she's a movie star too.

I am pretty much disgusted with him as probably you can tell from the tone
of this letter. I too feel that he has betrayed me. But let us forget about
him for a while and talk about you. Perhaps you feel that somehow you are failing
in your marriage, that maybe in some way you are partly responsible for the
failure. Perhaps you are, but the greatest failure is Salvi's moral failure.
It is not because of you or because of that woman but simply because of sin
itself. Cheap, dirty, sin has a great attraction to some people. They only
want to do things when they are sins. It's the thrill of evil that attracts
them. Salvi doesn't love that woman—he loves himself. To get back to you,
above all else try to look upon this affair of Salvi's as a moral sickness
of his, for that's what it is. He is to be pitied—not you. You can turn the
evil he does into good for yourself and for the children because God is just.
He thinks he's getting away with a lot, but he's kidding no one but himself.
Try to act as if he were insane, as if he were sick in the head. Your peace
of mind and soul should come from the knowledge that you are doing God's
holy will, that you are bearing a trial sent by God. By keeping in your mind
the thought that God is present at all your humiliations, that He sees all,
knows all, you will feel stronger in bearing up with them. Those who would
follow Christ to the glory of heaven must follow Him also in the shame and
humiliation that Christ had here on earth. You vowed to God when you married,
God will bless you a thousand times over for being faithful to your vow.
Carmela there is a great truth that we must all learn before we die and that
truth is simply this—God loves us and wants to be loved by us. Everything
that happens to us is intended to make us turn toward God. The more God
loves us, the more He makes us turn to Him and the more He separates us from
those things that turn us from Him.

You asked whether you are wrong to feel the way you do. Certainly, no.
But please try hard to keep from pitying yourself. It's a terrible shame
you have to bear and I wish some how I could bear it for you, to take it
upon myself. But it's your cross—sent by God. Be brave and bear it.
God will help you carry it.

I have been around long enough to know the kind of woman that has fascinated
Salvi. In time she'll find some one else's husband and Salvi will be forgotten.
As I said he is not the first she has had, but she is clever enough to make
Salvi feel as if he were a very special one. You see how stupid he is, how
much he is to be pitied. Both in this life and in the next he will pay for
his stupidity. He turned to God in a great fear of hell, but now he seems to
have forgotten hell. Remind him that hell still burns. You need not seek to
revenge yourself because God will do the revenging. Tell him that. Tell
him you bear no malice, but you fear God's vengeance on him.

I have cousins there in California. I don't think it's a good idea to
tell others about your personal family problems unless you know them very
well, so I hesitate to send you to my aunt and uncle. But, I tell you what,
I shall write to my cousin Victor's wife Mary. She's a fine girl and I will
ask her to call on you. I know she will protect your secrets.

Be sure of my prayers. You have been in my thoughts all day. May Jesus
and Mary comfort you and strenghten you. May Mary the Mother of God give
you all the grace you need. Pray the rosary often. You will find much
comfort in it.

Your cousin and brother in Christ,

fr. Dominic

**By the time this letter was written, we were
living in Los Angeles, CA.**

Ann R. DiMare

May God guide all of you with joy and peace Nov. 1, 1958

Dear Carmela

I was happy to receive your letter but was quite saddened after reading of your disturbed thoughts. One thing you must always remember is there is no hurt in this world that cann't be healed in time. At present your probably letting your imagination get the best of you. I'll admit I felt disturbed also, but error is not going to push us down, its only the human force, when we go to God's spiritual power nothing else matters. We have to keep and stick to good thinking and know that, God is still God's will be waiting with patience when we are disturbed. Jesus said, "For this world you shall tribulations sometimes through no fault of our own we are involved and then again, "Who are we to judge. How do we know its not meant for our penance. No one can escape some sort of trial. So please Carmela do not lack any faith in Salvy. Let the sunshine through your heart. I know and have complete confidence that Salvy will never do any wrong or hurt you anymore. Probably Salvy hasn't completely forgiven himself and has a complex. Suppose you try to appeal to his sense of justice, tell him you know something is disturbing him and you would

like to share his trouble. It is the will of God to share good and bad if we want to find happiness. I know he might not be telling you all because he fears to hurt you and in his way he's sparing your emotions. If you could give him your confidence with hope patient and understanding compassion that what ever he'll say you'll try to help him in love. Many & many people have gone through the same situation and later on have found a more richer and deeper contentment. What really counts is God's judgment. Salvy will not have peace any more if he should do wrong, because God has captured his soul, and his conscience will not rest unless it, rest with God. You see what I mean Carmela when we even up the score the persons that do wrong or harm, always end by punishing themselves. We make our own heaven or hell, thats why we have to be very careful on judging others. With the help of Our Blessed Mother you can certainly come to a good solution for the sake and love of your children. Salvy knows how to turn to God, he knows evil will destroy body & soul. Through prayers we find peace and mental stability. Believe me Carmela I know its not an easy road there are many thorns by the way before we can get to heaven. Always trying to express ourself with love in our heart will help us up the ladder.

3) Thats why I always say, never to do any thing to regret later. Try to write to Fr. Cremia ask him and Fr. Tom to write to Salvy. Thats their work. Don't worry Carmela and please try not to be or look disturbed fill yourself with confidence that every thing is going to be alright. I hope you can go to see your commore soon and probably you can with her son to your house some sunday. If you feel uneasy on account of the children when you go to Teresa house, maybe you shouldn't go, let her call on you. In time I know Carmela you'll have more friends that you can handle; through the parents of your friends of your children. I'm glad the children will be and are a lot happier by going to school. The pictures of them are real nice I shall treasure them. I wish I could see the place of the booklet you send me. The way it looks and as you describe it, it looks like one of the wonders of this world. One day this week Bella Rosie and I went to see Josie. Charlie took us.

Josie is very happy there, at first one of her little girls was very lonesome and was getting sick. Now she founde two little girl friends, they were hugging and kissing each other. one of them is a little Japanese girl. A young school teacher who lives across the street went to Japan and adopted her. The teacher happens to be Francis Chinese teacher in Medford. Connie DeMare called, asked me to go to Rosie with her, she gave me an envelope with Jimmy's wedding gift. Maria and her girl friend were dressing for halloween. one was a sailor and the other an army soldier, they were going to a halloween party. Pop is sleeping and "can't you hear him snoring? he must be tired he's allergic to his old traps. He's taking in and his eyes are so red, and is always sneezing, we have a steady music between him & me. I'm writing this while I'm sitting in bed. I hope you'll understand what I said and I mean to say everything with love. Its very late 10 minutes past 12 and I'm tired. Believe me Carmela there is nothing to fear. There is no greater evil than to lose faith in God. The unexpected will come to all of us, from time to time, but what does it matter. God expects us to do our part with his law, for we live for the eternal life. Our Blessed Mother will help you to joy and happiness she know how good you are. lass I can't write any more its so late. Love and kisses to you Salvy and the children. God Bless you all always and guide you his way. Let him lead you.

Letter from my grandmother Anne to my mother when we were living in LA Written November 1, 1958

223

MARY IMMACULATE SEMINARY

GLENCLYFFE

GARRISON, NEW YORK

Dear Carmela,   July 24, 1959

Your letter arrived this morning. I will write to Salvi, but what can I say? Words don't mean much to him, it seems. He's abused the grace of God and when people abandon God, God eventually abandons them. Their hearts become hard with sin.

I don't know what happened. Soon after you returned to Boston Salvi wrote me and even phoned me and it seemed that he was really sincere about starting his life all over again. Since he was 3000 miles away from that woman, I thought he would finally keep his word. But I guess that creature followed him back. She must be quite an evil thing. It makes me wonder if the Devil is not involved in her soul.

Carmela, what can I say to you? I don't know what's in your mind and in your heart. That's what matters. Do you still love him? Are you willing to suffer and wait—maybe years—until he gets tired of her or she gets tired of him? Many women have waited and suffered for their husbands and it seems it was worth the waiting.

You are both young. You got married too young. The fact that Salvi is so young is the reason that woman has such power over him and she'll have it until he matures, becomes an adult. It may be many years away. But if your heart is tired of loving him, then perhaps, you should give him the divorce or at least tell him that <u>you want</u> a divorce. Maybe he is too sure of you, maybe the sudden realization that you are completely fed up, will shock some sense into him. But you must make him pay you alimony for the rest of your life. As a divorced Catholic you can never remarry, as you know. I don't think Salvi would ever marry that woman even if he could. If he were free (legally) to marry her she would want to get married, then he would either have to marry her or get away from her.

He has not been much of a father to his children so a divorce would not do them any harm. Children need a father, but a bad father is worse than none at all. As long as he were forced to support you and the children, they would probably be better off. But—and this is the important thing—if you still love him, then wait and pray. Men like Salvi always come back. Sooner or later they come crawling home—perhaps their sick and their girl friend has deserted them or they're broke or they're just lonely; eventually they come back—are you willing to wait? You got married too young; those years that you should have waited maybe have to be made up now.

Carmela, pray as you have never prayed before. Ask Jesus for a clear mind to know what you should do and for the grace and strength to do it. God sent you this cross, He will send you the grace to bear it. All things happen for the best for those who love God. Someday you'll look back and understand

You are in my prayers always, love,

Fr. Dominic

Remember me to your mother-in-law and father-in-law and your parents. *You should have written to me sooner than this. Never hesitate to visit.*

By the time this letter was written, we had already returned to living in Winthrop.

CAPUCHIN FATHERS,
MARY IMMACULATE FRIARY,
Glencyffe,
GARRISON, N. Y.

Dear Carmela and Salvi,   Feb. 25,1961

God give you His peace.

I know it has been a long time since I last wrote to you.
There seems to be so much to do all the time. But you can
be sure that you have been in my thoughts and prayers.

Your Christmas card was not good news. But we must not
lose hope. Throughout our lives there are problems of
one kind or another—we just have to live with them and
try to make the best of them. Some people have problems
of health, others of money, others of family—so everyone
carries a cross.

I have a lot of faith in Salvi. The problems that you have
are not due to the fact that Salvi is just a bad man;
Salvi, like any other man, wants a peaceful and happy home.
He wants a place where he is loved, where he can find
rest for his tired body and soul. A good wife provides this
for her husband. She makes his home a happy place so that
her husband loves his home. One of the troubles with many
wives is that they don't make their homes happy places.
They nag their husbands, they constantly bicker and fight,
they make their homes battle grounds; there is no peace
there. When this happens a man looks some place else for
love and peace and sympathy. It is wrong for a man to do
this—but that is the reason he does.

A good wife must forget her own happiness and be interested
only in the happiness of her husband and her children. If
she looks for her own happiness instead—troubles come.
The trouble with most of us that we are too selfish; we
are too much interested in ourselves and not enough in
others. Real love forgets about self and thinks only of
others.

With God's help we can learn to love others—without
God's help we can only love ourselves. So I beg you
both to ask God's help, pray constantly, go to communion
often. Lent is a good time to do these things.

Be sure of my prayers for both of you. Remember me to
your families.

Love,

Father Dominic

This letter was written on my parents 10th Anniversary.

May 25. 1962

Dear Carmella and Salvi:

God give you His peace!

Thank you for your card and letters. Knowing how busy you are I appreciate your thinking of me all the more. You are very kind to me. For my part, though I do not write often I do think of you and pray for you. May God bless you and give you all that is good and just and holy.

I know no reason why Salvi should resent the fact that his father wants to remarry. He has a God given right to a home and a wife. It is not good for some men to live alone. When he returns with his wife, it is your duty to show her all the respect and love which is due to her. I trust you will perform your duties.

Salvi should be the last one to object. I am greatly disappointed that he has yet to break away from his illicit affair with that other person. How can he who has no respect for his solemn marriage vows object to his good father's desire to remarry? This seems like a cruel distortion of values. There is no shame to a remarriage, but the shame and scandal of impure love is one that God will revenge. If Salvi performs his duty and breaks away completely from that person I promise him I shall use my influence to get him back with his father's business.

As for you Carmella, God will reward your patience and your suffering. Because you have been faithful to your marriage vows God will be faithful to His promises to you. He will make it all up to you someday. Wait and pray. You will see.

Remember me to Diane Fazio when you see her. Tell her I shall write someday.

Pray for me. Ask the children to pray for me. Tell them I want them to do it.

My love to you all.
Fr. Dominic

Fr. Domenic was now living in Tokyo, Japan to open a monastery. My parents were still living together.

Feb. 1,1963

Dear Sal and Carmella,

God give you His peace.

I am very sorry to learn of your sister's untimely death. It is
especially sad when one realizes how young she was. But, God's ways
are not our ways and it is beyond our power to realize just why
God wills such things. But this much we know, God does not cease to
love and all he does is from His love of us. His love for your sister
is ultimately the cause for His taking her when he did. What trials
and sorrows he spared her from we will never know. She is now in
a better life, the life to which we are all destined. I shall keep
her constantly in my prayers. May God have mercy on her and bring her
to life everlasting.

I would be happy to receive the vestments and other items you mentioned. We will soon be opening up a new monastery here in Japan and they
will be of much use to us. Even though the vestments are both white it
will be all right. White is used more than any other color so it is goo
to have extra ones around.

My father is related to the Faro's. Carmella's grandmother and my
father were cousins. As a young boy I remember going to visit them at
Shirley St. I don't remember Carmella's sister. She was probably just
a baby at that time.

I finish school here in June and return to my mission on Okinawa.
Between now and then I have a tremendous amount of work to do. Just
pray that God gives me the strength to do it all. I am studying very
hard and I'm even teaching now, so I have a double job.

I pray that you two have once and for all settled that shameful proble
The word shameful is not strong enough for what I think of a man who
despises his solemn marriage vows. Marriage vows are a sacred thing and
the man who breaks them tramples a holy thing. God will have His revenge.

Love,

Father Domini

PAX MY MONUM

ST. JOSEPH FRIARY
20-4 MIKAWADAI MACHI
MINATO-KU AZABU, TOKYO

CABLES: FRANCISO TOKYO
TEL. 46 9947

March 14,1963

Dear Carmela,

God give you His peace.

As yet I have not received the package you sent, but
don't worry, it usually takes about six weeks or more
for a package to arrive here.

Carmela, the unhappy situation you find yourself in
is not an easy one to give advice about. You certainly have given him all the possible chances a man could
ever ask or have a right to. I'm surprised you let
him into the house at all.

As you know, there is no such thing as a divorce.
As far as the law is concerned it is possible, but not
as far as God is concerned. So, you are right in
refusing to give him a divorce. If he is leaving you
let him go and good riddance. He can't get a divorce
unless you agree. If he does file papers for a divorce
you will receive notice. At that time take the papers
to a lawyer and have him answer for you. Also it would
be good to bring the matter before the attention of the
pastor of your parish. He can get a formal permission
of the bishop for you to refuse to allow him into your
house again.

Also, I would go to the City Hall and bring the
matter before the Welfare people. Because your husband
has deserted you and the children, you are entitled to
help from the State and City. This is quite a bit of
money and it will need it. You will have to sign some
papers there. Since your husband has abandoned you,

he is a criminal according to the law. If he shows up
in court trying to get a divorce or trying to get married
he is liable to end up in the house of correction. A
few months in the house of correction may be just what he
needs.

Anyway, Carmela, get in touch with a lawyer as soon as
he leaves and also go see the parish priest for a formal
permission to keep him out of your house.

In time, he may come back. Eventually, that type of
man always comes back. They get fed up with their girl
friends, they get sick and lonely and they want to see
their children, so they come crawling back. When he does
come back, let him wait outside the door for a few weeks.

Your nagging is a terrible thing to live with for any-
man and I'm surprised you are not able to control it. It's
true you have a reason to be disturbed, but nagging is not
the way to correct it. A man wants to find peace at home
--even though he doesn't deserve it--and if he finds a
nagging wife only then he's going to get out.

It is a heavy cross you carry and God who gives such
crosses also gives the strength to carry them. Be faithful to Him. Spend your time in prayer rather than in
brooding over your fate. Start with the rosary. Say it
as often as you find yourself thinking about yourself.
Make of Jesus and Mary true friends. You will find great
peace and comfort for your aching heart in the Hearts of
Jesus and Mary.

Be sure of my prayers,always.

Father Dominic

**This letter was written on my 10th birthday,
the day my cousin Paul was born.
Dad was still having breakfast with us at this time.**

228

Jan 29, 1964

Dear Carmella,

God give you His peace!

Thank you for your card and gift. You didn't have to do that. I know that things are not easy for you. I would prefer you didn't do it again. I have some rich relatives who don't give me what you have given. It is a strange thing. The poor people give more than the rich. Heaven is only for the poor people I think.

I received the package about 7 or 8 months ago. It caused me a great deal of trouble because Sabi put the value of the things too high. I had to get an import license and pay all kinds of duties. It should have been sent as a free gift of less than $50 value. Also the ciborium was damaged (bent). That also caused trouble. But after it was all done, I was very very happy to get the package. The vestments are beautiful. I use them only on Sundays and big feast days. They are a real asset to my poor little mission.

Someday I hope your husband comes to his senses. Before it's too late. The evil that he does will all one day come down upon him and crush him to the ground. We pay for our sins — that is a fact! He will pay every penny. And if he should be struck dead before he has paid — he will pay forever in hell. You are a weak and sentimental woman to put up with him, Carmela. Nothing but pain and evil can come from such a man. Perhaps you just love to suffer? Some people do. But your weakness has been a source of security for him. You have made it easy for him to sin. I ask you

think carefully just why you have put up with such evil. Do you love him or do you love yourself and are too proud to lose him to another woman. You need not fear, Carmela. To lose such a husband to such a woman is no disgrace. The world is full of such men and women. Even this poor miserable island has thousands of them. Someday God will pay them back and He does. I see it every day.

Take care of yourself.   Father Damien

Dec. 29, 1964

Dear Camella,

God give you His peace and a blessed New Year.

Just a few lines of encouragment. I too am sorry I did not get to see you . There are so many problems. I could have stayed home for a year and not gotten around to all the relatives.

I did not know that you had taken him back. You didn't tell me. I was surprised to see you two togther but at the time I didn't want to make anything of it. You ought not to take him back. I told you this before. I feel bad that you would do it in spite of how much I urged you not to. You will gain nothing by taking him back—do you understand. Only misery will come to you. In you mind you must pretend that he is dead. Someday, when he is old and sick and that woman he lives with abandons him, he will return with tears and repentance—then if you have that much pity for such a louse you can take him back—but you need not. However, as long as he is keeping that woman—you must not take him back. Your softness with him encourages him to live like a beast. You must not give him any divorce either. Do not sign anything. Get your fifty dollars a week and as the children grown older insist on more and more. Keep him broke or force him to run away.

Camella, I insist that you never let him in your house again. You are young and it is difficult to live without love—but it is your cross and you must bear it. God will help you if you ask Him to. If you continue to do as you please and do not take advice from those who love you and want your peace and happiness, then you will be abandoned even by your friends. You must turn to God more than ever before in your life.

My prayers for you and the children,

Father Domini

This letter was written on my mom's 35th birthday.
By the time this letter was written, dad was living with Shirley.

Dear Carmela,   Dec. 27, 1965

God give you His peace.

I got your card and letter and I'm sending these few words to
you to comfort you and encourage you.

Years ago, when this business first started, I had hopes that
your husband would eventually smarten up and realize that his life
is that of an animal. But it seems that he is going from bad to
worse and that he has entered the long steep slide to hell.

If you can really get $20,000.00 for a divorce--which I don't think
your husband has--I suggest that you take it for the sake of the children.
If this new woman your husband has found is willing to pay $20,000.
for him--take the money. The boy is not worth the price to bury him.

I really mean it, Carmela. Take the money and put it away for the
children.

The ugly things that have been done in that business of Joe and
his brothers is a terrible thing. You have been hurt by evil and selfish
people, but some day God will make it up to you. There is an end to
suffering. The day comes when God turns toward us in love, mercy and
consolation. Sometimes one day of such joy is worth the price of many
years of suffering. So be brave. God is with you. Say your prayers
and bring your children up as christian lladies and gentlemen.

Be assured of my prayers. A blessed new year.

                              Sincerely,

                              Father Domini

**By the time this letter was written, dad was married to Shirley,
although not yet divorced from my mother.**

231

Ann R. DiMare

Dec. 28,1966

Dear Carmela,

God give you his peace.

It was good to hear from you again. I realize how much you have gone trough and I wish there was some way to help and comfort you. I am sure it must have been very very difficult.

I hope the settlement that you made with him was a good one and that you are now independently able to live a good life. I suppose some of the family objected to your giving him a divorce and they are perhaps surprised that I would give you that advice, but I think it is for the best.

There is no hope that he will become a decent man and there is not any good reason why you and the children should have to continue putting up with him. It is too bad, but there is nothing to be done. A bad man produces badness and those around him are always hurt by him. It is better by far to avoid such people.

He is still their father and I suppose your sons feel some loyalty to him, but I want you to tell them for me thay they too will be hurt by him. He will bring only sorrow into theirllives—as he has done up to, now. It would be better for them to leave him alone. But if they don't th ey will learn for themselves. He will betray them when they need him the most. He loves no one but himself.

Keep up your good work. God will someday reward you for all that you have suffered. Do not think that God is far away. He knows and He will someday settle all the accounts—sometimes it is much soonert han we think. Sometimes God's justice comes like a bolt of lightening—so fast and so terrible. Some people say God is dead—that is what they wish, but God is not dead, He is patient, terribly patient.

All is well. This year I will be home for a short time. Perhaps I can see you.

Remember me to your family.

God bless you,

By the time this letter was written, mom and dad were divorced.

232

*A*ppendix B contains excerpts from my cancer blog on CaringBridge.Com and a sampling of the support messages I received from friends and family who were following my blog.

On October 30, 2009, as a result of a surgical procedure I had earlier in the week, I learned I had a high grade (aggressive) endometrial carcinoma. I was in total shock as I believed myself to be fairly healthy for a woman my young age (56). How did this happen to me? Why did this happen to me? How could I fix it like I had fixed so many other things in my life before? Thus begins my journey to wellness.

My doctor immediately scheduled me for surgery on December 8, 2009. Later that day I requested the surgery be done earlier as I was having severe panic attacks. The surgery was rescheduled for November 24, 2009. I was supposed to be going to my condo in Florida for 3 weeks leaving on November 2nd and intended to continue with that plan.

On November 1st, my medical condition worsened, perhaps due to anxiety and perhaps due to God sending me a strong message. I cancelled my flight and called my doctor.

He moved my surgery up yet again so now I am scheduled for surgery on Friday November 13th! I am told the surgery will last 4 1/2 hours. My cancerous organs will be removed along with some lymph nodes to see if the cancer has spread.

The outpouring of love from friends and family has been incredible. Thank you everyone!

- Tuesday, November 3, 2009 5:29 PM, CST

Today was the first day I didn't cry. I went to the hospital to get a copy of my medical records and 2 pints of Barium Sulfate Suspension to drink prior to my CT tomorrow. The containers show a picture of berries on it and it's called "Berry Smoothie"! Yeah right! I am told it tastes terrible so I refrigerated it so it will go down easier!

I also contacted an e-patient cancer survivor to discuss ideas for getting well while living with a disease for which we had no training. His name is Dave. He had stage 4 kidney cancer, was given 24 weeks to live and is now showing NO evidence of the disease. He suggested I use the CaringBridge web site to document my journey. Good idea Dave. Thanks.

I researched my Gynecological Oncologist - whom I have not yet met. Dr. M. Adel Hamid is the Director of Gynecologic Oncology at the Boston Medical Center and a Professor of Obstetrics and Gynecology at Boston University. He will be assisted by my GYN of 10 years, Dr. Steven Dakoyannis.

I have lost 7 pounds since I learned I had cancer - 4 days! Not the way I wanted to lose weight but I'll take the good with the bad.

- Wednesday, November 4, 2009 7:52 PM, EST

I am overwhelmed by the many phone calls and messages of caring, love and concern. Thank you. Thank you. Thank you. I am spending time each day getting educated and learning all the things I can do to fight this disease. The way I am approaching it is to improve my physical, emotional and spiritual life to help me face the surgery and remove the cancer from my body forever.

Early this AM, I got a phone call from a gynecological oncologist from Beth Israel Hospital. One of Dick's friends had contacted him yesterday for a 2nd opinion. What an amazing man. He put my mind at ease as he confirmed the approach I am taking is appropriate. He answered many questions and actually gave me a few questions to ask my oncologist. He wants to continue talking with me before each step of my treatment plan (i.e., radiation or chemotherapy). He has heard all positive things about my surgeon.

I drank my Barium, as directed. It didn't taste as bad as I expected. I arrived at the hospital at 1:40 PM for my 2:00 PM CT Scan. I was the first one there! By 3:00 PM after everyone else there had their scans (5 other people); Dick asked the nurse if they forgot about me. Yes, they had and of course, they were sorry! It reminded me of college math FILO! First In - Last Out! I read 18 pages of a 93 page document I found on the American Cancer Society's web site. Document title is "11 Strategies to Focus on When Fighting Cancer...What the Medical Industry Won't Tell You About Treating Cancer.

The CT Scan was easy. I kept my eyes closed when they put the IV in and kept my eyes closed when they moved me in and out of the machine. So 15 minutes later, I was good to go!

We headed straight to the grocery store to find some "organic" vegetables, and then out to dinner. I learned you can ask for whatever you want to eat and they will give it to you prepared exactly as you ask for it. I had baked scrod and broccoli rabbi, the first full meal I ate since last Friday.

When leaving the restaurant, I saw my Senior Class Advisor from Winthrop High School. Since I have been helping plan our 40th high school reunion and he was one of the people we wanted to invite, I talked to him and got his contact information. He was amazed I had remembered him, as he didn't remember me!

When I arrived home, I found a floral delivery sent by my nephew Jake. Thank you Jake. I love you too!

I also found a letter from my GYN with two prescriptions and instructions for "bowel prep for abdominal surgery". Yikes, I think this is the same stuff I took for my colonoscopy 5 years ago! HELP!!!

So, all in all, today was a good day and I know tomorrow will be even better as I will be babysitting my grandson, Logan. He gives his Nana lots of love and affection!!!

- Thursday, November 5, 2009 7:00 PM, EST

Today was better than yesterday. The time flew by as I had my grandson here. We spent part of the day on the floor crawling around. He's getting really good at it!

I only lost a half a pound since yesterday as I am now able to eat without getting nauseous. I am accepting my "new food reality" and my new "life reality". I had Multi-grained Milled Flax Seed hot cereal for breakfast, tofu (for the first time in my life) with string beans for lunch and organic cottage cheese with ground flax seed and fresh pineapple for dinner.

This A.M., I got a call from a BCBS patient advocate. I didn't know they existed. She told me what my insurance covers and assures me she will be there to help me through the process. I am entitled to a visiting nurse when I get home for up to 25 visits per year. I am entitled to therapy visits as well. I guess my government plan is better than I thought.

At noon time, my GYN called to tell me my CT scan was "clear". I believe that is a good thing. Others who have had CT scans can let me know if I am doing wishful thinking or if in fact that is a good thing!

I went to the pharmacy to get my meds for next Thursday. It's going to be a "draining" day if you get what I mean! I need to drink 8 oz. of water with Magnesium Citrate Solution 6 times starting at 11:00 AM, can have only clear liquids or broths for that day. In addition, I need to take Neomycin and Erythromycin in four hour intervals three times each starting at 4:00 AM and ending at 9:00 PM.

I continue to be humbled by the outpouring of love, the phone calls and emails. I am getting stronger each day by your support. Thank you. Thank you. Thank you.

• Friday, November 6, 2009 7:56 AM, CST

Today I am going to post early as I have a full day planned. My daughter and grandson will come with me for my Pre-Op tests at 11:30 AM. I am guessing the testing will not include an EKG or a chest X-Ray as they did those two weeks ago prior to my other surgery. Today's tests should be easy so I didn't bother to study for them!

Last night, another of God's angels called me. My cousin's wife had been through Endometrial Cancer surgery in August this year and is now undergoing chemotherapy. She gave me reassurance we are not alone. She answered more questions for me and shared many feelings I also am feeling. Her 2nd opinion doctor was the same as mine. In addition, we talked about my cousin (her husband) who has been undergoing chemotherapy on and off for years as he has leukemia. They both keep a positive attitude.

After my tests, my daughter Cara will join Deana, Logan and me for lunch. Later tonight, Dick and I are going to see Loretta LaRoche at Cary Hall in Lexington, MA. I saw her years ago at the Volpe Center and remember leaving the auditorium with my face cheeks and stomach hurting from laughing so hard. I need a good laugh this weekend in preparation for next week.

I didn't sleep well last night as I awoke around 2:30 AM and played the **"Blame Game".** I don't drink, smoke or do drugs so I know they didn't cause the cancer in me, but what did? Perhaps...genetics...the environment...processed food...my acidic system (my kidney stones are uric acid)...my hypothyroidism...stress...creams I use on my body...cleaners to clean my house...the water I drink...the water I shower with... lack of exercise...being overweight...the prescription meds I took for kidney stones combined with the one I take for hypothyroidism ....sitting at a computer screen for so many hours in a day...cell phone use... pesticides... or the devil? This morning I came to the conclusion I don't know and probably never will know and it doesn't quite matter.

I know through the love and support I am getting from God and all of you that one day at a time, this too shall pass.

Thank you again.

• Saturday, November 7, 2009 10:00 PM, CST

Loretta LaRoche did it again! I left her presentation with my cheeks hurting from laughing so much. It is "just what the doctor ordered"! The name of her presentation and I believe her new book is "Lighten Up". So throughout the day, I did just that! If ever you get the opportunity to see her, please do. She is good for the soul! She talked about growing up Italian and how important "Love, Laughter and Lasagna" were. I always thought it was "Family, Friends and Food", but same idea!

I spent some time today making a list of questions for my oncologist. Do you think 41 questions are too many??? Actually, I divided them into Pre-Op, During Surgery, Post-Op and Future so I will only ask 26 questions on Tuesday and save the rest for later.

I also got a great package in the mail from the American Cancer Society. Thank you to Ed, Rene and Dave. It contained two books and an organizer. And everyone who knows me well knows I love organizers!

The bills for all the doctors, lab work, testing and first surgery arrived and the hospital already called for the co-pay for the next surgery. There is no price too high when it comes to being healthy. I'm happy to pay whatever it is.

Thank you again for all your messages.

• Sunday, November 8, 2009 4:27 PM, CST

Today we went to the 7:30 AM Liturgy, as we do most every Sunday. Normally one of the Catechists asks the family of the person the mass is being said for to present the gifts to the priest. For some reason, today they asked Dick and me to do it. I call that Divine Intervention! As we approached the alter Dick asked the Priest to say a special prayer for me. He said he would. I was praying for God to watch over my daughter's father-in-law (Larry) as he is having surgery tomorrow for kidney cancer that spread to his lungs, my girlfriend Rita who so bravely fought breast cancer over the last 6 months, my doctors to guide their hands appropriately on Friday as they do their work and for myself to surrender to God's will for my life.

Remembering what Loretta LaRoche said about "Lightening Up", I spent the afternoon watching the Patriots beat Miami. The Patriots are my favorite team but Miami has been my second favorite team for a long time. Years ago, I had a "crush" on Dan Marino.

I called Larry to tell him I was thinking of him and find out for how long he would be hospitalized. We agreed to celebrate over dinner when we are both healthy again. As soon as I hung up with Larry, Rita called me. More Divine Intervention!

Today, I feel strong and ready to take the next step. I will meet Dr. Hamid on Tuesday AM and ask for a copy of my lab work from Friday. I did quite a bit of reading today and want to compare my red and white blood cell counts from my previous pre-op (10/23) to my current pre-op (11/6). The materials supplied by the American Cancer Society are written in plain language and are so easy to understand. They also pertain specifically to my form of cancer making the information much more valuable. Thank you ACS and thank you all for your prayers.

- Monday, November 9, 2009 7:09 PM, EST

Today the sun was shining and the weather was beautiful (70 degrees) so my daughter Deana, Logan and I took an hour long walk around Lake Quannapowitt in Wakefield. We went by Cara's office and snagged her to join us for lunch.

Later, we got the news that Larry's surgery had to be abandoned due to unforeseen complications. I couldn't help but to think no matter how bad we think our situation is, someone has it worst than we do. Tonight my prayers will be for Larry.

Tomorrow A.M., I meet Dr. Hamid. Then I will be babysitting Logan tomorrow, Wednesday and Thursday. Time flies by when I am with him. He makes me laugh. When he kisses me, he's like a puppy lapping my face.

I ate more tofu today, blueberries and a pomegranate. I believe those are cancer fighting foods and therefore will be part of my new life's food choices.

I am blessed to have so many wonderful and amazing friends in my life. I appreciate the phone calls, the uplifting messages and the prayers. Please say one for Larry tonight. Thanks.

- Tuesday, November 10, 2009 4:13 PM, CST

I went to see the GYN-Oncologist today. Dr. Hamid was wonderful. He answered my 41 questions as best he could given he hadn't performed the surgery yet. He said my questions were good ones -- whew. I didn't want to upset him. He's going to use a knife while I'm asleep on the table!

ALMOST everything he said was POSITIVE! Positive: 1. the surgery should only take 2 1/2 hours 2. It's possible they will find no cancer as they may have gotten it all in the D&C when they removed the large polyp. 3. All my test results were clear except for a small polyp on my liver but that has nothing to do with the cancer 4. If no cancer is found they will still do a complete hysterectomy, take out 10-15 lymph nodes for dissection and remove my omentum. I didn't even know I had an omentum!! Had to "google" that one! 5. Gave me meds for a yeast infection. Not so positive: 1. If cancer is found, will most likely do 4-6 weeks of radiation followed by 3-4 treatments of chemotherapy. 2. Instead of a hairline cut under my stomach, he is going to do a cut from my belly button down to my hairline -- big zipper scar but I'm too old for bikinis anyways.

So far, I have lost 8 pounds. Dr. Hamid was not concerned about the weight loss. He said treatment will start 4-6 weeks after surgery and I should be able to return to my normal activities in 6-8 weeks.

Today I got a phone call from the wonderful people that have known me the longest in my life, my Godparents. My Godmother has always had a way of making things humorous so it was great to hear her voice. Perhaps I get my sense of humor from her. They are two of the most loving people I know.

I also heard from Helen Papulis. All my former colleagues know how wonderful she is. I was supposed to be visiting her in FLA last week. She was devastated to hear about my illness and that I had to cancel my trip. She turned 89 years old in October and is having her son, Father Doug, say some prayers for me.

My BCBS Advocate called again to be sure I was still on schedule for surgery. I can't help but wonder if the real concern is "the bottom line" or my recovery. Whatever it is, I will use only the resources I require as I've never been into wasting either mine or anyone else's $$!

And so, since I chased Logan around for a good part of the day, I am tired and going to bed early tonight. Logan will be back in the AM to give his Nana more loving.

- Wednesday, November 11, 2009 5:18 PM, EST

Last night after posting, I got a phone call from a friend who had a similar surgery over a year ago. From listening to her story, I realized "I Ain't Seen Nothing Yet". She had many complications during and after her surgery. As I said in a previous post, there is always someone who has it worst than we do. Kathy was helpful and gave me some pointers should I require chemotherapy and thus a "haircut and a wig"! She has definitely been through it all and is living proof that keeping a positive attitude will get me through it too. She said I have permission to cry from time to time but then need to pull myself up and keep on keeping on. Great advice Kathy - thank you.

Today, I lost another pound (9 pounds total now). I hope I don't find all those lost pounds later. They can stay lost as far as I am concerned.

Went to buy some "jammies" so I can be presentable during my recovery. I understand they are going to blow up my belly and I won't be able to wear pants for a while.

Since it was Veteran's Day, Cara had the day off. She spent it with me and Logan. We walked to our local Veteran's Day Parade for fresh air and exercise. A special Thank You to all our wonderful Veteran's keeping us safe!

I also had a visit from a former colleague. She brought me a "bear" to hug. Those of you who work/worked at the Volpe Center will remember Karen C and her bear collection. I named the Bear "Peaches" because I found out the cancer ribbon color for Endometrial Cancer is peach. What a sweet surprise.

Another special call came from my friend Patty. I met her in September 1971 on our first day as Freshmen in college. We have been friends since. Patty works at the Chem Center in Stoneham which is where I will want to go for my chemotherapy treatments. She said I will be treated special while there. I know that will be true especially if she is the person taking care of me.

I got calls and many special email messages and posts here in my CaringBridge Guestbook. I continue to feel blessed to have you all in my life. I have fond memories of special times with each of you. I can't thank you enough for making me feel loved and supported.

Tomorrow is "Draino" Day. I start taking meds at 4:00 A.M. and stay on a liquid diet throughout the day. Since I really don't have much of an appetite, I'm guessing it won't be too difficult! I'm also expecting to lose a few more pounds!!!!!

- Thursday, November 12, 2009 6:24 PM, EST

243

What a day! By noon time, I had taken 14 pills on an empty stomach. I've never had a stomach ache or head ache as I have today. I'm not in pain but nauseous and hungry. I just took my last cup of "draino"! Along with the water for taking the pills and Magnesium Citrate Solution, I had two cups of chicken broth and can't stomach the thought of having another.

I got many special phone calls, cards and emails today. My cousin Carla read me a prayer over the phone. My girlfriend Patty sent me the exact same prayer in an email - more Divine Intervention. My brother, Pastor Sal DiMare (East Wenatchee, WA) called and we prayed together. I also forgot to mention previously, my friend Helen Papulis (a Greek lady) knows that my GYN is a Greek man (both lived in Stoneham) so she asked me to have him do the Sign of the Cross with me before surgery. When I mentioned it to him, he said, "I'll do you one better. We will hold hands and say the Lord's Prayer." What more could I ask for?

I am thus heading into the surgery knowing I have done everything I can to properly prepare myself, physically (lost 10 pounds), mentally (researched, de-stressed and felt the love from you all) and spiritually (read the bible to Logan and said lots of prayers. I also know I have the prayers and good wishes of many loving and caring people. I have always gotten my strength from the wonderful people in my life and consider myself blessed. Thank you again for everything. I am sincerely grateful and appreciative for all the love and prayers.

The next journal update will come from Dick when he gets home from the hospital tomorrow evening (unless one of my daughter's brings their blackberry/I-phone to the hospital and I'm alert enough to log on.

- Friday, November 13, 2009 3:58 PM, CST (entered by Dick)

Annie's surgery, according to the doctors, went "exactly as we expected and everything looked fine with no visible signs of any additional cancer". They did say the lymph nodes and other samples removed would need to be tested to check if the cancer has spread and determine the stage of the cancer. She would be told about the results and further treatment next week. I did ask the doctors several probing questions and I'm comfortable with their answers that the surgery stage of Annie's recovery went according to plan and "no surprises" were found. I stayed with Annie for an hour after she was placed in her room following recovery and she was still understandably groggy; however, she did manage a smile when she saw Logan.

I'm sure I'm speaking for Annie as well when I say how helpful and supportive so many family members, friends and even new acquaintances have been these past two weeks. The well wishes, prayers, lengthy inspirational/informative conversations and journal entries were all extremely helpful in building Annie's strength for today's 2 1/2 hour procedure. She couldn't have done it without each of you and the valuable information she received from the American Cancer Society and the Caring Bridge service. We both know the road ahead for full recovery will be long and difficult however, a big positive first step was accomplished today.

I'm sure you'll hear from Annie soon for more updates. She's expected to remain in the hospital for 3-4 days before heading home.

Thank you to everyone and please keep praying for Annie's full recovery!

Dick

P.S. Annie, I am so proud of you today and I love you very much.

- Saturday, November 14, 2009 10:16 PM, CST (entered by Dick)

Annie had an "up and down" day today, which is understandable since it's her first 24 hours after a complex surgical procedure. She only had 2 hours of sleep last night (Friday) since the nurses where dutifully monitoring her every 2 hours. Also, we were told it was an unusually busy evening after 12 midnight with emergencies which created several ambulance sirens and "code 99" announcements on the intercom throughout the night. Since her room is in close proximity above the emergency room entrance, she awoke several times during the early morning hours. I blamed it on Friday the13th. The nurse was able to get Annie more comfortable with some suggestions and kind words by about 8:30AM. Logan brightened her morning by arriving at about 10AM with Mom (Deana) & Dad (Sean) followed a few minutes later by Cara and David. As expected, Annie was experiencing a lot of discomfort and bouts of pain from the surgery, but, her biggest concern was how Logan felt after getting his flu shot this morning. Telling her it was "normal" to have discomfort didn't make her feel any better, but we all did our best to comfort her. By the time the doctor arrived at about 12:15PM, she was feeling better. The Doc gave her a private exam, made some adjustments to her medication and instructed her to work on her breathing exercise to strengthen her lungs. Everyone knows Annie is a Type A personality, however, the Doc is a Type A+ so she listened and followed his directives. He's competent and professional in his approach and most important, Annie trusts him. At about 3:30 the staff got Annie out of bed and into a chair where she sat upright for an hour. She did wonderful and I could see she was making progress, however, after 60 minutes and given only two hours sleep the night before, I asked the nurses to return her to bed to rest and re-connect the pain medication again. The really good news for Annie was the Doc letting her have 30cc of water every hour. After that perk was allowed, I gave Annie her "H2O champagne" every hour and it definitely starting making a positive impact. She's really is a terrific, cooperative patient.

During the day there were a few phone calls and visitors, however, Annie needs her rest, so she couldn't speak with anyone on the phone. I think she needs at least another 24 hours of complete relaxation to focus on the duties expected of her from the hospital staff. Tomorrow morning she will start her walking and I feel she will be ready. She's determined (no surprise here) that she will show the Doc solid progress when he visits her tomorrow (Sunday). I've known Annie for almost nine years now and she still amazes me with her determination to succeed, no matter what the obstacles presented to her. During the later hours in the day, she did mention some somber thoughts about her condition, pain and lack of movement; however, we openly discussed how less than 30 hours beforehand, her main concern was surviving the surgery and all of a sudden we both realized how fortunate and blessed she was to be on the road to recovery, even with all the associated difficulties ahead. A guestbook posting today by Dave D said it best about the reality of her progress and I'll make sure to read this and all the other postings to Annie tomorrow. BTW, I read all of yesterday's guestbook postings to Annie this morning and they all brought smiles to her face so please keep sending them.

Warmest regards to all,

Dick

- Monday, November 16, 2009 7:00 AM, CST (entered by Dick)

On Sunday, Annie had a better day compared to her first two days after surgery. She was able to walk three times with assistance and the Doc took her off oxygen. She was able to go to the bathroom as well during the day. The Doc told her today, "I did my job (re: surgery) now you need to do yours." Annie is doing a good job at walking and doing the breathing exercise. She's still uncomfortable and needs pain medication however, she's making progress. The Doc also placed her on a clear liquid diet so that made her feel better. Getting enough sleep has been a problem for her so she's tired all day, however, physically I'm seeing progress since Friday. No definitive word yet on when she can leave the hospital as the Doc just said "probably in a few days".

She's still not up to having visitors, outside of immediate family, or phone calls and everyone has been terrific understanding she needs her rest. Thank you.

We expect the Doc will provide Annie the test results this week, so that will be the next big step in the process. The results will tell her the cancer stage and prescribed treatment.

I'll do my best to provide an update tonight.

Dick

• Tuesday, November 17, 2009 6:54 AM, CST (entered by Dick)

Annie will be discharged from the hospital today (Tuesday) and although we anticipated her stay to be a few days longer, her initial concerns about leaving the hospital earlier than expected have turned to relief that she'll be going home to continue her recovery. Both her doctors made us feel comfortable leaving the hospital at this stage was best for her recovery. We both agree and now Annie is anxious to be "in my own home". The Doc said her test results will be available next Tuesday, Nov 24th, and she will be told at that time about follow-up treatment based on their findings. The doctors said she will be required to get rest at home, especially for the next couple of weeks, as she's still experiencing pain and remains uncomfortable. Please keep the well wishes and prayers for Annie coming her way.

Annie did great in her days after surgery at doing what the medical staff recommended every step of the way. Every nurse that came into her room yesterday commented how "great" she looked and mentioned that she was a terrific patient. Now the next step in her recovery period begins and we're hoping her progress will continue. Thank you all for your support.

Dick

• Wednesday, November 18, 2009 5:50 AM, CST (entered by Dick)

Annie is home and that's good news. Shortly after her arrival, it became apparent to both of us that we had some challenges in getting the house comfortable for her. It should have been obvious to me that houses are not normally built for caring of "patients" recovering from major surgery. We have her settled in the family room, close to the kitchen and bathroom. The Doc told Annie to just concentrate on resting, doing her breathing exercise, walking, staying inside, minimize visitors and taking her medication as prescribed for the next two weeks. Although we had to cancel our Thanksgiving plans with family, we both know it's in her best interest to focus on gaining her strength back. I'd like to thank everyone for being so understanding about not calling Annie or expecting an immediate return call and/or email as she's still tired from last Friday's surgery. Hard to believe it was only about 100 hours ago that Annie had cancer surgery. She's doing excellent and, again, being a terrific patient. She is showing me great patience even though my expertise is not healthcare, for sure! I keep telling her, "we'll figure it out" when we need to make her feel more comfortable or solve any unexpected new issue.

This morning Annie mentioned she had a good night sleep and her spirits are good. The Doc changed her pain medication and the itching has gone away from the previous pain med, so that's a relief. Today I'm hoping Annie has a quiet day and gets a lot of rest. Thank you.

Dick

- Thursday, November 19, 2009 6:26 AM, CST (entered by Dick)

Annie had a mixed day yesterday. She did get some rest and she's eating better. However, she's still having difficulty with mobility and the pain is still there though subsiding somewhat. Her new pain medication is working better for her. It's humbling after major surgery that one cannot do the "simple" things in life, such as, sneezing, coughing, laughing, getting off the couch, standing up straight, sitting at the kitchen island that are parts of everyday living. She'll get there and I do see progress, however, it's obvious to me that it will be several more days before Annie is feeling better enough to do some of the normal things during her day. I'm getting better at knowing how to make her feel comfortable in certain situations and we're both collaborating on the tougher issues as they occur. I did call the surgeon yesterday to ask a few questions and we'll be following up with him today. I'm realizing that no issue is too small if it means Annie can be more comfortable if I get it done.

On a non-health issue, the main TV in the family room has not worked since 12 Noon yesterday which means "Annie's room" has no entertainment. After calling Comcast and being told they "may have a technician show up Friday some time", I had a "friendly discussion" with the Comcast service rep about how important it was for the cable signal to be fixed and all of a sudden an opening was available today. See, miracles do happen! So, I expect this issue will be solved today or there may be a big satellite dish on the roof this afternoon.

Speaking of miracles, when Annie and I were somberly speaking about her current pain and lack of mobility, we were enlightened by openly discussing and remembering her plight last Friday and our fear that the worst could happen. Yes, she's uncomfortable and will remain so for another couple of weeks at a minimum, however, her determination to get 100% back to a healthy state is evident. The doctors and healthcare professionals did their job during the surgical process and the long road to recovery is just beginning. Again, thanks to everyone for allowing Annie to get her rest as it's what the Doc said is most important for her now. Optimistically, Annie is hoping to have visitors by the second week of December and I'm sure she will let everyone know. We'll learn more next Tuesday when her test results are provided and she speaks with the Doc. Thanks for your understanding and patience. Your prayers, cards and thoughts are all so much appreciated.

Thank you

Dick

- Thursday, November 19, 2009 6:59 PM, CST (entered by Dick)

Annie finally got some needed sleep today. We both realized today how exhausting the past several days have been for her. I guess it was just time for her body and mind to get re-charged and catch-up with the reality of the situation. Her lack of mobility and pain are basically the same as yesterday and I'm expecting she'll improve slightly tomorrow since I made her a pot of homemade Italian chicken soup with escarole. Annie's appetite differs throughout the day and she still eats relatively light since Tuesday. We have to keep remembering that the Doc stated it would take "six to eight weeks for her to recover" and it's only been six days since her surgery. I'm hoping the Italian soup will make it closer to six weeks vs. eight, but we need to plan for eight weeks. Annie's approach has been to "listen to her body" and react accordingly. She has been realistic what she can and cannot do so far, and I'm confident

she will continue this process of a patient recovery while
following Doc's orders.

Please know that Annie has been reading EVERY message
on Caring Bridge and she and I are touched and grateful
for the kind words and prayers. Thank you, again, Dave for
recommending this terrific supportive resource. Frankly, it's
been a blessing for Annie to access everyone's messages every
day, as well as, allowing us to provide a single update daily
knowing that family and friends are reading about her progress.

We're hoping Annie will soon feel up to writing and responding
to the emails being sent her way. Good news.........Comcast
repaired the TV cable problem. More good news.........Logan
visited for an hour today and brought much needed sunshine
into the house for his Nana. He's only seven months old,
however, there's an obvious connection already with his Nana
as evidenced by the instant smiles on both their faces when
they are in the same room. He was the best medicine of the day!

Tomorrow will be one week since Annie's surgery and only four
days until she receives the test results. Please keep Annie in
your prayers as they definitely have helped her through this
difficult process. Thank you.

Dick

• Saturday, November 21, 2009 7:36 AM, EST

I'm back!!!! And, God sent yet another angel.

I feel a little better today than I have for the past week. Some
of my body functions are coming back to normal while others
still aren't. The Dr told me it takes a long time (6-8 weeks) since
basically the anesthesia shuts down all the functions when
they do abdominal surgery. I won't bore you with the details of

what's working and what isn't. I am taking it a day at a time so as not to relapse and/or catch a cold or the flu.

"Peaches" (my new teddy bear) has been incredibly helpful. Yesterday was the first day I could get off the couch unassisted. I tucked "Peaches" into my belly and rolled onto her. She has been right by my side since then. It's humbling not to be able to take care of myself.

Dick has been an amazing, loving and caring "male nurse". I couldn't have asked for a better life partner. He did have to go back to work yesterday so my daughters (and Logan) shared the care for the day and even washed my hair for me.

During the day yesterday, I got a phone call from one of my tax clients (God's Angel of the Day). After I was done answering her questions, I asked one of my own: "Aren't you a Registered Nurse?" Long story short - she is coming over today to change my bandages as I have an aversion to seeing what lies beneath them. I will be able to be cleaned "professionally" and have my vital signs checked.

I am reading all your messages on a daily basis but haven't been sitting up long enough to update my journal. Also, I felt Dick was doing such a great job that I saved my limited energy for taking in liquids and pain meds!

I can't thank you enough for the messages, prayers, cards, and flowers. I am using all your expressions of love and caring to bring me the strength I need to deal with whatever the doctor orders on Tuesday.

Love, hugs and kisses,

• Sunday, November 22, 2009 6:15 AM, EST

Yesterday was physically and mentally uplifting for me. For the first time since surgery, I climbed the stairs in my house and made it into my bathroom for a sponge bath and new jammies. I had taken a pain killer before I went on my journey but must admit I was exhausted by the time I was safely back on my couch.

My "angel" nurse arrived at 9:30 AM. She took my vital signs, listened to my heart and lungs and changed my bandages. I asked her to take a picture of my belly and to count my staples. I feel like a baked stuffed lobster where they took the stuffing out instead of putting it in and then put me back together with 28 staples. Since the Docs took so much out of me, it's hard to understand why I look like I have a football stuck in my stomach. Nurse Peggy said it is because of the swelling that will go down in time. It was mentally comforting to hear my incision looked clean and dry, my heart and lungs were clear and my blood pressure was only 134/80.

I spent the rest of the day on the couch watching football and sleeping. Today, I expect to do more of the same! Dick will go to the Pats game today. My daughters, sons-in-law and Logan will come over to be with me. Dick made an awesome Italian dinner for them and is leaving me with a plate of fish and veggies. It's nice to have a personal chef and a personal nurse!!!!

Thank you to everyone for all the loving messages.

• Monday, November 23, 2009 4:27 PM, EST

Today, I did some walking around the house without my walker. Because of the pain in my stomach, I did keep myself on pain killers all day and held my stomach up as I walked.

Dick went to work so I was left to care for myself. Actually, Dick made a "lunch" plate and a "dinner" plate so all I had to do was make my way to the refrigerator to get it. He put them on a low shelf so I could reach them without stretching!

The rest of my day will be spent in prayer thanking God for the many blessings in my life. I am optimistic the doctor will give me good results of the lymph node tests and this too shall pass one day at a time.

Thank you again for all your love and support. It has carried me through the dark days!!

Ann XOXOX

• Tuesday, November 24, 2009 2:25 PM, EST

I went to see Dr. Hamid at 11:15 AM today. First order of business was to remove my staples and put "steri-strips" in their place. While he was removing the staples, I implemented the LaMaze Breathing method to diminish the discomfort. Dr. Hamid asked, "Why are you breathing LaMaze?" He asked if I knew what LaMaze was. I told him I certainly did and I use it all the time. I breathed "LaMaze" when I delivered both Cara and Deana as back in the old days, it was popular instead of having meds to ease the pain of child labor.

I can now take showers again as the steri-strips are plastic. With my binder back in place, we were able to discuss my questions "du jour" and the next steps in my recovery.

The good news is the Cancer was Stage 1A which means the Cancer was limited to the Endometrium. The Lymph nodes tested clear. Based on this part of the pathology testing, Dr. Hamid is recommending 2-3 "treatments/rounds" of vaginal radiation. I put "treatments/rounds" in quotes because Dick heard "treatments" and I heard "rounds" and neither of us knows if there is a difference in the two.

255

Dr. Hamid said they are continuing with the pathology testing of the uterus as they want to be sure there were no more tumors on it. Dick and I will meet with him again on December 8th when he is confident he will have the full pathology results. IF the uterus HAD additional tumors, Dr. Hamid will recommend 3-4 "treatments/rounds" of Chemotherapy as well. If the uterus did NOT HAVE any additional tumors, Chemotherapy will not be required.

If the Uterus DOES HAVE additional tumors, Dr. Hamid is going to set me up for a Consultation visit at one of the Boston Hospitals. He specifically mentioned Dana Farber or the Boston University Medical Center but said I could go to any hospital, basically for a second opinion on the Chemotherapy as chemotherapy is considered "aggressive" for this type of cancer. Dr. Hamid has 36 patients with Endometrial Cancer . Only four of them have the same kind as mine. Of the four, three have opted NOT to have the Chemotherapy. He said with the Chemotherapy, I would have a treatment and in the first week would feel tired and sick. During the next two weeks, I would feel better and in the fourth week, we would start the cycle again. This would occur for 3-4 cycles. The Chemotherapy would increase my chances of survival by 10% and decrease my chances of recurrence by 10%. He specifically stated I would go from 70% to 80%. He also said I would lose "some" hair!

Prior to my leaving the office, I gave a urine sample to be sure I don't have an infection as my urine flows like a leaky faucet, sometimes taking about 10 minutes to empty my bladder. I will call tomorrow for those test results.

Once again, I was pleased with Dr. Hamid. He has allowed Dick to be a total participant in my visits, examinations and consultations. It's extremely helpful having that second set of ears listening and eyes watching. Today, Dick asked the questions I was too afraid to ask!

I must continue to recover from the surgery and listen to my body - still no driving, no lifting, no strenuous activity and most important, I need to continue to stay healthy and cold/flu free.

Thank you again for all your prayers and well wishes. May you enjoy the upcoming Thanksgiving Holiday weekend with those you love and those who love you. Be sure to count your blessings. I know I will.

Love,

Ann

• Wednesday, November 25, 2009 5:33 PM, EST

Greetings everyone,

Turns out I did have an infection and will be on new meds to clear it up. Today I slept for most of the morning and then sat up for a couple of hours to enjoy Cara and Logan. Cara was extremely helpful in getting the house in order for Thanksgiving. She even got a couple of XMAS decorations out of the basement and got a tax client's file out of the attic. I've decided the XMAS decorations Cara put up will be the only ones I use this year as I need to save my energy for sitting up and walking. Tonight for the first time since my surgery, I will try sleeping in my bed. Climbing the stairs and climbing into a bed with a thick mattress may be challenging!

This year more than ever, Thanksgiving has a special meaning to me. I am so thankful for the life God has allowed me to continue living. I am thankful for the prayers, love and messages from each and every one of you. I am thankful for having the wonderful love and support system I do in Cara, Dave, Deana, Sean, Dick and Logan. I am thankful for the terrific team of doctors and nurses that continue to guide me toward recovery. I am thankful for the loving heart my mother brought me up with that has allowed me to love so many and have that love returned to me.

So, please have a Blessed and Happy Thanksgiving. Remember, you are what you eat so go easy on the "Bird"!!!

Love, Ann XOXOXO

- Thursday, November 26, 2009 6:29 PM, EST

Happy Thanksgiving everyone,

I took my first shower today and suffered for it afterwards. I should have had Cara wash my hair yesterday so I wouldn't have to stand for so long. I also slept in my own bed last night but found myself terribly congested this AM as I was lying down all night instead of sleeping in a sitting position. I will bring another pillow to bed this evening. So I was up from 7-9 AM today, back on the couch until 2 PM, then up until 4 PM and popped another pain killer. I took pictures of Logan on his 1st Thanksgiving. Deana cut up turkey, peas, carrots and mashed potatoes and he fed himself. So cute!!!

The kids didn't take any leftovers so I am all set for food this week. We had plenty of vegetables and turkey. And, Cara made a sugar-free pumpkin pie for me. Delicious!

My first "CURE" magazine arrived. Tony and Rita, thanks for the subscription. It's packed with great information. BTW - since I am eating healthier, I am still losing weight. Am now down 13.5 pounds.

Hope you all had or are continuing to have a fabulous day. God bless you all and keep you safe over the holiday weekend.

- Saturday, November 28, 2009 8:52 AM, EST

I spent yesterday on the couch, mostly sleeping. Only took one pain killer yesterday. I am hoping to do more of the same today. Dick ordered me a shower chair so that should help with the grooming once it arrives. Still can't stand for more than a few minutes but am comfortable with my progress knowing it has only been two weeks post op. At least the pain has subsided! Now I'm just uncomfortable but that could be from the binder which the doc put on real tight!

- Monday, November 30, 2009 7:20 AM, EST

I spent the entire weekend sleeping and relaxing on the couch. I don't think I have ever seen so much football in one weekend. I am almost done reading Genesis in my bible and will start Exodus later this week.

I had a couple of big lumps on my right side so last night, I slept on my left side and now the lumps are gone. I am wondering if it was a "floating" body part that just needed to fall back into place.

I am down to one pain killer a day and am hoping to be off them by the end of this week. I lost another pound (now down 14.5 pounds). One day at a time, one pound at a time, I will get to a healthy weight for my height.

It was one month ago today I found out I had cancer. Today I feel so blessed to be alive and on the road to recovery. I'm so thrilled I didn't ignore the signs and pushed to have the surgery moved up. It's so important we listen to our bodies. Many of the illnesses that run in my family I have gotten with the one exception being diabetes. And now, with the cancer, I have sworn off sugar/white flour products also.

Most important, over the past month, I have felt so loved and cared for by all of you who have signed my guestbook, sent cards, prayers, flowers, fruit, emails, and had masses said on my behalf. I couldn't have asked for a better support system. Thank you everyone from the bottom of my heart.

Love, hugs and kisses

- Tuesday, December 1, 2009 8:24 AM, EST

Yesterday was the first day without any pain killers. I am having severe back aches but I believe it to be from not being able to stand up or sit up straight yet.

Yesterday, Dick went to FLA as his dad had a stroke on Monday AM. We both felt it was important for Dick to be there to help his sister. Angelo/Dad is 89 years old and based on preliminary reports, the blood clot in his head is inoperable because of his age. So last night my prayers were for him as God has been so good in answering all your prayers for me.

Deana, Sean and Logan came by in the evening to be sure I was fed and tucked in. Tonight, Cara and Dave will do the same. I am so blessed to have the wonderful daughters I have. They have always been there for me and are willing to help in any way they can. Of course Dick left us with plenty of food. Feeding the girls and their families is a cheap price to pay for such great nursing care!!!

- Wednesday, December 2, 2009 8:50 AM, EST

I spent yesterday resting on the couch. It was much needed since I hadn't slept the night before. Last night, I was up at 10, 12, 2, 4 and 6. Perhaps I need something to help me sleep or perhaps because I am sleeping through the day, I am staying awake at night. I do have a few pain killers left so perhaps tonight I take one and hope it works as a sleeping pill would. My back is still aching so I am making a conscious effort to sit up straight and walk up straight.

Dick's dad is stable. They are working to get him into a rehab center to help with his speech, eating and mobility. It isn't easy getting old but it certainly beats the alternative. I'm still hoping to be healthy enough to visit with him the day after XMAS. I think our hugging each other will be good therapy for both of us.

I started Exodus today. I always wanted to read the bible from cover to cover so I feel I am being productive in doing that.

Cara and Dave came by last night to get my dinner for me and bring my "high chair potty" up to my master bathroom. Cara came back this AM to bring it back down so I don't have to do stairs during the day.

I am thankful to God every day for all of you and for my daughters and Dick who so lovingly take care of me without reservation

- Thursday, December 3, 2009 8:34 AM, EST

I had a rough day yesterday so decided to get to bed early and take a pain killer to help me sleep. Unfortunately, I didn't fall asleep until after 11:00 PM but did sleep until 5:00 AM so at least I got six straight hours!

Whoever said, "When it rains, it pours" certainly knew what they were talking about. On Tuesday, Dick's Step-Mom (Jean) fell and cracked her pelvis so now she is in the same hospital as Dick's Dad, one room away. Dick is going to come home later today and if I am healthy enough, we plan to go back the day after XMAS.

Ann R. DiMare

With the exception of my grandson being born, my making new friends through the American Cancer Society and my re-connecting with so many wonderful friends from Winthrop High School, 2009 has been a trying year for us. We are anxious for 2010 to begin and are praying for a better year.

God bless you all for being in my life! I get my strength from your prayers and messages.

- Friday, December 4, 2009 7:38 AM, EST

I got a great night's sleep last night (9:00 PM - 5:30 AM). Thank you pain killer!! It's amazing how good one feels with sleep.

My girlfriend Rita suggested I spend my days without the binder on as well. I took it off an hour ago and already feel so much better. It was squeezing me so tight and making me sweat.

Today is grooming day for me. One of my girlfriends is coming over to take the gray out of my hair and my shower chair has arrived. I'm so looking forward to a daily shower. I know it will help me to feel better.

Cara, Deana and Logan are also coming to visit. And, Dick arrived home last night so things are getting back to normal slowly but surely. Today is 3 weeks post-op. I'm almost half way through recovery!!!!!

Enjoy the weather and enjoy the weekend. Next week, I see Dr. Hamid on Tuesday for more test results.

Love, hugs and kisses to all.

- Saturday, December 5, 2009 9:28 AM, EST

Yesterday was a great day for me. Deana assembled my shower chair so I took a much needed shower and was able to just enjoy the water flowing on me as I sat there - kind of like a water fall. I then dressed in a jogging suit -- only the second day post-op without jammies on.

Susan arrived (from NH) with a whole kit of grooming items. She came prepared to give me a manicure, pedicure, hair coloring and leg and foot massage. Since my pre-op pedicure was still ok and I had given myself a manicure earlier in the week, we just did the hair coloring and leg and foot massage. I am back to being a brunette and I look 10 years younger than when she started. Also, my skin was so dry that the lotion Susan used on my legs and feet was absorbed quickly into my skin. Thank you Susan. God bless you!

I spent the afternoon sleeping while Cara wrote out her Christmas cards.

Today, I got dressed again. That's progress - two days in a row, I had the strength to get dressed. I am feeling physically stronger every day. I am not wearing the binder as my skin is itchy and flaking underneath it from lack of oxygen. I do have to hold my stomach when I walk still but am practicing sitting up taller when I sit.

• Sunday, December 6, 2009 8:20 AM, EST

Yikes - I am thinking of suggesting to Dr. Hamid that he allow me to develop a "Recovery Expectations" booklet. I would simply state week by week what one might expect to happen.

Yesterday I was feeling great in the AM and so I sat up for a while writing thank you cards and email messages. Then my steri-strips started pinching, burning and itching. I thought I would go out of my mind. Just the feel of my clothes on them

263

was so irritating. I spent the afternoon on my back literally blowing cool air onto my stomach. I wanted to rip the strips off but knew I shouldn't. I went to bed at 9:00, took a pain killer and am doing better today.

I am enjoying looking at the snow glistening in the sun. I'm looking forward to watching the Pats game today. The adult kids and Logan will be coming to watch with me. And, Dick will be cooking something fabulous for sure!

Enjoy your day.

• Monday, December 7, 2009 7:30 AM, EST

The itching and pinching continues. I am dealing with it as best I can. I have been told the itching means I am healing so that is a good thing. I have a terrible rash from scratching so much but I know Dr. Hamid will give me something to clear it tomorrow. I am going to spend today resting knowing tomorrow will be a more hectic day.

• Tuesday, December 8, 2009 2:10 PM, EST

Dr. Hamid removed the Steri-strips. He suggested a 1% Cortisone Cream for my rash. He said the rash looked like an allergy as opposed to a bacterial or fungal infection.

Dr. Hamid gave me a copy of the Operation Report (3 pages) and the Pathology Report (5 pages) from the body parts he removed. He said they found "residual traces of the cancer" on the uterus and for that reason he was going to make an appointment for me to see Dr. Anthony Russell (Radiation Oncologist) at Massachusetts General Hospital (MGH). Dr. Hamid said in his opinion, I should have 2-3 rounds of Vaginal Radiation Therapy (one per week, each an hour and a half long) followed by 3-4 rounds of Chemotherapy. Dr. Hamid's opinion is "if it is there, treat it".

He said Dr. Russell has the most experience with Endometrial Cancer and therefore Dr. Russell will set me up for the Vaginal Radiation Therapy at MGH and discuss his views on Extended Pelvic Radiation and/or Chemotherapy with me. Dr. Hamid believes Dr. Russell will "most likely" suggest Chemotherapy but "maybe" he will suggest Pelvic Radiation instead. If Dr. Russell suggests Chemotherapy, I will meet with Dr. Nasima Khatoon (Hematologist/Oncologist) at Commonwealth Hematology and Oncology 41 Montvale Avenue in Stoneham for the Chemotherapy. If he suggests the Pelvic Radiation, I will go to the Chem Center at 48 Montvale Avenue in Stoneham for treatment.

I am waiting to hear from Dr. Hamid's office re: my appointments with Dr. Russell and Dr. Khatoon. I will be seeing Dr. Hamid again at 11:00 on December 22, 2009.

I also intend to follow up with the doctor from the American Cancer Society as a "third" opinion.

As far as daily activities are concerned, Dr. Hamid said "Do not lift anything over 10 pounds for at least 3-4 months and do not move any furniture."

I am a bit disappointed as I was hoping there would have been no traces of the cancer left on the uterus and therefore I wouldn't have needed the Chemotherapy but am done dreaming and am back to the reality I most likely will need the Chemotherapy. Again, I feel blessed and happy to be alive so will continue to take one day at a time and do what is prescribed by the experts.

Dr. Hamid, did say I was lucky to have caught this Grade 3 cancer so quickly and was even luckier it was only a Stage 1A cancer. He said it was a good thing I didn't go to FLA and that FLA will be there next year! How right he is.

265

And so, my recovery continues one day at a time! Thank you again for all your prayers and love

• Wednesday, December 9, 2009 1:39 PM, EST

It's amazing what a difference a day will make! Without my steri-strips, I feel like a new person. My tummy feels like shoe leather where the incision was made -- perhaps scar tissue! I was able to sit up quite a bit longer today and even wrote out some XMAS cards, paid some bills, and talked to a few awesome people on the phone.

I haven't heard from the doctor's office re: my appointments with Dr. Russell and Dr. Khatoon. I did hear good things about Radiology at Mass General and Chemo with Dr. Khatoon so thank you Eileen and John. Am excited about the valet parking at Mass General - need to find out more about it!

Cara came by last night to borrow my car. My battery was dead (since the car has been sitting there for over a month) so we called AAA. After they had started the car, Cara accidently turned it off so this time, we called David and her father-in-law for assistance. It was great to see Larry and learn about his chemotherapy. He takes a pill each day. He looks great and says he feels fine. How uplifting is that?

Today, the car gave Cara more trouble so she is at Sears now getting me a new battery. What an awesome daughter. She has Logan with her so will be coming over to visit when they are done.

Today is also the third day in a row I got dressed in something other than pajamas so I suspect I will be dressing every day from now on.

Tomorrow I will be missing my "Income Tax Update" course. I have taken the course for many years with Cara but will have to pick her brain instead this year as I know I couldn't sit for the entire 8 hours. Also, I still need to be careful about catching the flu or a cold. Speaking of the flu, Dr. Hamid wants me to get the H1N1 shot. Does anyone know where I can get it in the Saugus area?

Time for my afternoon nap! Love, hugs and kisses to all the wonderful people cheering me on. I couldn't do it without you. XOXOXOX

- Thursday, December 10, 2009 8:15 AM, EST

Yesterday morning, I faxed my operation report and pathology reports to the American Cancer Society doctor (my 3rd opinion Dr. Chris). He called me back last night to discuss his thoughts. Basically, he said he agrees 100% with the treatment plan suggested by Dr. Hamid. He said it is the best plan to be sure I don't have a recurrence of the cancer as if it does recur, it most likely would recur in my upper abdomen (bladder, kidneys, etc.). This would be more serious to my life expectancy.

I had already made up my mind I was going to go with the opinion of 2 of the 3 doctors so if Dr. Russell and Dr. Chris said something different than what Dr. Hamid said, I would have gone with their plan. Since Dr. Chris already agrees with Dr. Hamid and I am assuming Dr. Russell will as well, I am now committed to doing both the radiation and chemotherapy. I must admit, I did spend a good portion of last night crying. I am so afraid my weak immune system will become more weakened by the chemotherapy. Dr. Chris assured me that won't happen.

So, my medical appointments for the rest of this month are:

Fri. 12/11 10:00 AM Melrose-Wakefield Hospital Mon. 12/14 9:00 AM Medford Dentist Wed. 12/16 11:00 AM Mass

General Radiation Dr. Russell Thurs. 12/17 9:30 AM Chemo Center Stoneham Dr. Khatoon Tues. 12/22 11:00 AM Melrose Dr. Hamid Deana is taking me to the first two appointments. Dick will take me to the next three.

I will start Radiation and Chemotherapy after January 3rd. I know the radiation will only take 3-4 weeks going once per week. The Chemotherapy is expected to go on for 12 weeks, one week on, two weeks off for 3-4 cycles. Dr. Hamid said I will lose "some" hair once the Chemotherapy starts. I'm not excited about it but will do whatever it takes to survive.

I'm going to continue praying God helps me through this. And, as always, I appreciate your continued prayers as well. Thanks so much. With love, Ann XOXO

- Friday, December 11, 2009 4:51 PM, EST

Today was a busy day for me. Deana and Logan brought me to see my dietician at Melrose-Wakefield Hospital. When she saw that I had lost 16 pounds since my last visit she asked how I did it. When I told her about the cancer, she understood. Instead of discussing how I could lose weight, we talked about foods to eat to avoid cancer and foods to eat while undergoing chemotherapy to help with the nausea and vomiting.

We then came home, had lunch and waited for Cara to arrive. Today was "Christmas Cookie" baking day. I would like to say I helped but the truth is, I napped/slept. I awoke to an awesome smell of cookies baking but couldn't bring myself to eat one. I had a small nibble. Sugar is one of the foods that aren't good for me so I am avoiding it at all costs.

OOPS - forgot to pick Cara's brain about what she learned at the Tax Update course. Will have to do that next week!

Thank you again to everyone for your loving messages. Have a safe and warm weekend! Love, Ann

- Monday, December 14, 2009 10:41 AM, EST

On Saturday, I escaped cabin fever by doing some XMAS shopping with Dick. We visited Logan for about 20 minutes. I slept the afternoon and then for the first time since Nov. 11th, we went out to dinner. After sitting in the restaurant for a couple of hours, I was totally wiped out. I was excited to go out but more excited to come home! I ran into a couple of friends in the restaurant. It was great to see Elia D., and Dan & Jude P.

On Sunday, my younger brother came to visit and brought his new "love" for me to meet. It was a short and sweet visit. Thanks Dom and Linda.

I spent the rest of the day watching the Patriots beat Carolina and sleeping. I'm amazed by how much sleeping I do and how being in the reclined position still feels the best after a month.

Today, I went to the dentist and learned more about Chemotherapy. My hygienist told me about her husband's experiences at Dana Farber. She promised me the fear of the chemo is far worse than the treatment itself. I hope she's right!

- Tuesday, December 15, 2009 6:03 PM, EST

Dick teases me about taking two steps forward and one step back. I understand what he means. I was feeling a lot better this AM so I sat up and paid some bills (all medical bills), wrote out a few more Xmas cards, wrapped a couple of gifts, got dressed and folded a load of laundry. Then when I was going "potty", I found blood in my urine. I called the doctor and patiently waited for my return phone call back. When

269

Dr. Hamid called, he asked me to go to the office and leave a "sample" for testing, then he ordered a prescription for me.

I spent the rest of the afternoon on the couch. I am waiting for Cara to come deliver the prescription. I'm hoping it will correct the situation. I will call the doctor's office tomorrow to find out what the testing showed to be sure I am using the right prescription for the problem.

Tomorrow, I will also meet with Dr. Russell at MGH at 11:00 AM. They sent me a registration package where I learned I am not eligible for the "valet" parking program since most likely, I won't be having radiation on a daily basis for 6 weeks. That's actually good news. This year, I have paid out of pocket over $8,000 for medical expenses. It looks like next year is going to be an expensive one too!! At least I am alive!!!!!!

• Wednesday, December 16, 2009 3:37 PM, EST

It was a long day. We left the house at 10:00 AM and didn't get home until 1:30 PM.

As expected, Dr. Russell was wonderful. After talking to me about the radiation therapy, he answered my 16 questions and then gave me an exam to check my incision and check my "size" for the medical equipment needed to do the radiation. The doc told me I was a "9" out of "10", whatever that means. We scheduled my 3 sessions of radiation for January 4, January 11 and January 20.

I can have radiation at the same time I am having Chemotherapy. Dr. Russell said if I were to have the Chemo at MGH, they would give me 6 cycles as that is what they do as a matter of course. So, it will be interesting to see what Dr. Khatoon says tomorrow re: the number of cycles I will need.

Cara brought Logan over in the afternoon so I got to play with him for a while. He is cutting his first tooth so I kept singing "All I Want for Christmas is My Two Front Teeth". He loved it. There's nothing like the excitement of children around the holidays!

Let's hope tomorrow brings as good news as today did. I was expecting 4 treatments and only have to do 3. That's 25% less --- works for me!!

- Thursday, December 17, 2009 12:29 PM, CST

Today I met Dr. Khatoon and Nurse Karen at the Commonwealth Hematology-Oncology (CHO) Center in Stoneham where I learned I will need 3 cycles of Chemotherapy. Since I expected 3-4 cycles, I was delighted to learn it would be only 3 cycles. Dr. Khatoon was extremely thorough and answered my 8 questions. While there, I had blood work done and got my H1N1 Flu vaccine. In preparation of the Chemo, I will need a PET Scan and 24 Hour Urine sample. I've done the 24 Hour Urine samples many times before following each occurrence of kidney stones.

They will use two drugs during the Chemo sessions: Taxol and Carboplatin. Prior to each Chemo treatment, I will take medication to control nausea and vomiting. Each treatment will be from 9:00 AM until 4:00 PM. The day after each Chemo treatment, I will be required to return to the office for a shot.

Next Tuesday, I will meet with Nurse Karen for a 2 hour Chemotherapy Education program. At that meeting, I will ask what the shot is for since right now I don't know what it is. Also, I will ask why the treatment is from 9-4 and should I be bringing lunch with me. If anyone has any other questions, please feel free to post them for me. At the Tuesday meeting, I will be "fitted" for a wig. Nurse Karen already suggested I have my hair cut short to accommodate the wig.

So, here is the schedule:

Dec. 21 Urinate into a jug for 24 hours
Dec. 22 Drop urine off and have blood test done at MWH
Dec. 22 8:00 AM - appt. with Karen at Chemo Center
Dec. 22 11:00 AM - appt. with Dr. Hamid
Dec. 23 7:15 AM - 10:30 AM at MGH in Chelsea for PET CT Scan
Dec. 23 11:00 AM - Cut hair short
Jan. 4 - 9:30 AM Radiation at MGH
Jan. 5 - 9:00 AM - 4:00 PM Chemo at Chemo Center
Jan. 6 - 4:00 PM Shot at Chemo Center
Jan. 11 - 9:30 AM Radiation at MGH
Jan. 20 - 9:30 AM Radiation at MGH
Jan. 26 - 9:00 AM - 4:00 PM Chemo at Chemo Center
Jan. 27 - 4:00 PM Shot at Chemo Center
Feb. 16 - 9:00 AM - 4:00 PM Chemo at Chemo Center
Feb 17 - 4:00 PM Shot at Chemo Center
I'm guessing there will be some follow-up appts. with Dr. Hamid, Dr. Russell and Dr. Khatoon in between and after these appts. And, I will need to go for a "wig" fitting somewhere too. If you know any places for wigs, let me know.

Right now, I feel overwhelmed and exhausted but it appears there is light at the end of the tunnel as most of the treatments will be done by mid-February at with time I would have done everything possible to prevent the cancer from recurring.

Thank you again for your prayers and messages. They mean a lot to me and brighten my every day.

• Friday, December 18, 2009 5:12 PM, EST

Today I did a lot of reading and learning about the two drugs they will use for my Chemotherapy. I realize my fears of the treatment are probably unfounded and promised myself I would laugh at my being "bald", however, since I never felt any pain from "the Cancer", I now believe I was in denial that I ever had it. Having my hair fall out is going to bring home the reality that yes, I had cancer!

I remember when my friend Sheila was diagnosed with Breast Cancer, she told me she didn't want to lose her breasts or her hair as those were what she believed to be the assets by which others knew her. As I fought back the tears when Sheila was refusing treatment, I would hug her and say, "I know you for your loving heart, intelligent mind and beautiful smile". I am hearing Sheila's words when I too thought people identified me by my hair, especially in the day when I wore it long and straight down to my waist. But, those days are gone and soon my hair will be too. And, I would much rather people know me and remember me for my loving heart and beautiful smile too.

So, I am going to grin and bear it and although I may cry on Wednesday or on January 5th when whatever hair I have left begins to fall out, I will think of the others (Kathy, Allison, Joann) that went before me and so bravely faced themselves in the mirror. I'm hoping to put the smile back on my face quickly.

Today, I also lined up rides to and from all my current appointments. Thank you Dick, Cara, Deana, Karen, Priscilla and John. Also, my darling Patricia (who works at the Chem Center across the street from where I am having my Chemo treatments) called and told me she will come visit me while I am having my treatments. What awesome people I have in my life! Thank you all.

Have a great weekend and keep warm. I will watch the snow fall by the fire place!

- Monday, December 21, 2009 11:53 AM, EST

I was extremely grateful this weekend that I didn't have to go out in the snow. I enjoyed watching it fall and looking out

273

the window at the frozen pond across from my house. I also enjoyed watching the Patriots beat Buffalo. This would have been the weekend we go to Syracuse to visit Dick's beautiful granddaughters but we were unable to make the trip because of my health. I am sitting for longer periods but sitting for 10 hours in a car over the weekend would have been too much for me.

Last night, I got a call from my wonderful Cousin Jimmy. He wanted to assure me I would be able to deal with the Chemo by taking one day at a time. He has done it several times himself and is now watching his wife do it. We agreed that cancer hits good people, perhaps because we will deal with it by giving more good. Everyone he has met through his disease, his wife has met through hers and I have met through mine have been so loving and caring. Since I was diagnosed (Oct. 30), I have never been hugged by so many doctors and nurses in my life. It amazes me how they treat each patient as if they were their only one. It also amazes me how many people have rallied behind me through Caring Bridge and other media. I wish there was something I could do to repay the kindness to you all.

Today I printed my tax client letters and stuffed the envelopes. I will send my annual mailing out the first week in January. Once I send the mailing, my phone doesn't stop ringing with people making appointments. My daughter Deana (CPA) agreed to help me with data entry this year if I can change my business model. In the past, I would sit with each client for an hour and enter their data as we caught up on the past years events. This year, I will be trying to get people to send me their information so Deana and I can do the data entry at our leisure.

I am grateful it appears my chemotherapy will be done by the middle of February as then I can concentrate on the business and perhaps still squeeze my March trip to FLA in.

Happy Winter Solstice to all! Enjoy the day!

- Tuesday, December 22, 2009 3:42 PM, EST

Dick and I spent 2 hours with Nurse Karen today at the Chemo
Office as she educated us about what I need to do before,
during and after chemotherapy. It seems "little" things keep
popping into the equation that I hadn't counted on. So, today
I need to start taking 2 Vitamin B-6s per day, 1 Vitamin B-12 per
day, and 1 Prilosec now per day and 2 Prilosec on my treatment
day to decrease my stomach acid. Then the day before my
chemotherapy treatments, I need to take 5 Decadron in
the evening and an Ativan to reduce anxiety. On the day of
treatment (Day 1), I need to take 5 Decadron again (with food),
and an Ativan. The day after treatment (Day 2), along with
getting the shot of Pegfilgrastim to rebuild my white blood cell
count, I need to take 2 Decadron in the AM and 1 Decadron in
the PM. On Day 3, I will be taking 1 Decadron in the AM and
one in the PM. On Day 4, I will take 1 Decadron in the AM and a
half of one in the PM and on Day 5, I will take a half a Decadron
in the AM. Decadron is a steroid and thus the weaning
process. Since there is so much preparation required for the
Chemotherapy, it's really a 6 day process. No wonder people
get exhausted. And remember, for my first chemotherapy, I
will be having radiation the day before, which is also supposed
to be tiring. My guess is that once they put the IV for the
chemo into me, I will pass out from the Benadryl and the Aloxi
(to control nausea and vomiting) that will be administered with
the Carboplatin and Taxol. Oh joy!!!

Some of the common side effects from chemo include: feeling
queasy or sick to my stomach, diarrhea, anemia, infection,
alopecia (hair loss) and appetite loss, neuropathy (tingling or
numbness), mouth sores, and muscle or joint pain.

Nurse Karen believes I will lose my hair so she gave me a
prescription for a wig along with the prescriptions for the

other three meds. I felt overwhelmed when I left her office and headed for my check-up with Dr. Hamid.

Since I am 5 1/2 weeks into recovery, Dr. Hamid did a pelvic exam and told me I was recovering as expected. He saw two "dark spots" that concerned him so once I am completely healed, he will do a biopsy on the spots. He set my next appointment with him for April 13th. He said I could resume "NORMAL" activities. I'm sure he meant the new "NORMAL" as I still can't lift more than 10 pounds and they still don't want me driving, bending, stretching, or exerting myself.

So, after going to the pharmacy, I came home and baked brownies for my guests tomorrow. Tomorrow will be a busy day as first I will be having a PET Scan, then am going for my first short hair cut in 33 years and finally, my friend Dave is coming over with his darling daughters. Gabrielle and Jaclyn want to play with Logan and since Cara is babysitting Logan tomorrow and she is my ride home from the PET Scan and to the hairdressers, we will come back to the house and "hang out" for the afternoon.

I finished Exodus in my bible reading so I will start Leviticus tomorrow. I'm thankful to God for answering my prayers and all your prayers for me as I believe by the time Spring comes, I will be healthy again and have far more energy than I do today. My friend Elia wants me to write a book about my experience. What do you think?

- Wednesday, December 23, 2009 1:38 PM, EST

Whew, what a day (so far). At 6:30 AM, my son-in-law Sean picked me up for my trip to the MGH in Chelsea. After filling out more questionnaires, I was sent to a dressing room to get my "doctor's pants" on. Then I was brought into a room where I could drink 2 bottles of Barium and shiver. They had to cover me with three blankets to get me to stop shaking. I read for an hour and then was brought in for my PET Scan. That took 30 minutes of being absolutely still while they moved my body in and out of the machine. Once that was completed, they shot my body with an IV of a solution that caused a tinny taste in my mouth and a burning sensation throughout the rest of my body. They did my CT scan and I was on my way by 10:30.

We then went to the hairdressers. Josephine had dealt with cancer patients before as her mom and her sister both had cancer (kidney and breast respectively). So, we both cried a little and then she cut my hair short, knowing two weeks from now, I will most likely be back for a complete head shave!

From there, Cara, Logan and I went to Panera's for lunch and now are home. I'm ready for my nap so I will be ready to receive my company. I did try to upload the picture of the "new Annie" but Caring Bridge said the file was too large. If anyone has any ideas of how I could reduce the file size, let me know.

I just realized, I am done with medical appointments for this YEAR!!! That's awesome!!!!!!

- Thursday, December 24, 2009 12:01 AM, EST

I forgot to mention I was able to post the picture of me with the short hair. It reminds me of when I was a "little girl"!!

- Thursday, December 24, 2009 8:08 AM, EST

My dear friends David, Susan, Gabrielle and Jaclyn came by yesterday for a visit. We had a wonderful time catching up and watching the girls play with Logan. Logan's a "typical" guy. He flirted with the girls and grabbed their hair and faces! We cut our visit short as Dick's daughters arrived to celebrate Christmas so Dave et. al. promised to come back soon.

277

I'm spending today organizing and getting ready for my trip to FLA. Dr. Hamid said I could go as long as I did it via wheelchair so that is what I am doing. Dave, Cara, their nieces, Dick and I will fly out late Christmas night and return right after the New Year. That should give me time in the sun to rejuvenate, walk and do plenty of relaxing by the pool.

My girlfriend Priscilla will be coming by for a visit and is bringing her grandson Henry. Henry was born in August 2009 but lives in Las Vegas so this is his 1st visit to Boston. Priscilla was one of the wonderful people who was instrumental in helping me raise my daughters as a single mom. Priscilla lived next door to me (in my former home). Her daughter Jennifer is Deana's age so the girls grew up like sisters always in and out of each other's houses. Isn't it ironic that both Jennifer and Deana also had sons in the same year?

Dick and I will go to the 4:00 Mass and then head to Deana's house for XMAS Eve dinner with her in-laws. Dick and Deana are sharing the cooking responsibilities today. We will have a typical Italian XMAS Eve with fish. Italians have 7 kinds of fish on XMAS Eve. This year, we will have 2 different kinds of shrimp (cocktail and fra diavlo), scallops, lobster, mussels, calamari and haddock.

This is a special XMAS Eve for me as it is the first since Deana was 4 years old that I will get to spend with her. As part of my divorce agreement, Deana and Cara spent XMAS Eve with their father's family and Deana continued to spend it with them until this year as her paternal grandmother died while I was in the hospital having surgery in November. It's also special because we are blessed to have Logan with us and because I am on the road to recovery!

Tomorrow, we will have Christmas dinner at Deana's as well. Dick, Cara and Deana will do the cooking. I will watch from the couch! Then we are off to the airport!

May you all have a blessed and Merry Christmas. I am so thankful to God for all I have in my life and to all of you for your continued prayers and well wishes.

- Friday, December 25, 2009 10:01 AM, EST

To my CaringBridge Family and Friends,

May you all have a blessed and Merry Christmas. I continue to be grateful for all the love and caring you have given over the past couple of months and was reminded, while sitting in church, that but for the grace of God, I wouldn't be here today.

God bless you all,

Love,

Ann

- Sunday, December 27, 2009 8:27 AM, EST

Christmas Day was wonderful. We spent it with Cara, Dave, Deana, Sean and Logan. It was so much fun watching Logan get excited about his new toys.

We left Logan Airport at 9:15 PM and arrived in Orlando at 12:30 AM on Dec. 26th. We checked into a hotel for the night. Yesterday Dick's sister (Darlene) picked us up at the hotel in the morning and we were with the rest of the family by noon time. Dick's dad looks frail but is mentally as sharp as a tack. Dick's step-mom was in good spirits and seemed to enjoy playing cards with us. We played a game called "45s" which is popular in the Merrimack Valley, which is where Dick grew up.

The temperature here is in the mid-60s. We understand the temperature in Fort Lauderdale is 10-15 degrees higher so

Ann R. DiMare

I'm sure I will have a relaxing time sitting in the sun starting tomorrow!!! I am also anxious to see my wonderful FLA friends. It's been way too long. I usually have the pleasure of spending Novembers with them but this year, God had other plans for me!

Stay warm and enjoy the day. I'm thrilled to be here and out of the cold weather. Unfortunately, I lost my "cancer" bracelet. Perhaps that's a sign that I soon will be cancer free.

God Bless you all

- Monday, December 28, 2009 9:21 PM, EST

Today we had lunch with Darlene and her family, went to see Dick's dad and step-mom to say our "goodbyes" and then made our way to Fort Lauderdale. I haven't been at my condo since March so was overjoyed to see my FLA condo friends and am looking forward to seeing my FLA FAA friends this week. Dick suggested I invite everyone for a New Year's Day buffet! Works for me! What a great way to start the New Year. So, tomorrow after running some errands, I plan to sit in the sun and watch the boats go by, as it is supposed to be in the 70s here.

Tomorrow would have been my mom's 80th birthday so in some ways, it is a sad day for me. My mom died in 1994 so she never got to see my condo. She would have loved it here as she hated the cold weather in Boston in the winter. I will try to take some pictures so you can see why I call this Paradise!

I also understand we are having a "Blue Moon" on Thursday night. One of my favorite restaurants here is the Blue Moon!!!! http://www.bluemoonfishco.com/index1.html It's on the Intercoastal. They offer two lunches for the price of one providing each person buys a beverage! Go figure!

- Tuesday, December 29, 2009 4:53 PM, EST

We had lunch at the condo. My girlfriend Rita came by for a hug and a visit. It's been amazing for me to see people who have gone through the same ordeal I am going through and seeing them healthy helps me know I will get there too. We laughed and we cried together but that's normal for us. Actually, we usually laugh so hard, we cry. This time our tears were tears of joy for having our lives and having them void of cancer. We are two of the lucky ones who found it fast enough to get help.

Rita, her mom (89 years old) and her husband will be coming over on Friday to celebrate the New Year. My girlfriends Roberta & Beverley will also join us. I can't wait to see what Chef Dick comes up with!!

I posted a picture of the view from my living room window. They call my unit the "Fishbowl" because I have water on three sides of me, the Intercoastal on the East and the South, the swimming pool on the West. The temperature was only 69 today but it felt like 79 in the sun so I only sat out for an hour or so. My skin is so light now compared to how I usually am. This summer was not a good one for tanning and without coming down in November, I need to go easy with the sun.

Stay warm. I am thinking of you all!

- Wednesday, December 30, 2009 8:21 PM, EST

Every year I buy myself a Christmas gift and a birthday gift. This year, I bought a new refrigerator for the condo. Dick and I went to a great store called Brandsmart in Deerfield Beach. Since we got there at 9:00 and they didn't open until 10:00, Dick treated me to a manicure and pedicure while we waited. So now, my fingers and toes look pretty for radiation and chemo.

The new refrigerator will be delivered tomorrow, just in time for Dick to go grocery shopping for the New Years Day dinner party.

As of this evening, Chef Dick will be preparing ravioli, chicken cutlets, veggies and a salad. He said he may switch the chicken cutlets to baked stuffed shrimp or he may make both!!!

I sat in the sun with my friend Beverley for a couple of hours. She shared her experiences with her past cancers (breast and endometrial). Bev turned 80 years old in July so I am totally convinced --- there is life after cancer. Bev is a vibrant, energetic and busy lady. She takes care of a lot of people, mostly elderly people in the 90s but she also takes care of me. When I find geckos or critters in my condo, she comes to get them out for me!!

Dick and I did something we haven't done before, we went out to celebrate New Year's Eve on the eve of New Years Eve. Most restaurants in Fort Lauderdale are booked solid. They have a limited menu with 2 distinct seatings. They rush you in and out and the food isn't as well prepared as usual. So we went to the Blue Moon, sat outdoors next to the water and watched the mega-yachts come and go. It was in the low 70s here today with a warm breeze so it was enjoyable. We haven't yet figured out what we will do tomorrow night but we may just eat in.

Whatever you do tomorrow night, please enjoy and keep safe. I wish you all a happy and healthy 2010

- Friday, January 1, 2010 9:25 AM, EST

Happy New Year Everyone!!! I hope you all had a wonderful evening last night. I know we did! Dick made scrod, salad and lobster bisque --- all delicious. We started to watch TV but both fell asleep. We woke up at 11:45 PM, waited for the "ball to drop" in NY City and fell fast asleep again.

Dick and I just got back from Mass. They renovated our church here (St. Pius X). It's absolutely beautiful with marble everywhere. I should have taken a picture.

The Chef is in the kitchen making breakfast and soon will be starting on the lunch. I will set the table and take care of the ambience! There will be 7 of us for lunch. My biggest decision today will be whether to use the Christmas dishes or the regular ones. I have a feeling the Christmas ones will win out. Why save them. It is still Christmas season -- correct? So, today's guests include (Rita - recently done with radiation for breast cancer, Roberta - her mom passed away two weeks ago, Beverley - had breast and endometrial cancer, Rita's mom (89 years old), Tony (Rita's husband) and Dick (my sweetheart).

Yesterday, I learned that one of my FB friends has breast cancer so please add Brenda to your prayer list. She lives on Martha's Vineyard and will be going to Dana Farber for treatment. That reminds me of how lucky I am to live close to some of the best hospitals in the world. Brenda --- if you need a place to stay during testing or treatments, my house is open to you and Chucky!

Today, I will pray that in 2010, God keeps you all safe and healthy. And, I also pray that I get to see each and every one of you for at least one visit in the new year.

Love,
Ann

- Saturday, January 2, 2010 3:56 PM, EST

It's a bit chilly here today so we did some shopping. They have a Carter's Outlet store in the mall so I got Logan a bunch of clothes for Valentine's Day and his 1st Birthday! I can't believe he is almost a year old. Where does the time go?

We then went to the Fort Lauderdale Art Museum to see a Norman Rockwell exhibit. It was educational and interesting.

Tonight, we plan to eat leftovers for dinner (baked stuffed shrimp, asparagus, ravioli and chicken cutlets) and stay in. Tomorrow, we clean the condo then head to the airport for our trip back home. It's bittersweet for me. I miss Logan but am going home to face what I suspect will be one of the toughest weeks of my life.

I suspect the weather in NE may present us with a difficult and lengthy journey tomorrow so I will post again on Monday when I get home from Radiation and Wig Shopping!

See -- I'm still "Lightening Up" as Loretta LaRouch would say!!

• Monday, January 4, 2010 12:16 AM, EST

Yesterday, fearing the snow storm would leave us stranded in Charlotte, NC, Dick and I changed our flights to direct flights to Boston. Our new flight was scheduled to leave Fort Lauderdale at 3:30 and arrive in Boston at 6:30 so that also would give us more time at home to get ready for our busy week of medical appointments. Since the weather in NE didn't quite cooperate, our 3:30 flight left FLA at 7:00 PM and arrived in Boston at 10:00 PM. At least we didn't have to change planes.

Deana, God Bless her, smartly paid someone $60 of my money to shovel the 3 feet of snow from my driveway so we could get in the house when we got home. Thank goodness she is a smarty! It would have totally ruined our vacation if we had to shovel our way in so late at night.

When we got home, there was a stack of mail. There was also a box of goodies sent by another angel. My cousin Donna, a dental hygienist, sent me a package of mouth care products for people who are having chemotherapy. Thank you, Donna. I'm sure they will be helpful.

This A.M, Deana and Logan picked me up for my 1st Radiation Session at MGH. We arrived early since there was no traffic. Dr. Russell and staff were prompt and efficient so by 10:15, we were on our way. We went to the "Wig" store on the 9th floor of the MGH (Yawkey Bldg.). Since we didn't have an appointment, we were unable to get me fitted for a wig. We made an appointment for next Monday after my next radiation session.

Radiation went as advertised. I didn't have much discomfort. The only discomfort was from the positioning on the table with legs in a stirrup for 20 minutes. A friend of my girlfriend Patty's (Tom) came by to meet me and visit for a few minutes. What a way to meet someone (with legs in a stirrup). Also, since Dr. Russell and crew told me they would be watching me on the camera/monitor positioned toward me, I decided to make some faces at them. We all got a laugh out of it.

I did walk out of the hospital feeling exactly as I had walked in but am getting tired now (as they told me I would).

Tomorrow is my first Chemo session. I am already taking meds for it so I am really not sure if my exhaustion is from the radiation or the chemo meds. I still wish someone would wave a magic wand and tell me I didn't need the chemo but I don't believe that will happen by 9:00 tomorrow so I will show up as planned. And, based on what I heard from different other women who had chemo, I should have a naked head by this weekend. I know my hair will grow back and I know there is nothing to be afraid of, but I am still feeling anxious about this whole Chemo thing! So, tonight before going to bed and tomorrow before going to chemo, I will pop more of those anxiety pills they gave me!

- Wednesday, January 6, 2010 3:26 AM, EST

Yes, it is 3:26 AM and I cannot sleep so I figured this would be a good time to update my journal.

Yesterday, after my taking 14 pills for Chemo Day #1, we left the house at 8:00 AM for my 9:00 AM Chemo appointment as we had a couple of errands to run. We arrived at the Chemo center at 8:30 AM.

While waiting for my 9:00 AM appointment, my wonderful girlfriend Patty came to visit. Patty brought me a beautiful card filled with many of the experiences we shared starting in September 1971 when we met at our first day at Boston State College. She also brought me a "smiley" face on a stick and a heart necklace. What a blessing to have such a wonderful friend.

At 9:00 promptly, a nurse came to take my blood while Dick and Patty talked about what we would do for lunch! Prior to any Chemo treatment, they take blood to be sure the white blood cell count is high enough to tolerate the procedure. Since mine was high enough, the next step was to meet with the Doctor. Dr. Khatoon was on vacation in Bangladesh so her associate Dr. A. Sattar Menon (from Brown University) spoke with me. It appeared my file was "empty" as when Nurse Karen sent my records "off shore" for transcription (14 days ago), they didn't come back in time for my appointment. Dr. Menon called Nurse Karen, who was at their Quincy office for the day, and she relayed much of the information to Dr. Menon from her written notes. The rest of the information we recreated by Dr. Menon interviewing me again. Since I wasn't prepared to postpone the chemo treatment, I was a patient patient! Normally, I would have suggested they change their office procedures to capture the data electronically on the initial intake to save money from having to send the information "off shore" but that was my FAA thinking coming out and just not how they did it in this office!

At 10:45 AM, they hooked up my IV and we finally got started with the pre-med portion of the treatment. The first three bags of solution contained Benadryl, saline and Decadron (steroid). At 12:30 PM, Patty returned with an awesome salmon lunch with rice and vegetables. Soon after, my friend John C. came to visit and delivered a CD player with the Seinfeld Season 4 and Catch Me If You Can DVDs. Unfortunately, it was so busy and noisy there that we were unable to watch them, but they will be much appreciated tonight.

By 1:00 PM, I was finally on my way to receiving the Taxol. This is the Chemo drug that causes the hair loss. It took 3 hours to administer the whole bag and they immediately switched me to the Carboplatin, which took one hour to administer. They scheduled me for three follow-up appointments (Jan 12, Feb. 2 and Feb 23) and by 5:15PM, we were ready to leave the center. We were the first in and last out (FILO) again.

I went home thinking, "that wasn't too bad". Actually, the worst part was the needles from the blood work and the frequent urination from all the liquids I was given via IV and from drinking water.

By 7:00 PM, I had severe stomach cramps, feeling queasy, diarrhea, nausea, severe chills, slight fever, dry mouth, metallic taste, burning eyes and exhaustion. I ate a small dinner and went up to bed where I also noticed I had a large lump on my hand at the sight of the IV incision.

At 8:00 PM, Dr. Menon called to see how I was doing. When I told him my symptoms, he suggested I put ice on my hand and suggested a med to stop the diarrhea. I played some Sudoku and passed out! The good news is, so far no hair loss, no constipation, no neuropathy, no mouth sores, no muscle or joint pain, no painful urination and no bleeding. But today is another day so one never knows what will come my way. I clearly am having difficulty sleeping.

Today, I return to the chemo center for a shot of Neulasta to help rebuild my white blood cell count. I understand the side effects are bone pain for which they will give me either Tylenol or Vicodin. PLEASE I'M BEGGING THEM --- NO MORE DRUGS! Did I ever tell you I hate taking any kind of meds?

Oh yes, and the medical bills keep coming in. Thank goodness tax season is starting soon. The government BCBS and pension just doesn't cut it when one has a major medical setback like this! I am grateful for what BCBS does cover but it's amazing what it doesn't even when I am using all preferred doctors and facilities.

Thank you all for your continued messages and prayers. I pray we are coming down the home stretch in this race for the cure.

- Thursday, January 7, 2010 8:41 AM, EST

Yesterday afternoon, Dick and I went to the Chemo Center for my shot to increase my white blood count. I reported all my side effects from the night before to Nurse Karen. She said they were all related to the Decadron. She cut my doses for the rest of the week to wean me off faster and additionally cut my doses for my two subsequent Chemo treatments. They will not administer the Decadron in the IV on the next two Chemo treatments.

Dr. Menon came by to see my wrist/hand and suggested I continue using ice to reduce the swelling and to get the internal bleeding to stop. They will not use my wrist/hand for the next doses of IV. Instead they will use the back of my left arm.

Next Tuesday, I will go for a follow up where they will check my vital signs and take blood to be sure my white blood count is up where it should be. So each Chemo Treatment is actually three visits or $90 in co-pays using the 2010 co-pays set by Blue Cross. The price of the plan went up. The co-pays went up. The prescription drugs went up and since we didn't get a federal cost of living adjustment, my pension went down! But life is still worth living and I'm happy to be alive whatever it costs!

I was speeding through the day yesterday thinking I could leap tall buildings in a single bound. At 7:00 PM, I crashed. I got more done at home than I had since Oct. 30th when I just cried while staring at the walls for days. Now I know why athletes aren't allowed to take steroids. They make you feel like a Super Woman/Man!

I slept until 11:00 PM, stayed awake until 3:00 AM and slept again until 5:30 AM - That's 6 1/2 total hours, better than the night before! Nurse Karen told me I would be "hitting the wall" when I am completely off the steroids. Since I am still on them today, I will get some of my bookkeeping work done in preparation for tax season.

Thanks again for all the prayers and well wishes. I am 1/3 done with both the radiation and Chemo treatments. I still have my hair although Nurse Karen said it should start falling out in a week or so. Thus, I am still on schedule to have radiation on Monday and will order my wig after my radiation appointment.

• Friday, January 8, 2010 8:18 AM, EST

I'm still smiling. I haven't lost any hair yet and am still on steroids. I am buzzing around doing lots of things I haven't done in 8 weeks. YES, today is 8 weeks from when I had my surgery so supposedly, I am fully recovered from the surgery. And, I feel physically so much stronger than I did 8 weeks ago but I recognize it could be the steroids. The test of my strength will be to see if I can pick up Logan later today. He's probably a little over 20 pounds. I am so anxious to babysit him again but I can't until I can pick him up.

I am also cleared to drive as long as I am not on the Decadron or the Atavin so I am going to make my way to my doctor's appointment alone next Tuesday. Today, I cut the Decadron to a half pill in the AM and a half pill in the PM. Tomorrow, I will take a half pill and the AM and then be off it until the day before my next Chemo session (Jan. 26).

On Saturday, we will celebrate Cara's 33rd birthday. She was away and I was in Radiation on 1/4 so we will have a family dinner on Saturday evening. On Sunday, I am hoping I am well enough to go to the Patriots playoff game. IF my "hitting the wall" occurs on Sunday, I may sleep though the game but if it is an exciting one - I may just stay awake! I just hope the Patriots don't "hit the wall" as I would love to go to Superbowl Weekend in FLA!!(20 minutes from my condo).

My cousin Donna and Aunt Mary are coming to visit today. I am thrilled as they will get to meet Logan and I will get some much needed family hugs!

Thank you all for your continued hugs. I am certainly up for company so if you are ever in the area and what to stop in for a visit, just let me know. It gets hectic here from Feb. 1- April 15 but there is always time for loving friends in my life and my tax clients are awesome people who are patient with disruptions!!

Stay warm and enjoy the weekend. GO PATS

* Monday, January 11, 2010 2:09 PM, EST

The weekend presented its challenges. Since I was still on steroids (1/2 pill) on Saturday, I felt fairly good in the AM. I had tingles throughout my arms and legs the previous evening but they had gone away so I figured I was in good shape and potentially had overcome or escaped any side effects from the chemotherapy. I got up early and baked Cara a birthday cake and brownies. On Friday, I had started the outline for my book. Yes, I am going to write a book. It may take years but I figure it will be therapeutic for me to get my life and lessons learned down in writing and perhaps others can either be inspired by it or watch for the pitfalls that lead to repeated problems (i.e., loving the wrong people too much). Also, several people recently and through the years have suggested I write a book so I figured there is no time like the present to get started.

On Saturday evening, after going to bed, I started to experience chest pains. Nurse Karen said I could get tingles, chest pain and/or back pain from the shot they gave me on Wednesday. Since they hadn't occurred by Saturday, I thought, "NOT ME!!" Not so soon Ann!

I knew Sunday was the day I was supposed to "hit the wall". Dick would be going to the Patriots game, I decided to go with him as I figured I would be better off in the fresh air (appropriately bundled up of course) than I would be home alone on the couch. And since I was getting chest pains on Saturday night into Sunday, it was even more important to me not to be alone. So dressed with thermals, hand warmers, toe warmers, turtle neck sweater, down storm coat, hat, scarf and mittens, I went to the game. Needless to say, it was a disappointment but for Pats fans, it's been that way for a couple of years now. I certainly was warm enough and felt good throughout the day with the exception of when I was walking. My hips were hurting and I could feel shooting pain in my lower back and thighs. I was home and in bed by 7:00 PM but spent the rest of the evening getting up and down to take Tylenol for my severe back spasms and pain. There was nothing I could do to get comfortable so I cried! Finally, at 3:00 AM, the pain subsided and I fell asleep.

Today, I had my second radiation treatment. Deana and Logan picked me up for our trip into MGH. Radiation went as expected. It certainly doesn't affect me physically the way the chemotherapy does. After the radiation treatment, we went to order my wig. I stuck with brown hair, similar style as my new haircut. Although I wanted to "lighten up" and be able to laugh at myself with a wig, for some reason, I just didn't find the humor in it --- not today anyways. I still want to take pictures of me with my "hairless" friends but that will come later.

- Tuesday, January 12, 2010 12:30 PM, EST

This morning, I had an appointment at the Chemo Center to have blood drawn to determine if my white blood cell count actually did rise again. Since I was having the back spasms yesterday and the day before, Dick drove me to my appointment. While there, they took my blood and vital signs. They tested my blood and yes, I am progressing nicely. That's a good thing. Also, my blood pressure is getting better (140/80). I asked about how long the Chemo drugs would stay in my system as I am extremely fatigued and generally feeling weary. I also asked again about the hair loss as I was thinking perhaps I could beat this part of the program! I was told that once I felt tingling in my head, it would be falling out soon. As soon as I got home, the tingling started. I just finished reading Kelly Tuthill's (Channel 5) blog on her battle with breast cancer (for the 2nd time) and I am trying to gather strength from her experience. She's an amazing woman. I feel fully equipped with great support from all of you and I know I will beat this too. I just wish the roller coaster ride would stop! On a lighter note, when I got home, I made myself an ice-cream float to lift my spirits. I haven't had one in years – delicious and worth the calories just for today!

I am still not sleeping as well as I would like but that is giving me quiet time to write my book. Early this morning, I wrote some sections about my birth and my early childhood, living in Winthrop, MA. Winthrop was an amazing place to grow up as people cared for their own children and their neighbors as well. My friend's parents treated me like their own. As a child, adolescent and young adult, I faced an incredible amount of challenges, that others may have considered insurmountable. My learning to cope with them and how I dealt with them is what made me who I am today and allowed me to succeed in life almost against all odds. I am therefore using the writing of this book to be therapeutic and informative so others will know they too can succeed. I trusted in God to guide me and hold my hand when others didn't or chose not to because of their own situations. My mentors through the years were incredible as well, but I will save all that for the book.

Thanks again for your continued prayers. I am now officially half way done with my treatment program -- or so I think!

- Wednesday, January 13, 2010 8:11 AM, EST

For some reason, today I woke up thinking about the "numbers". When I went for radiation on Monday, it occurred to me that there were about 50 people in the waiting area at the MGH Radiation Center. For each person, radiation takes about 20 minutes or to be conservative, we could say a half an hour between undressing, treatment and dressing up. When I arrived I saw all different faces than when I left. So, if this scenario goes on all day for 5 days a week, I figure, MGH alone is treating between 4000-5000 people a week. I strongly believe there are thousands of radiation centers in the country as I know there are over a hundred in the state. Therefore the numbers of radiation patients alone is overwhelming. Now, let's add the chemotherapy patients to the mix.

At the CHO in Stoneham, there were at least 25 people in and out the day I received my chemo, the day I received my shot and yesterday when I went for my follow-up appointment. I know there are 10 CHO Centers in Eastern Mass so again, multiplying the numbers, there is an incredible number of people having chemo treatments on a daily basis.

Today, I am gathering my strength from the numbers, just knowing there are so many out there that have overcome far more serious cancers than mine. Thank God, we have made great strides in cancer research. I know 14 survivors (Allison, Kathy, Larry, Bob, Marie, Beverley, Rita, Josh, Jimmy, Kevin, Brenda, Kate, Georgie and me). YES, I will be a survivor. Today I feel better than I have in a long time...no doctor's appointments...no chemo meds...no poking and probing.

Last night I had head and feet tingles but both were tolerable without Tylenol. I'm still taking one day at a time but must say I am getting excited about tomorrow. My little man "Logan" will be coming for a pajama party tomorrow night!

• Thursday, January 14, 2010 9:18 AM, EST

I have been up since 4:00 AM and am finding myself full of energy despite my having back spasms yet again. I'm sure I will crash later today. Anyways, I wrote about 5 pages in my book, mostly the circumstances surrounding my mother's death. It's amazing how time can clarify things. Things my mother predicted would happen in the days prior to her death have actually happened. She was wise beyond her years.

Last night I met two girlfriends for dinner. It was good to see Ann Marie and Donna. Ann Marie is a nurse so the discussions centered around my treatment program. It's always reassuring to hear I am doing the right thing by having both the radiation and chemotherapy. We agreed that "whatever the doctor orders" is the best approach, especially since I am blessed with a team of doctors that are the "heads" in their respective hospitals.

Tonight Logan arrives for our pajama party. Yesterday was a quiet but busy day, getting ready for tax season.

• Friday, January 15, 2010 8:01 AM, EST

Ouch - the roller coaster ride continues.

Logan arrived yesterday afternoon at 5:30 and after his dinner and a "tubby", he was sound asleep in his crib by 8:00 PM. The little angel slept until 6:00 AM! What more could a Nana ask for?

I was another story. I was up until well past midnight and couldn't sleep until I took a few Tylenol. I had severe back spasms along with stomach cramps. I may be doing it to myself with all the fruits and veggies but am just trying to eat healthier than I used to. So, I was up at 5:00 AM and spent way too much time on the "potty". Thank goodness for Sudoku!

Forest Gump said, "Life is like a box of chocolates, you never know what you are going to get". Jackie Gleason said, "How sweet it is!" Am hoping today sweetens up and brings me some chocolates! Enjoy the day.

• Saturday, January 16, 2010 6:31 AM, EST

Yesterday Deana, Logan and I went to get my wig at MGH. If you see someone with an "Erika" style wig in Chocolate Brown, it could be ME!

We met Deana's Godmother, my awesome friend Joyce and her sister Liz for lunch. Logan was our entertainment. Earlier in the day, I taught him how to kiss by putting his lips together instead of licking my face. I told him to give Nana a "fish kiss". Throughout lunch, Logan gave "fish kisses". Joyce and Liz took the opportunity to teach Logan how to do "pig" noises and other barnyard noises. He's a copycat so he had us in stitches. Laughter is such good medicine. I was belly laughing for the first time in a long time and it felt so good.

Yesterday was another day of back spasms and dysentery. I had gained a little of my weight back while on steroids so am losing it again the unnatural way! I also broke out in a terrible rash all over both my arms and hands. Overnight, I had more

295

dysentery and a bloody nose. I am going to hydrate today as I believe I may be dehydrated (ammonia smell in the urine)! I wonder what is next!

Enjoy the weekend and keep safe. XOXOOXOXO

· Monday, January 18, 2010 7:45 AM, EST

Yesterday Dick and I went to mass and prayed for all my friends who have cancer. From there, we went to Sabella's to buy some chicken soup. Anyone that lives in the area knows how delicious Sabella's chicken soup is. Usually Dick makes his own but HE was the one feeling sick yesterday so he bought it. To give him as much rest as possible, I went to my daughter Cara's house for a few hours. Her in-laws were there so I got to see Larry (my son-in-law's father) and Gene (his grandfather). Both are currently going through chemotherapy for cancer. The three of us talked about our experiences! It's obvious for everyone, the experience and the side effects are different. I am still having back spasms and am starting to lose my hair. Larry and Gene aren't experiencing that but have other side effects of their own.

Yes, I am starting to lose my hair. This morning it came out in clumps in the shower and there was plenty of it on the bathroom floor as well. Since I have thick hair, I have a ways to go before I will have any bald patches. I am being extremely careful when I comb/brush it. My head is also feeling tender, kind of like it is black and blue.

Yesterday I wrote about 10 more pages in my book. I am up to 50 pages already. I didn't realize I had so much to say! I also started scanning vital documents from my parents past. I have their birth certificates, military discharge papers, divorce decree, etc. It will be nice to have everything in one place.

Today, I will stay warm inside while the snow falls. I "may" attempt to use my electric snow thrower when it is done to clear my driveway. I felt good yesterday and feel good today, perhaps because I am not on any meds.

- Tuesday, January 19, 2010 1:06 PM, EST

I spent most of the day yesterday and today adding to my book. I have 70 pages and am still going strong. I'm scanning in a lot of pictures as well. Unfortunately most of my childhood pictures were lost after my mom's passing but I have a few to include.

I refilled my "pill" box this AM and was troubled to have to put the Decadron and nausea pills back in. I will start taking the Decadron again on Monday as I will be having chemo again on Tuesday. I know I have said it before but I will say it again --- I hate drugs! I know they help in some cases but I would just rather be healthy so I wouldn't' need them.

Tomorrow is radiation. Based on my last two encounters, I am expecting it will be uneventful. The worst part is getting there in the Boston traffic but Deana showed me the back roads so even that isn't too difficult.

Yesterday I talked to a childhood friend. Karen is the sister of two guys I graduated high school with. I was close to her family for a long time. Karen has survived stage 3 breast cancer for 4 years now. She gave me some pointers to get better sleep at night and to help with itching. She also encouraged me to join a support group in Winthrop called Survivors by the Sea. The group started with a few ladies from Winthrop that were breast cancer survivors. They now have over 100 people in the group. It got me wondering if all the jet fuel that was dumped over the ocean (from planes landing at Logan Airport) that we swam in as kids, cause for all our cancers? Just wondering!!

Winthrop is a small town and there are so many people living there with cancer.

OK - back to my writing and scanning! Who wants to play me in the movie?

- Wednesday, January 20, 2010 12:27 PM, EST

I just got back from my last radiation session. This one was easier than the others as I only had to be on the machine for 8 minutes. The problem was, I got to MGH at 9:15 and the girl at the front desk forgot to tell them I was there despite my arriving on time and despite giving me my hospital bracelet. So, when I didn't get called by 10:00, I found Dr. Russell and Dr. Wakefield. They told me they were waiting for me to arrive and were just about to call my house. After checking with the desk and finding out how long I had been waiting, they offered me a "nutrition" voucher for my troubles. Nutrition vouchers need to be spent on food at MGH, so after I got my instructions for using my new vaginal probes (to be sure I don't get any scar tissue), I made my next appointment for March 5th and went to the MGH food store. My girlfriend Priscilla drove me today and had a great idea. Since it wasn't time for lunch, she suggested we get items to take home. So we left with a shopping bag filled with: 2 bagels, 1 muffin, 2 bags of chips, an orange juice, a chocolate milk, a bottle of iced tea, a box of cheerios, a cup of yogurt, a cup of cantaloupe and a cup of strawberries and a good laugh. Great idea Priscilla - thank you.

We did a little shopping for Mr. Logan (outfits for FLA) and went to Prince Pizza for lunch. And now, it's time for my nap!

In my bible readings, I finished Leviticus and will be starting Numbers tomorrow. I took a glance at the first Numbers reading. It talks about The First Census of Israel. Since its census time in America too, I thought my timing was impeccable.

Have 78 pages in the book and still have a lot more to say so will continue with the writing after my nap. Logan will be with me all day tomorrow and for portions of Friday. We are having our next pj party on Saturday night this week.

God Bless you all for getting me through 2/3 of my treatment program. I only have 2 more chemo sessions left. Hugs XOXOX

- Friday, January 22, 2010 7:59 AM, EST

Wow - yesterday was the first time I had Logan alone for a whole day. Actually, he had slept over the night before so I had him for 24 hours!! Suffice it to say, I passed out on the couch as soon as he left. He's so much fun and such a good boy but wants 100% of my attention when he is with me.

Yesterday, I shed so much hair that I now understand why people shave their heads. I found hair on everything. In fact, my jersey had so much hair on the back that it looked like a gorilla. I saw how much was falling forward but didn't realize how much was on my back until bedtime. It's still falling out today at a rapid pace but I am going to just hang in there for a while with what I have left. I have lots of scarves and have learned how to make turban hats but plan to see if I can find something today that I can easily put on that I don't have to worry about it falling off.

I spent quite a while on the phone yesterday with my uncle Joe, validating family history for my book. As I write each section, I am trying to be sure I am 100% accurate on things and thus I am including scanned copies of original documents to validate my content.

I am thankful to God for all the wonderful people in my life that have kept me strong through these trying times.

- Monday , January 25, 2010 8:17 AM, EST

The weekend flew by. On Saturday, Logan came over at lunch time. He loved the spinach calzone we gave him. After his nap I dressed him for Carmen's birthday party. He had a great time eating (mac & cheese and chicken fingers) and playing with the other kids. He passed out on the way home which made it easy to put him to bed! Since he's a good sleeper, I had a good night's sleep too. On Sunday we took him to church with us. The priest blessed him while walking up the aisle and then again at communion time. He was a good boy in church, eating his cheerios, drinking a bottle, doing his baby talk to my friends Donna and Charlie and singing the hymns!

Sunday afternoon, my daughters and their husbands came to dinner along with my wonderful nephew Jacob. Jacob hadn't met Logan yet so it was fun to see them interact. Logan is a friendly baby. He'll talk to anyone! He loves to perform for people too so he did his repertoire of words (hi, ouch, quack) and facial expressions for Jacob. Jacob gave Logan some stuffed animals and me one of his mom's old WHS yearbooks (1972) so I enjoyed looking at that. Jacob's mom has been deceased for four years now. She was only 51 years old when she died of MS.

Dick made us a fabulous dinner, as always and Logan had his first meatball and eggplant parmigiana. My son-in-law Sean has competition with Logan for the food. It's amazing to watch him eat.

The rest of the afternoon, we spent with Jacob and my daughters reading portions of my book and watching football. I got the "thumbs" up from all three of them so I will continue writing. Jacob had some good advice for me. He said to write the book for myself and I can't go wrong. I feel that is what I have been doing and will continue doing that. Thanks Jacob. I love you.

Tonight I will go to a wake for Dick's sister-in-law's dad, then I will come home and take my pre-chemotherapy meds. Thus starts the roller coaster ride again. I know they are meant to help me but I believe it is all the meds and the drugs from the chemo that made me so sick the last time. I did have some reprieve last week but since that was the week I lost my hair, it was fairly traumatic for me too.

Today, my Facebook friend Brenda is having breast cancer surgery. As I will be completing my therapy next month, Brenda is just starting her journey to wellness. Please send some prayers her way. Thank you all and God Bless You.

- Tuesday, January 26, 2010 7:57 PM, EST

Well, I made it through another day of chemotherapy. I now have only ONE more treatment left --- YIPPIE.

So far so good. They did NOT give me the Decadron in my pre-meds so I suspect I will sleep well tonight as I won't be speeding as I was the last time. Also, since I had one less bag of fluids, I was out of there by 4:00 PM instead of 5:30 PM and I didn't spend as much time on the "potty"!

Dick and my wonderful girlfriend Patty came with me again today. Since the treatment room was so crowded, they had to limit their visits and sit in the waiting room. Patty works across the street, so she was able to return for lunch. She brought me and Dick a sub sandwich at Angelo's' on Main Street in Stoneham - delicious!

When I got home, I had 6 phone calls and a few emails to return for tax appointments. The schedule is filling up. I'm trying to book people around my babysitting schedule too so Logan doesn't feel neglected when the clients are here. I'm guessing at some point, I will start teaching him taxes as I did his mother and his aunt so perhaps we can have a large family tax business some day. I can see it now, "Logan, Nana, Mom & Auntie" all working together! Perhaps at that point, I just do the FLA clients and leave the rest to them!

Tomorrow, I was advised to cut my Decadron even more than last time and take two Tylenol before going for my shot at 3:45PM. Then I am going to the hairdressers for my buzz cut and wig adjustment. I am praying I don't get the same side effects from the shot as I did last time. It was horrible. Since they put the IV in my arm this time instead of my hand, I don't have any bumps or black and blues so that too is better than last time.

Am going to upload and post the picture we took this AM of me leaving for my second Chemo Treatment. Promise not to laugh at my hat!! XOXOXO

• Wednesday, January 27, 2010 7:10 PM, EST

I have been up since 3:00 AM and am busy. I am having similar side effects to the last chemo treatment but not to the intensity as last time. Since they didn't give me any Decadron in the IV yesterday and I was able to cut back on the amount I took today, I am starting to get tired now but still need to take another Decadron before bed. Wish I could just take the Ativan and call it a day.

In any case, being up for so long allowed me to get more of the book done and get two client returns started. That's all good since my schedule gets really hectic for the next couple of months.

Today, I went to the Chemo Clinic for my shot. I then went to the hairdresser for my "buzz" cut and wig adjustment. I am posting a picture with my new "do". Please don't laugh as that is what I will be looking like for the next 6 months. They are telling me the hair will start growing back in 6-8 weeks after my last chemo. That is on Feb. 16th so I will be "wigging" it until the hair is long enough to go without the wig and if it grows back in gray or blonde, long enough for me to be able to color it! I'm being told I might end up with curly hair. My hair was naturally wavy anyways but since I wore it so long, it appeared straight. So check out the photos and let's pray I don't get those terrible back spasms again. That was the worst part of it all besides the amount of time I spent in the toilet!

For those facing chemo or radiation, I am SHOCKED at the amount I pay out of pocket for each treatment. The chemo is costing me $589 per session OUT OF POCKET x 3! The radiation is costing me $618.78 per session OUT OF POCKET x 3! I called Blue Cross today. They told me once I go over $5000 for this year, everything else will be free as catastrophic protection. Amazing and OUCH!

Thanks again for all your well wishes and cards. They mean so much to me. They keep me smiling during these tough times. Oh and I didn't cry when the hairdresser shaved my head since this morning, I cut off most of my hair myself and laughed as I was doing it.

- Thursday, January 28, 2010 4:52 PM, EST

It's been a long day for me so far. I have been up since 3:30 AM again but am feeling no side effects from the chemo so that is a good thing.

I got a lot done on my book again today and actually finished a "first cut" at my taxes. Am still waiting for paperwork to verify the numbers I put on the return.

I enjoy reading every message and am blessed to have you all in my life.

- Saturday, January 30, 2010 6:33 PM, EST

Another wild few days! I had Logan yesterday and today. Gosh - boys are active! I also was on a lower dose of the Decadron so am almost hitting the wall, and of course, add some tax clients to that mix and Annie's a tired lady! Logan was 10 months old today so we sang and clapped.

Even though it is only 6:35 PM, I am hitting the couch and am guessing it will be for the night! I feel so old! But I know I am coming down the home stretch and this too shall pass in time. Stay warm and God bless you all.

- Tuesday, February 2, 2010 5:17 AM, EST

It's 5:17 AM and I just got back from driving Dick to South Station for his business trip to NYC. It's a good thing we are both morning people. My day started at 3:45 AM as it has for the past three days. The "drugs" they give to assist with the chemo seem to be my problem. I'm getting those terrible back spasms again and will spend today on Tylenol. I see Dr. Khatoon later today to determine if the shot last Wednesday did what it is supposed to do (raise my white blood count). I suspect it did.

Last night I met a wonderful group of ladies from Winthrop, MA. All 8 of them are cancer survivors. Their group name is Survivors by the Sea. They have a website if you are interested: www.survivorsbythesea.com . They picked me up for dinner and brought me a "goodie" bag to help with getting through treatments. Each of them had their own different story as I now have mine, but the one thing we all agreed to is how a person changes once they have had cancer! I know I have changed. It was amazing to see faces of ladies I had gone to high school with and actually remember them and have them remember me, even with my wig! They started the group with 2 people and are now over 150 strong. I plan to participate in as many activities with them as time allows.

I felt like I was coming down the homestretch with putting the cancer behind me but last night I was told "NOT SO FAST". Each lady told me it took them a year to feel better and not to expect so much or be so hard on myself. It's tax season so that's hard to do. I did 8 returns yesterday and have 5 already scheduled for today --- and am anxious to see what the rest of the day brings.

We are heading to FLL for some sun this weekend so that will be my rest time!

Happy Ground Hogs Day to Everyone!!! XOXOXOX

- Wednesday, February 3, 2010 5:10 AM, EST

I'm back on the roller coaster -- I spoke too soon yesterday. Since my blood counts (white blood and platelets) were fine after my 1st Chemo, I thought they would be after the 2nd, especially considering my side effects from the 2nd weren't as severe as the 1st. NOT!

I got to Dr. Khatoon's office at 9:45 as I knew they needed to draw blood before I saw the doctor. My appointment was for 10:00 as I always ask for the first appointment of the day. When I arrived, the office was packed with people. I thought, "This can't be good!" The nurse immediately took my blood and put me in a room so I was second guessing myself. Forty-five minutes later, Dr. Khatoon arrived and told me my platelets were low. They are supposed to be 150. Mine were only 94. She wants to see me AGAIN next week --- cha ching cha ching. IF my platelets don't come up by next week, she wants to postpone my last Chemo until they do come up. My white blood cell count was fine.

When I called for my follow up appointment, I told them my ONLY available slot of time is next Wednesday at 10:00 AM as my first client on Wednesday is at noon. After some haggling, they agreed I could come then. So, I ask the following: Aren't

I the person that needs to be accommodated at this point? Why is the doctor's work schedule more important than mine? Can't someone else check the counts when they are done? What are they giving me to assure my counts come back up (answer - nothing)? Since they are only going to draw blood again (and the doctor isn't the person doing it), what's the problem with my arriving before the doctor gets there? Why does the doctor get to be 45 minutes late for my appointment? Didn't they appreciate the $514.00 I gave them when I got there for my 1st chemo session? And, aren't they going to appreciate the $514.00 I will have to give them for each of the second and third chemo sessions?

So, my back spasms continued, probably due to stress. Tax clients came and went and by 8:00 PM, I was passed out on the couch. I love this time of year though. I get to see people I haven't seen for a year and I get a lot of hugs and $$.

I hibernate. People come see me and they pay me to visit with me! What could be better than that? Answer -- GOOD HEALTH!! Have a great day and stay warm. God Bless you all.

- Thursday, February 4, 2010 11:00 AM, EST

I'm spending today being thankful for my life...my family... my friends...my doctors...my nurses. I'm helping my "platelets" do what they are supposed to be doing by being sure I get plenty of rest this weekend. I'm anxious for my next chemotherapy to go on time.

Dick and I are heading to the sunshine state. We got our tickets in September, wishing and hoping the Patriots would be playing in the Superbowl. Since I had to cancel my Nov. trip, we decided to do this one anyways. Stay warm. Stay safe and enjoy the weekend. I'll take some pictures to post next week with me in my turbans.

Hugs to all and I hope the Saints Come Marching In!

- Saturday, February 6, 2010 7:07 AM, EST

For those of you who haven't flown "SPIRIT" Airlines, let this be a fair warning -- cheap tickets, no leg room, no monitor, no music, flight delayed THREE HOURS and a lot of drunk people on the flight heading to Super Bowl!!! We arrived on 2/5 at 1:00 AM. We were supposed to be here on 2/4 at 10:00 PM. By the time we got to the condo and into bed, it was 2:30 AM. The entertainment on the flight was one man vomiting and another passing out. They asked, "Is there a doctor on the flight". A brave doctor stepped forward and asked for a stethoscope and a BP cuff. When the flight attendant handed them to him, he said, "What's this crap?" He found a pulse on the man although his BP was low, so they literally packed him in ICE to try to get him to come to! Plane landed two hours later, the man was still out COLD!! He was 2 rows behind us so we had decent seating to watch it all.

Yesterday I was exhausted but the temperature was 80 degrees although it was cloudy all day. A few of my neighbors came by to visit and check out my "Chia pet"(new wig) and my turbans. One suggested I eat steak for dinner to help with the platelets. So Dick took me to Ruth Chris's Steak House for dinner. It was the first time there for both of us. Steak was good but nothing like Jackson's Steak House here in Fort Lauderdale. For the travelers, you read about Jackson's in all the magazines as being one of the top 10 in the country and it is.

Anyways, I slept like a baby last night - first time in a long time and today I feel so much better than I have in a long time - but then, it's the second week after Chemo and I felt good last time when it was second week after Chemo.

So, we learned the NFL is staying less than a mile away from us at the Westin FLL Beach and this afternoon from 4:00 - 9:30 PM, they are hosting a massive FREE rock concert on Fort Lauderdale Beach followed by fireworks at 9:40 PM. The Bare Naked Ladies will be one of the groups performing so after dinner with our wonderful FLA friends this evening, Dick and I will walk to the beach and see who these Bare Naked Ladies are! The sun has already risen over Sunrise Bay so it looks like it is going to be another beautiful day in Paradise. Keep warm and enjoy the rest of the weekend.

- Wednesday, February 10, 2010 11:44 AM, EST

I have been busy catching up on being away for the weekend. Today I had my blood drawn to be sure my platelet count was high enough to go ahead with the chemo treatment next Tuesday. Thank goodness it was. I had read on the internet that by eating molasses, one can rebuild their platelet count so naturally I got a jar of molasses and have been eating a tablespoon a day!

I'm feeling good this week but know once I start the Decadron again, I will be back on the merry-go-round. Notice I didn't say I would be on the roller coaster. Since I now know what to expect, I think the ride will be smoother.

God Bless you all. Keep safe and warm in the storm that is about to hit NE.

- Thursday, February 11, 2010 10:52 AM, EST

And the ride continues..... I woke up at 2:00 AM with a severe stomach ache, back ache and the terrible urge to vomit. I gagged for a couple of hours and then passed back out. I'm taking it today easy alternating between clients, the couch and the bathroom. The aching and the urge to vomit continue so I took a pill to help the situation. Am hoping tomorrow is a better day!

- Monday, February 15, 2010 7:10 PM, EST

I'm hoping tomorrow goes on as scheduled so I can put the treatment part of the cancer behind me and concentrate on getting healthy again. My journey to wellness continues as I have been sick this week with terrible stomach problems, back aches and also a cold (drippy nose, burning eyes). I have been taking my Ativan to sleep and have been taking my Prilosec for my stomach but nothing seems to help. Is it possible my body is getting used to them so they aren't working anymore? Tonight before I go to bed, I start the steroids (Decadron) again. I'm weary but will continue to do as the doctor orders.

I'm hoping the snow stays away long enough to get us to the chemo center. Tomorrow at this time, I will either be rejoicing that the treatment is over or disappointed that it isn't. Stay tuned!!!!

Thank you again for all the support. I hope to see you all and thank you over the next year. With much love for all your support. XOXOXO

- Tuesday, February 16, 2010 4:28 PM, EST

HALLELUJAH! YIPPIE! YEAH! AWESOME! INCREDIBLE! YES! OK!!

I started the Decadron last night and got little sleep. This morning, I took the Decadron again and was able to disguise my sneezing and cough long enough for them to check my blood. My platelets and white blood counts were exactly where they should be so at 9:45 AM - they HOOKED me up for my last Chemotherapy!!! Chemo lasted until 3:00 PM as they didn't give me the Decadron via IV since I had done better last time than I did the first time.

They were concerned about the sick stomach all this past week and attributed it to my stress (from doing 74 tax returns in 15

309

days), my diet (from eating too much sugar) and my lack of sleep. So, I am going to take 2 Prilosec a day and 1 Ativan a day until I stop getting that sick feeling. Also, the nurse was concerned I wasn't eating enough and that could have caused the stomach cramps. My thought was if I ate more than I did, I would have vomited it up. The nurse also gave me Biafine to put on my bald head to get rid of the dry itchy scalp. Another nurse suggested when the hair starts to grow back, I use coconut oil on my head to keep my scalp moist and stimulate the hair growth. Has anyone ever heard of this before?

At noon time, my wonderful girlfriend Patty brought me and Dick lunch again and she came back at 3:00 PM with a bouquet of tulips and a box of chocolates. Patty is an amazing, incredible friend. We met at Boston State College in 1971 and I know we will be growing old together!!!! I LOVE YOU PATTY!!!!

So, I go back to the Chemo Center tomorrow for my shot, Tuesday for a follow-up visit and then they will schedule me for another PET/CAT Scan in three weeks. Dr. Khatoon doesn't know I go to FLA for 2 weeks in March so she is going to be surprised when I tell her we need to do the scans on MY schedule. If they aren't done by March 12th they will have to wait until April!

I'm keeping my fingers and toes crossed the next two weeks bring me fewer side effects than the past and am keeping my chin up looking for flowers to bloom and the sun to shine.

Thank you all again for your love and support. I couldn't have done it without you! When tax season is over, I want to concentrate on walking, my Italy trip, my 40th WHS class reunion, finishing writing my book (I have 159 pages) and seeing ALL OF YOU somewhere somehow!

- Wednesday, February 17, 2010 7:47 PM, EST

I spent the day chasing Logan which totally tired me out. He loves to climb stairs even though he can't walk unassisted yet. At 4:00, we went to the Chemo Center for my shot of Neulasta to help rebuild my white blood count. I asked about scheduling my PET/CT scan. We are aiming for March 12th. They will call me back tomorrow to let me know if they got it.

On the way home from the Chemo Center, I got a call from my Urologist. It seems I have a UTI so he prescribed Ciprofloxacin to be taken two times a day for the next 5 days. He did relieve me of having to have several XRAYS (KUB - kidney, urethra, bladder) and a chest x-ray as he is going to use the PET/CT scans from December to see if I have any kidney stones at this time. My guess is the chemo and radiation killed everything and anything left inside of me so I should be stone-free!

Dr. Khatoon suggested I keep my annual mammogram exam as scheduled so for the next couple of weeks, these are my dr. appointments:

February 23 Dr. Khatoon
March 1 Dr. Rubenstein - Urologist
March 2 Mammogram
March 5 Dr. Russell - Radiation Dr.
March 12 PET/CT Scan

Although it appears my visits with doctors is nearing an end, it's really not! Good thing I am retired and have time for this! Oh yes, and today's bills were for $343.07, $285.32, $509.06 and $337.05 along with the co-pay for yesterday ($30) and the co-pay for today ($30). The original bills were for over $16,000 so I shouldn't complain that I only have to pay $1474.50 of it!

Cha ching cha ching cha ching!! I understand we are not getting a COLA again in 2011 -- Guess I will just have to get more tax clients!! No wonder, I am losing my hair!! JUST

KIDDING - they tell me it should start growing back in the next 3-6 weeks! I took a picture and it turns out, I have a perfect EGG HEAD with fuzz on it! I could probably decorate it for Easter!

- Friday, February 19, 2010 7:19 AM, EST

Yesterday, I was expecting to be "soaring" as I am still on the Decadron, however with adding the UTI meds, I was hurting and had many side effects from the Neulasta. So, I did 12 tax returns with an aching back, upset stomach, chills, watery eyes, drippy nose and constipation! I went to bed at 10:00 and woke up at 3:00 AM with the same aches and pains I went to bed with. So by 4:00 AM, I knew it was time for prune juice! Am feeling slightly better now but wish I could see today's 9 clients while lying on my back!

Logan is coming by this AM. He will lift my spirits and put a smile on my tired face! I continue to believe the best is yet to come and will take it one day at a time. I know I need sleep to feel better - perhaps next week when I am off the steroids!

- Saturday, February 20, 2010 8:38 AM, EST

I made it through the day yesterday but went to bed at 7:30 PM last night and didn't get up until 5:30 AM today. My side-effects continue...aching stomach...nausea...back ache... drippy nose. I know it is just a matter of time and wish it were bedtime already again so I could try again tomorrow.

I realize how blessed I am. Two of yesterday's clients brought me gifts along with paying me to do their taxes. Who does that? Special people that's who! My friend Susan made me a beautiful peach crocheted shawl and Joan brought me perfume. Thank you ladies! Today should be easier, I only have 5 returns to do and will hit the couch. I will also be hitting the wall as I am coming off the decardon. Once the side effects go away, I know I can become more "upbeat" and continue the journey to wellness!

Tomorrow, my aunt, uncle and cousin are coming for a visit. I haven't seen them for a while so I am looking forward to the loving and hugging. God bless you all and keep you safe.

- Tuesday, February 23, 2010 12:13 PM, EST

I've been having a bad week and am still trying to stay upbeat but I feel like I am breaking down slowly. I went to see Dr. Khatoon today to see if my blood counts had come back. They hadn't. So now, I have low white, low red and low platelets.

I knew something was wrong as I have had severe back aches, severe stomach aches, and the chills. Dr. Khatoon took a blood culture. She thinks I may have a blood infection. Oh joy - just what I need! So next week, she wants me to go to Melrose-Wakefield Hospital for another blood culture to either confirm or deny her suspicions.

She believes the stomach aches were caused by the Cipro to clear up the urinary tract infection. She wants me to take a double dose of vitamin B and yogurt twice a day for a while to see if that settles my stomach. I have never felt so sick or so weak in my life.

And of course, all this comes with another follow up to her office at the end of March. When do all these meds and visits slow down or stop? So for the next month:

March 1 - blood work at MWH
March 1 - Urologist
March 2 - Mammogram
March 5 - Dr. Russell at MGH
March 12 - PET/CT Scan at MGH

March 29 - Kr. Khatoon
March 29 - Dentist appt.

I'm still happy to be alive and sorry to be complaining! Keep warm with the storms coming our way and thank you for your continued prayers.

- Thursday, February 25, 2010 3:20 PM, EST

I'm breathing again. I am definitely on the other side of whatever it was eating my stomach away. I'm still not sure if it was the UTI meds, the stomach virus or the combination of the chemo, chemo meds, UTI meds and stomach virus. All I know is TODAY, I feel better!! Thank you God!!!

Dick and I are excited to be going to see his son, daughter-in-law and 2 gorgeous granddaughters this weekend. Jenna turned 6 last week and "her Annie" missed seeing her for her Happy Birthday! I am taking a break from taxes so we can head out of town tomorrow and relax for a couple of days. I need some time off and I am going to take it. See - you can teach an old dog new tricks! Normally, I don't relax during tax season!!

Speaking of relaxing, Logan's taking a nap so I am going to take one too. Love to all. Stay warm this weekend and keep safe. XOXO

- Monday, March 1, 2010 4:35 PM, EST

I had a great weekend with lots of loving from Dick's granddaughters Sophia and Jenna, son Marc, daughter-in-law Tina and Tina's whole family. It was great to see everyone and get all those hugs! Naturally, I got little sleep which set my body back a bit but last night I climbed into bed by 8:00PM and slept until 5:30 this AM. I felt good when I got up with the exception of the numbness in my feet (neuropathy).

At 7:00 AM, I was giving blood at MWH and at 9:00 AM, I visited with my Urologist where I learned I have NO KIDNEY STONES for four years in a row. That's great for me since I was producing 1-2 a year for a long time. I guess the lithotripsies I was having on a yearly basis taught me a good lesson!

I called the Chemo center to see if they have something to relieve the neuropathy but was told to call back tomorrow so I will do that. Gosh - what a medical education I am getting.

I did 5 tax returns today, visited with Logan and am heading to the couch in a few minutes. I'm guessing I will hit the sack early again this evening. I need all my energy for my "little man's" visit tomorrow. He amazes me with all the words he says and how smart he is for 11 months old! I'm trying to teach him "Happy Birthday" so he doesn't get scared when people sing to him. He says, "HAP HAP HAP"!!!

• Friday, March 5, 2010 2:12 PM, EST

I had a busy week with doctor's visits and babysitting Logan! I talked to the folks at the Chemo center yesterday. My test results (blood and mammogram) were all good. I have no signs of blood issues or any breast cancer! YIPPIE!!! I do however have neuropathy that will require the attention of a Neurologist so I have made an appointment to see a Dr. Fischer in Melrose. My appointment is at the end of May so perhaps the symptoms will subside by then. Dr. Khatoon prescribed Gabapentine (300mg) that I can use at night if the neuropathy throbs or causes enough pain that I can't sleep. After reading the warning signs associated with the med (drowsiness, dizziness, suicidal tendencies, physical impairment, must wear medical identification when taking this med, etc.), I have decided to take it as a last resort! Tylenol usually works really well on me. I don't want to add any more powerful drugs to my system.

Also, Dr. Russell suggested I see a dermatologist for a black stripe I have in my left thumb nail. I expressed concern to him about my father having melanoma in his right thumb and it was detected by a black stripe he had in his thumb nail. He specializes in GYN so thought it best I see a dermatologist. Good call. He also told me he had neuropathy 10 years ago and saw a Neurologist and there is little they can do to help with the condition. He said he has just learned to live with his and believes I will learn to live with mine too. Goodness gracious --- what else will the chemo have done to me before this is all over? I understand Taxol is the drug that causes the neuropathy. Perhaps some researcher out there will find a substitute for the Taxol as it is also the drug that causes the hair loss.

By the way, my hair has NOT started growing back in yet. Am hoping I have enough hair by the summer time as I don't want to be wearing hats all summer.

The bills keep rolling in - I am at $3854 out of pocket so far this year so I should be hitting my "catastrophic" $5000 soon. I'm anxious to see if the rest of the year is really FREE or if that is another one of those things Blue Cross "gets" you on when the time comes. Last year, I spent $3799 out of pocket for the whole year, most of which was in November and December.

I heard the weather in NE is going to be incredible this weekend so while I am doing tax returns, please ENJOY YOURSELF.

- Saturday, March 6, 2010 11:48 AM, EST

This AM I was thinking about how "I AM NOT ALONE". I have so many wonderful people in my life that have been recently (AFTER ME) diagnosed with cancer. They have so many different forms of cancer and are just beginning their journey to wellness.

Tonight, Dick and I are having dinner with his good friend Jim, who was recently diagnosed with cancer but still isn't sure which kind. We are hoping to give Jim some laughs. Perhaps when he sees the Chia pet on my head, that will do it or perhaps when he sees that I have even less hair than Dick, that will do it.

I have tried to stay "upbeat" throughout the whole surgery and treatment. That is just who I am and how I have lived my whole life. I will go back to writing my story/book once tax season is over. Once it is finally published, there will be many that may be amazed or shocked by some of what I lived with throughout my life. My way of dealing with it was to just acknowledge "it is what it is", say some prayers and move on.

So if there is anything I can do to help those of you reading my blog to deal with your new found cancer, please let me know. YOU ARE NOT ALONE either. As I get healthier and healthier, I will be able to do even more and if you want some laughs, I can bring Logan along. He is great medicine. I am posting a picture in the photos section of him sucking on a lemon. It's priceless!

Enjoy the rest of your weekend. I see the sun shining outside and inside my heart.

- Tuesday, March 9, 2010 6:07 PM, EST

I'm keeping busy with taxes and Logan. I'm trying to get as many people completed this week before I head south to my FLA clients. Speaking of my FLA clients, one of them Leah, has breast cancer. I got word yesterday that the cancer has spread to her brain and she is now in hospice care. I am devastated. Leah is only 44 years old. She will turn 45 on Tuesday. She was planning to join a group of us for dinner on Friday night at Shooters Restaurant. My understanding is that won't happen now. Leah grew up in Revere, MA and is my cousin's best friend. My cousin used to babysit my daughters when they were babies and from time to time, she

317

would bring Leah along so I have known her for years. My cousin and I will visit with Leah on a week from Friday, God willing and give her some hugs. Please keep Leah in your prayers.

The neuropathy in my right foot hasn't changed. My left foot isn't feeling as numb as it was so I am holding out hope my right foot will follow suit. I am walking but am anxious for "sandal season" to come as I believe sandals will be more comfortable then my sneakers have been. I know I will learn to live with it if it becomes a permanent part of the "new me" but am hoping to see it disappear over time.

Enjoy the beautiful weather while it lasts. I believe we are in for a rain storm this weekend and some snow on Monday. I'm hoping the snow holds out long enough for my plane to take off! I am wondering if I should do the full body scan at the airport or the old system. I know I will be carrying a card telling the TSA I had a PET/CT scan on Friday as the Barium may "light me up" as I go through security. I carried a similar card for my Christmas flight. God Bless you all and keep you safe.

- Thursday, March 11, 2010 1:02 PM, CST

Tomorrow I will go for my PET/CT scan and keep my fingers crossed the results show no visible sign of cancer. When they called to "pre-register" me, they told me to be sure I wasn't in the company of any babies or pregnant people for 10 hours after the test as I will be emitting radiation. That means I will drive myself as originally Sean was going to drop me off and Deana was going to pick me up. Since Deana will have Logan with her, we can't do that. I wish they had told me this when I had my last PET/CT Scan in December as that day, Cara and Logan picked me up!

I have finished reading Numbers in my bible and will be moving on to Deuteronomy soon after tax season ends. I am so overwhelmed with work right now.

- Friday, March 12, 2010 2:37 PM, CST

Nobody ever said it was going to be easy! Today was another roller coaster ride day. When I learned yesterday that I couldn't have my daughter pick me up from my PET/CT scan appointment, Dick offered to take me and pick me up. Isn't he absolutely amazing? He has been my rock through this whole ordeal. So, we left at 6:15 for my 6:30 appointment and after filling out paperwork, they took me and got an IV line hooked up and gave me my two bottles of Barium. Last time I had raspberry. This time there was no flavor which made it extremely difficult to take in -- but I did it. They gave me 24 minutes of "machine time" for the PET scan, injected the dye into me and gave me 5 more minutes for the CT scan.

Dick then took me out for breakfast and back home so I could rest as my first tax client wasn't scheduled until 2:30 PM. I was literally on the couch for 5 minutes when the telephone rang. It was my PRIMARY CARE PHYSICIAN's office calling. Dr. Feygina wanted to see me IMMEDIATELY. I knew it couldn't be good news so I went to see her.

She was impressed with the speed in which the PET/CT scan results came in and annoyed I was going to FLA on Monday. Why you ask? The answer is because I have a LARGE BLOOD CLOT in my STOMACH that needs to be dissolved ASAP. So, she ordered two prescriptions. She had me go to the pharmacy to get them and come back to her office. Since my local pharmacy didn't have both prescriptions, I had to go to a second pharmacy (Walgreens) to get the second.

I returned to the doctor's office as directed and was instructed on how to self-administer a shot into my stomach. Dr. Feygina did the first shot. I need to do the rest -- or find someone that is willing to do it for me!! The needle is LOVERNOX which I will take for the next 5 days. I am also now on WARFARIN which is the same as Coumadin. Initially, I will take 5 pills a day in the evening then on Monday while in FLA, I will have my blood tested at Quest Diagnostics (THANK YOU ROBERTA for making my appointment - YOU are the best!!), fax the results to my doctor and call her at 4:00 PM for further instructions!

In the meantime, I need to stop all vitamins, stop my baby aspirin, stop GREEN vegetables and cancel my dentist appointment for my cleaning!

THE GOOD NEWS --- she didn't tell me to cancel my trip to FLA. That would have put me over the edge!! She was a little upset I wouldn't be going to her office for the blood work but understood my need to get away -- to do taxes and get some much needed sun and rest.

Now all I have to do is get the guts to stick myself with a needle or find a willing candidate to do it for me! I know I have people in FLA in my development that are nurses so am guessing I just need help for the next two days and Dick may have a stronger stomach for this kind of thing than I do!

I'm hoping to get off the roller coaster soon and believe this too shall pass ---- one day at a time! Stay safe and HEALTHY until we meet again. Lots of love and hugs to you all. XOXO

• Saturday, March 13, 2010 7:33 PM, EST

God sent me more angels. My girlfriend Joyce came to give me my shot. I still can't see myself sticking a needle into my stomach. I turn away when they draw blood and covered my arm throughout the chemo so I wouldn't have to look at the IV in my arm. Now, I have two black and blues on my belly. By the time I am done, I will have six!

I also got two phone calls that helped put my mind at ease about blood clots. Thank you Brenda and Karen. Having both had cancer, they can identify with how I am feeling and how depressing it really is to continue to have setbacks.

Since I am back on meds again, I am exhausted and am about to climb into bed. Gosh, it's Saturday night at 7:45. How boring am I?

Tomorrow I have to get up early for church. In the afternoon, my daughters, their husbands, Logan, my nephew Jake, our friends and Dick's brother and sister-in-law are coming over to celebrate my "HEINZ 57" birthday. We are thinking of using the bottle of catsup as the centerpiece!! Dick's doing the cooking so I am sure it will be delicious! The rain is nasty out there! XOXOXO

- Monday, March 15, 2010 7:36 PM, EDT

I had an amazing birthday and an incredible birthday dinner cooked by Chef Boy-R-Dick. He made Italian wedding soup, Fuseli with meatballs and sausage, veal cutlets, chicken piccata (my favorite), chicken parmigiana, a salad and asparagus. I got some terrific gifts, each of which was definitely "me"!! But for me, the best part is always the people. It was great to see everyone and share the day with them. This was Logan's first time at "Nana's" Birthday so Dick made sure he put Annie - Nana on the cake. How thoughtful! I have been teaching Logan "Happy Birthday" so he doesn't panic when people sing it to him in two more weeks so he appeared genuinely shocked when they starting singing to me! He just says "Hap Hap Hap".

My son-in-law Sean was my "angel of the day". He gave me my shot and was gentle. He wants to be "son-in-law of the year" since he was willing to give me the shot and David wasn't! I love how they compete for that position! We get a lot of laughs out of the things they do. I always tease and say, "What have you done for me lately"?

Today was a long one. I got up at 4:00 AM for my 6:05 flight and learned at 4:30 my flight had been cancelled. My thought is always to get to the airport and take the first available flight out. So by 5:00 AM, I was there. The line at JetBlue was wrapped around the building and down the hallway from Terminal C to Terminal B. I was shocked to see so many people there so early in the AM. It turns out many of them had spent the night since flights on Sunday were cancelled. When I arrived at the front of the line (6:15 AM), they offered me Fort Lauderdale on Tuesday at 2:15 PM, West Palm Beach on Monday at 8:30 PM or Orlando at 8:30 AM on Monday. I took the Orlando option and since the flight left late, I didn't get to Orlando until 12:30 PM. I had called the car rental agency and told them my dilemma so they changed my pickup location for only $25. That was awesome. I changed my Quest Diagnostics appointment to have my blood drawn to Tuesday at 1:00, got in the rental car and headed to FLL. The speed limit on the FLA Turnpike is 70 so I was able to make it to Fort Lauderdale by 3:45 PM. I walked into the Quest Diagnostics' lab and they drew my blood although they wouldn't give me my shot for fear of bruising me. My stomach is totally black and blue so I didn't understand their issue but whatever! I got my friend Bev to give me the shot at the condo when I arrive there at 5:15. The Doctor's office called at 5:30. Since they didn't get the blood test results by then, they told me NOT TO TAKE any Coumadin tonight. Sounds good to me!

So tomorrow, I start my vacation. I have a condo board meeting and will do 3 tax returns but then there will be time for some relaxing in the sun! I am going to bed! Nighty night and keep dry. I understand it's still miserable in the Boston area.

• Thursday, March 18, 2010 5:35 PM, EDT

Three days have passed since I have been here and I haven't sat in the sun yet. Logan and his parents are arriving tonight so I am committed to spending the weekend with them and relaxing. It is supposed to be in the high 70s and sunny the entire weekend. Tuesday, I did three tax returns and went to a condo meeting. Yesterday I did one tax return then my girlfriend Roberta spent the rest of the day helping me. We washed half the condo floor, put together a pack and play for Logan to sleep in and converted my daybed into a King Sized bed for Deana and Sean. Then we went to the Hard Rock Casino to have dinner with friends and gamble a little! It was great to see my former FAA friend Mark, his wife Eileen and my former supervisor Jim. Since we parted ways after dinner, they don't know I won $274.25. It's definitely going toward my medical bills as each evening when I talk to Dick he tells me more bills have arrived!

Today I went to have my blood drawn again at 7:00 AM. Then I ran some errands (grocery shopping, donated clothing, banking, laundermat) and then met up with a friend from Winthrop. I hadn't seen Henry since high school. I met him and his wife for lunch then we visited another high school friend. Joel is a hairdresser in Pompano and from what Henry tells me, he is also a famous hairdresser on Newbury Street in Boston. Has anyone ever heard of "The Will Charles Salon"? Perhaps when I grow some hair I will pay Joel a visit! We talked about our 40th high school reunion next year --- that's right 40th! I must have graduated when I was a baby as I don't even think of myself as being over 40 years old!

Tomorrow my cousin and aunt from Naples are coming to visit. I know they want to see me but they also want to meet Logan and I am thrilled about that. Tomorrow will also be Logan's first time in a swimming pool and Saturday he will go to the beach for the first time.

So, back to the medical -- the neuropathy is definitely getting better. I'm done with the "belly" shots. My stomach is totally

black and blue. Tuesday night I took 10 Coumadin, last night
7 1/2, and tonight I was told to take 5. I am in contact with my
PCP EVERY DAY. It's so weird to me that they call me every day
with a new dosage of Coumadin.

So, now I am praying that I am finally on the road to recovery
and that there are no more setbacks. I want to send my prayers
to Lis, Jim, Brenda and especially Leah, who has now been
moved to Hospice in Boca Raton. God Bless them all as they go
through their treatment plans and let go and let God help them.

- Saturday, March 20, 2010 7:43 AM, EDT

Logan arrived at 11:00 PM on Thursday and since he slept on the
plane, he thought it was time to explore Nana's condo when he got
here. I went to bed at midnight. Logan went to bed at 1:00 AM.

Yesterday, Logan spent the day relaxing in the pool. He was
amazing as he floated around in his baby seat. He ended up
taking a two hour nap which allowed me ample time to spend
visiting with my cousin and my aunt. It was great to see them
both but unfortunately my cousin gave me the bad news about
Leah's passing. She passed on St. Patrick's Day, one day after her
45th birthday. Her wake and funeral are next week in Revere, MA.

Last night 11 of us went to dinner at Shooters. It's a fun
restaurant located on the intercoastal. It was great to see Jim,
Barbara and Flossie. Flossie is 95 years old and lives alone here
in FL. She is mobile and says she is just losing her eyesight.
She's amazing. It was also fun to have my FLA friends meet
Logan. He entertained them with eating his lemon and
showing them where his belly is!

I also heard from my doctor re: my Coumadin. Last night, tonight
and tomorrow, I will be taking 7.5 pills and then have my blood
retested on Monday. The neuropathy has definitely subsided

since I have been in FLA. I have no idea what's going on with my blood but I guess that is why the doctors get the big bucks!

Today and tomorrow are supposed to be sunny and in the high 70s so we are going to the pool today and the beach tomorrow. I know the NE weather is great this weekend to so enjoy the weekend and stay safe.

- Monday, March 22, 2010 5:02 PM, EDT

I took Logan and his parents to the airport early this AM and was terribly sad to see him (and them) go. Yesterday we took him to the beach. He loved the sand. It was so delicious! When we got home Deana made a wonderful chicken fajita dinner and left me with enough leftovers for the next two days. Thank you Deana!!

I had my blood tested again today and was instructed to take 7.5 Coumadin again tonight since the results of the blood test won't be ready until tomorrow. My stomach is now black, blue, orange, green and yellow. I think that means its healing!

I had lunch with a friend I hadn't seen in 8 years. It's always fun talking about the good times from the past but sad to realize how many people are not with us anymore.

I'm hoping to get some sun tomorrow. It rained for most of today. Keep warm. I heard it cooled off in NE!

- Tuesday, March 23, 2010 9:08 PM, EDT

Today, I did one tax return, then went shopping and got three pair of shoes and three pair of Capri pants! The clothes and shoes are so much cheaper here for name brands than in the Boston area, it's amazing. So I will bring my new stash home to use over the summer.

This afternoon I sat by the pool and got some serious vitamin D! I looked red today but tomorrow I will brown up! I have Olive Oil in my skin that helps me cook faster than most. I was wearing SPF 30 but I still got tanned!

My doctor called. Tonight I am taking 8.5 Coumadin. Starting tomorrow until next Tuesday, I take 8 Coumadin each night. I would love to know how they determine the amount and why it changes on a daily basis. Why wasn't tonight 8 just like the rest of the week? I will have my blood tested in Saugus next Tuesday (Logan's 1st birthday), then see Dr. Khatoon to find out more about my PET/CT scan. After that, I will go to lunch with Logan, his mommy and his auntie Cara, then home and bake him a choo choo train birthday cake!!

It's 9:15 and I can't believe I am still awake. Last night I went to bed at 8:00 and didn't wake up until 5:30 this morning. So, even though I am enjoying watching American Idol, I am going to bed as tomorrow is another day in the sun!

• Tuesday, March 30, 2010 5:25 PM, EDT

What a day! Today Dick took me to my PCP to have blood drawn to determine my Coumadin dose. Since I also had an appointment with my Chemo Doctor, the Phlebotomist took three vials of blood and gave me one to bring to the Chemo doctor so they wouldn't have to stick me with another needle just an hour later. When I got to the Chemo Doctor's office, they were a bit perturbed that I had the vile of blood with me as they said they like to draw their own but since my name and birth date were on the vile, they agreed to accept the blood.

I spoke with Dr. Khatoon for about 10 minutes. She read my PET/CT scan report and told me I appear to be cancer free but they are concerned about the "MULTIPLE" blood clots in my stomach. So they are keeping me on Coumadin for 6 months.

She checked for hernias, checked my heart and lungs and scheduled me for another CT scan on June 30th at MGH and another visit with her on July 20th. She also suggested I have MGH send the PET/CT report and films to Dr. Hamid as I will be meeting with him on April 13th.

Twenty minutes after I left Dr. Khatoon's office, she called and asked me to come back and have more blood drawn or to go to the MWH tomorrow to have it drawn. I agreed to go to Melrose tomorrow. Cha ching cha ching cha ching!!!

Cara, Deana and I then took Logan to the Macaroni Grill for lunch to celebrate his birthday. He loves eating so he enjoyed his birthday lunch. We then went back to my house to bake him a cake. He was so exhausted from eating that he (and his mommy) took a two hour nap while I baked the cake!

I also called MGH and requested the PET/CT report and films be sent to Dr. Hamid. They want the request in writing. I didn't have to put it in writing the last time I requested the reports but this time I do. They can't seem to make anything easy. I will put the request in writing tomorrow.

I also called my dentist as they want to prescribe some kind of medication as the hygienist says the radiation and chemotherapy cause teeth problems and since I had to cancel my regularly scheduled cleanings (because of the Coumadin), they want to have me on a med. The hygienist wasn't there today so she will call me back tomorrow and I will find out what the med is!

Dr. Feygina's (PCP) office called to tell me I should take 8 Coumadin for the next two weeks and have my blood tested two weeks from today again!

I started making dinner as Deana, Sean and Logan were going to eat with me and then have birthday cake. However,

Deana got a call from Sean. He needed help at home. Water was seeping into their basement from the storm. We postponed dinner until tomorrow night. Fortunately, the only tax client I have scheduled for tomorrow night is Deana's Godmother so we can all celebrate Logan's birthday and eat the "choo choo train" cake I made prior to doing her taxes!

The rain is still falling. I understand we broke a record in this area. The last time we had this much rain was in March 1953, the month and year I was born.

- Tuesday, April 13, 2010 11:53 AM, EDT

I have been refraining from writing because nothing new was happening and frankly, I didn't want to bore you with more old news!

Yesterday, I went for my dental cleaning as the hygienist said she would stop cleaning at the first sign of blood. Since I bled far less than I usually do, she was able to complete my whole cleaning.

Last night Logan and I had a pajama party. He slept for 9 1/2 hours ! He's such a good boy, it's hard to get upset with him when he throws his food off his tray and just smiles, says "oops" and laughs at me. When I ask him "what would mommy say if she saw you doing that, he replies by shaking a finger at me and says "no no no"!

Today, first I went to Dr. Feygina's (PCP) office. They drew two tubes of blood: one to test my levels for the Coumadin and one for my six month checkup for the hypothyroidism. They will call me later today to tell me how many Coumadin to take and for how long before I need my blood tested again.

Then I went to see Dr. Hamid (my surgeon). He said he hadn't received the report from MGH re: my PET/CT scan and the blood clot in my stomach. After all I went through to get them to send it to him, I'm surprised he didn't' get it. OR did he get it but he didn't have time to read it? I did see a FEDEX package in my folder. DUH - I wonder what that was!!! In any case, he examined me (from the waist down) and said he wants to postpone doing anything about the bump/nodule/tumor (or whatever it is) on my stomach and the biopsy he was going to do on the bumps further down! He said if he tried to do a biopsy now, I could bleed all over the place because of the Coumadin. So, we scheduled my next appointment for October 12th and he sent me on my way! He did suggest I start eating vegetables again and leave it up to Dr. Feygina to adjust the Coumadin based on my eating veggies. When I told him I was already taking 8 a day, he said, "Hum, perhaps you should wait then!" I miss my green veggies!!!

Dr. Hamid also said the neuropathy is from the Taxol. So, it was the Taxol that caused the baldness and the Taxol that caused the neuropathy. I bet it was the Taxol that caused the blood clot too. Oh well -- it is what it is!! I guess it is all good news since Dr. Hamid didn't find anything wrong. Now I just have to wait to see how many Coumadin I take and pray there are no blood clots in my June 30th scan so perhaps I can get off the Coumadin.

So I am now officially a "Chia pet". The fuzz on my head is growing back. It doesn't look or feel like hair but more like a cotton ball. Some people have told me they shave the first crop and let the second one grow in. Now I know why! Since I am so anxious to have at least a little hair for the summer, I think I will keep whatever it is I get and be happy with it --- at least for now!

Thank you to all of you who have been emailing me asking about my condition but as you can see, I am progressing as expected and am realizing there will be life (and lots of it) after cancer! I'm so looking forward to this summer and getting back in the swing of things with my friends and family.

Much love to all and thank you for standing by while I have fought the toughest battle of my life. Ann XOXOOX

- Sunday, April 18, 2010 6:33 AM, CDT

It's amazing what some hugs can do for someone. I spent the whole day on Friday with Logan. Deana and I took him for his 1 year pictures. What a ham!

On Saturday, Dick's son Marc, daughter-in-law Tina and granddaughters Sophia and Jenna arrived. We will be celebrating Easter with them today! Dick is making all the Polish Easter goodies today! They will be staying until Wednesday as the kids are on school vacation. Deana will spend Monday with us and I will be babysitting Logan on Tuesday so it will be fun to watch him interact with Sophia and Jenna. We are heading into Boston on Monday to enjoy the Patriots Day festivities.

Last night I went to my cousin's daughter's wedding. My cousin and his wife have both experienced life after Chemotherapy. Allison just completed her treatment in December. She and I were "wigging" it for the night and everyone said we both looked great! It was so nice to see my mom's entire family and get those much needed hugs. At one point, I thought I would never see everyone again. What a great celebration of love and life. Thank you Jim and Allison. It was an honor to be invited.

- Tuesday, May 11, 2010 6:46 PM, EDT

I haven't posted anything in a while since not much has changed in my medical condition. Life with Logan has definitely changed now that he is walking!

I finished my final tax clients yesterday and am heading for a much needed vacation in FLA. We will be visiting with Dick's Dad in Palm Bay to celebrate his 90th birthday. I am bringing

Logan along with us. It should be a fun trip. When we return to Fort Lauderdale, I will spend a week with Deana and Sean relaxing by the pool and teaching Logan how to swim.

When I return to Boston, I have an appointment with the Neurologist to see what I can do about the Neuropathy. I wish I could say it has changed but it hasn't. On Tuesday I will have my blood tested again so the doctor can adjust my Coumadin level if needed. I have been on Benadryl this week because of a cold I developed. I am always freezing and wearing sweaters even when I sit in the sun. That's not like me. It's difficult to get a tan with a sweater and long pants on!

I finally feel like I am on the road to recovery. My latest pap test came back normal. YIPPIE! My next CT scan is in June.

My thoughts now are with my friends that also have cancer and are continuing with their treatments. It's so important they stay the course and stay positive. YOU WILL BEAT IT TOO. I promise!

I'm looking forward to seeing lots of people this summer. Logan and I are up for lunch and short walks. With my neuropathy, I can't go too far without my feet hurting but I am willing to try! God Bless you all and keep you safe until we meet again.

• Monday, May 24, 2010 2:06 PM, EDT

I met with the Neurologist and he confirmed what I already knew - I have neuropathy of my feet and my hands. Since it is better now than it was when I made the appointment to see him (6 weeks ago), we decided to forego taking meds to ease the pain. Instead, I will have more blood tests tomorrow to see if there is something else going on inside me. The doctor wants to cover all the bases! They will check for Lime disease, Diabetes and Vitamin B deficiencies! I doubt I have any of those three as I am truly feeling better with each day. The doctor says it's important to walk and keep moving so despite the uncomfortable feeling I have from extended walking, I will walk!

I am going to sit in the sun to get my dose of Vitamin D. Am reading "The AntiCancer" and learning a lot. Hugs to all.

• Wednesday, May 26, 2010 4:13 PM, EDT

I had more blood work done yesterday to determine my next Coumadin dose. It turns out I will continue taking 7 mgs for the next month and have my blood retested on June 21st. June 30th is my next PET scan and if the blood clot is gone, the Coumadin will be too!

I am feeling so much better than I did for the longest time. I know the sun and the heat have something to do with it. I feel so much more physically "able" in the heat! And so, since I don't expect any major changes over the next month, I will wish you all a happy Memorial Day Weekend. Enjoy the rest of the springtime and I will report back after the tests in June. Love to all.

• Monday, June 7, 2010 3:22 PM, EDT

Will the ride ever end?!?!? Yesterday I had deep red blood in my urine so I called my oncologist. He suggested I go to the Emergency Room at MWH ASAP. He was concerned the Coumadin was too high a dose and perhaps making me bleed internally.

Although Dick and I had other plans for the day, we immediately did as we were told. Upon arrival at the ER (2:00 PM), I was seen by one nurse (triage). She took my temp (97.6) and my blood pressure (158/89). Then I was sent to a record keeper to update and verify my information on file. Then we sat for over an hour when Dick came up with a brilliant idea. He suggested I tell the nurse I had to urinate and unless they gave me a cup to give them a sample now, I may not be able to produce one later for them!

It worked like a charm. They gave me a cup and at least the process was started. When I gave them back a full cup of blood, they were concerned. Because of the lack of any other symptoms, they decided the best course was to get me into a "Johnny" and seen by a doctor. So the Phlebotomist came and took some blood, then the doctor came to check my heart, lungs, kidneys and stomach for any signs of pain or swelling. He asked many questions related to burning, itching, pain, etc. Absent any other symptoms, they decided to make us wait for the blood and urine test results (another hour).

At 4:45 PM, they told me the blood red and white counts were good but that the Coumadin count was 3 (which I was told is borderline high). They found bacteria in the urine and since they didn't know what the real problem was, they gave me a Cipro tablet, prescribed Cipro (2x per day for 5 days) and sent me on my way. They told me to have a follow up visit with my Urologist and my Primary Care Physician. The Urologist was supposed to determine what the real problem was while the Primary Care Physician was to determine if I need an adjustment to my Coumadin dose.

So, later in the evening, I went to the pharmacy to get the prescription filled. The pharmacist was alarmed I was prescribed Cipro given I am on Coumadin. She immediately called the hospital to find out if they knew I was on Coumadin. When they confirmed they did, she filled the prescription but suggested I call my Urologist before taking my morning dose as she believed Cipro was NOT THE RIGHT MED TO TAKE!

At 9:00 AM, I called the Urologist and waited patiently for a return call. When none came by noon, I called my primary care physician. She said to ABSOLUTELY NOT TAKE THE CIPRO and to visit with her tomorrow at 1:45 PM. At 3:30 PM, the Urologist called back and said to TAKE THE CIPRO but stop the COUMADIN and make an appointment to see him! He also ordered a PET scan and a CT scan. When I told the nurse I had a PET/CT Scan already scheduled for June 30th, she told me she would talk to the doctor tomorrow and get back to me! I also told her I had spoken to my PCP and she told me NOT TO TAKE THE CIPRO! She said, "ok". She will talk to me tomorrow.

So, as you can see, the roller coaster ride continues! It scares me to think I am given different instructions from each of my doctors. The ER doctor puts me on Cipro. My PCP says NO CIPRO. The Urologist says NO COUMADIN. And, everyone wants to scan me and see me --- cha ching! Only now, since I have already paid $5,000 this year out of pocket, they are going to be doing it all for free --- unless of course BCBS pays them. I really don't know how it all works!

And so, I will most likely update again tomorrow when I know more. The good news is Dick and I were safely in the hospital when the storm went through. When we left the hospital and saw all the downed trees and power lines, we were shocked at what we saw. It appeared the area got hit by a bomb. So, I pray you are all safe and had no damage to your property or yourself. When we got home, we saw we did lose power, our yard furniture was all over the yard, and our potted rose bush was thrown across the lawn. Stay healthy and safe until we meet again. XOXOXO

• Tuesday, June 8, 2010 6:38 PM, EDT

Today I went to see Dr. Feygina, my PCP. While waiting in the waiting room, I overheard the nurse talking about my daughter. How weird was that? Next thing I know, they asked me if I wanted to go sit with my daughter while she was having her blood tests done. I didn't even know she was there and she didn't know I was there! So, I sat with her and she offered to sit with me but I sent her on her way as she needed to return to work!

Dr. Feygina went through the detailed events that led me to the ER on Sunday and then decided she too wanted a CT scan within the next three days, just as the Urologist wanted. I told her I was willing to do one if I could combine the CT with the PET so I wouldn't need to repeat the same tests on June 30th as I am already scheduled for both then. The purpose of the June 30th tests is to determine if the blood clots have dissolved. The purpose of the current CT scan would be to see what's going on in my abdomen (kidneys) and pelvis (stomach) areas that is causing the bleeding in my urine.

Dr. Feygina took another urine sample and the blood is still there. Since she had ruled out kidney stones and urinary tract infections, she lowered my Coumadin by 1/2 pill per day so now I will take 6 1/2 until June 20th and retest my blood at that time. I'm hoping the CT scan shows no more blood clots so maybe I will be off the Coumadin in a short while.

Dr. Feygina called Dr. Khatoon and discussed how each can get the scans they want in a timely fashion. They made the decision to reschedule the PET/CT scan ordered by Dr. Khatoon for September 27th and I will have a CT scan this week --- day TBD tomorrow by the Melrose-Wakefield scheduling department. Dr. Rubenstein (my urologist) will get the results along with Dr. Feygina and Dr. Khatoon. I hope between the three of them, they will solve the mystery of the blood in my urine sans other symptoms. I feel fine but am naturally concerned about the cause of the blood.

This afternoon, I had a wonderful visit with my island (MV) friend Brenda. Brenda is staying in Malden as she undergoes

Radiation at Dana Farber. She is in her third of six weeks of radiation for breast cancer. We were amazed at how many similar experiences we had growing up. We both grew up in Winthrop but the similarities were with our family situations as opposed to our town. Amazing!!

I am still writing my book but after speaking to the publisher am most likely going to change it to "My Memoires"! He explained the pros and cons of a book vs. memoires/manuscripts. Once I am finished, I will have an editor review it, have an attorney review it, then call the publisher back. He will then tell me the next steps. Since I am busy this summer, I am guessing I won't finish until the fall.

• Thursday, June 10, 2010 5:51 AM, EDT

My CT scan is scheduled for tomorrow morning at 8:00 AM at MWH. Later this evening and early tomorrow morning, I will drink a Barium Sulfate Suspension. They call it Berry Smoothie to hide the chalky taste of it. Since I have done this before, I knew to refrigerate it so it will go down easier.

I am still bleeding heavily and therefore am becoming more and more concerned. I still have no pain but my whole body is aching. I attribute that to the damp weather though.

My urologist called back and is pleased we rescheduled the CT for Friday (from June 30th). He scheduled me for a follow up with him on June 28th.

When I first got cancer, my friend Kathy and my cousin Allison told me to expect a year's worth of medical issues. I am in my seventh month so perhaps I only have a few more months left!

And to make matters worse, when Logan woke up from his nap yesterday, he was burning up with a fever (101.3). Deana took him to the doctors. They want us to watch him for mouth sores or rashes. We will keep him on Tylenol to help him to rest and heal.

- Friday, June 11, 2010 9:30 AM, EDT

I just returned home from a nasty CT scan. I got to the hospital at 7:30 and was taken in at 7:50 for my 8:00 appointment. So far, looking good!

The first two pictures were taken with no problem. Then they had to insert an IV with the dye in it - the one that makes you feel all warm and fuzzy! Since the first nurse tried on my right arm and didn't succeed, she called a second nurse in for help. The second nursed tried my right arm and didn't succeed either so she tried my left arm. That was worse. They then called for help from a Cardiac Unit Nurse as I was clearly in distress from the ordeal and they didn't know what to do to get the IV inserted. The Cardiac Nurse tried unsuccessfully in my right arm. After wiping away my tears from the pain of it all, I suggested they use the veins in my hand. They told me they couldn't do that as they needed to inject the dye at a fast rate and it should go close to the elbow for some reason. My thought was "if the elbow veins are collapsing, you obviously need to try something else". How hard was that? After one more unsuccessful attempt, they agreed to use my right wrist and within 5 minutes the test was done. I had the IV taken out and had to wait 8 minutes for the last set of pictures.

Now I have a big black bruise on my left arm, 3 bruises on my right arm and a gauze style bandage on my right wrist. I'm going to a wedding tomorrow and definitely look like I have been beaten up. And to be honest, I feel like I have. That could be the damp weather or it could be that I tried exercising yesterday after not exercising for the last 6 months. Now I wait for the results while I hope and pray for the best. Thank you to everyone for your prayers and love. I will post something as soon as I know more. XOXOOX

• Tuesday, June 15, 2010 12:41 PM, EDT

After three phone calls to my PCP's office, I just now got a return phone call with the results of my CT scan from Friday.

I called yesterday morning at 10:00 and was told the doctor had the results and would call me back as soon as she had a chance to read them. I then called back at 4:30 PM and was assured I would hear from the doctor later on. When I went to bed last night at 9:00 PM and she still hadn't called. Dick tried to assure me everything was most likely fine so there was no urgency to call.

This AM, I waited again until 12:00 PM and called again. The nurse knew I had been waiting since yesterday so she said she would ask the doctor as soon as she finished with the current patient. She called me back at 12:30 PM and said, the CT Scan showed no tumors in my abdomen or pelvis. The doctor therefore wanted me to follow up with a Urologist. She then referred me to a Urologist and said I would most likely need a cystoscopy. Since I have my own Urologist and I already have an appointment scheduled with him next Monday, I am going to stick with him. It just so happens he is the partner of the man she recommended. The good news is I have no tumors. The bad news is they still don't know what is causing the bleeding.

Today I was able to stain the vertical risers of my front stairs and continue writing my book. I am up to 223 pages now and am writing the section about meeting my half brothers (1992) and the wonderful times I have spent with them. My relationship with them and their families bring me much joy.

Since it is beautiful outside, I may take the afternoon off and just go read on the deck. So, now we play the waiting game again with respect to my health. I have posted a picture on this sight showing the bruise on my left arm. I must warn those with a weak stomach, it's ugly!

Thanks to those who keep reading and praying for my good health. I received a Mass card today for one year of masses to be said for me. It came from my father's cousin. She wrote a loving note about praying for me and said, "I am sure your Grandmother, my beloved Auntie Annie is praying for you from heaven too!" I was deeply touched to see someone remembering my wonderful grandmother. Naturally, I cried! God bless you all and keep you safe. XOXOXO

- Thursday, June 17, 2010 8:30 AM, EDT

Yesterday I woke up feeling great. I had Logan for the day and I had more energy. I decided to walk Lake Quannapowitt in Wakefield. When I was half way through the walk, I turned back as Logan was getting fussy in the stroller and my feet started hurting. We visited Cara at her office, then came home and played in the back yard. After lunch, we went grocery shopping. At 3:00 PM, we both passed out but I wasn't surprised. We had a busy day.

Deana picked Logan up at about 5:00 and by 5:30 PM, I was in excruciating pain! I emailed Dick and he left the office immediately. By the time he got home, I was doubled over holding my left side and my left back. We called my PCP and without a return call from her, immediately left for the ER at MWH AGAIN. I was there June 6th and now was going back on June 16th. Obviously, they (and I) were missing something!

I arrived at MWH at 7:39 PM. After my registration questions, one of which was "How did you get that terrible bruise on your arm?", the nurse checked my CT scan results from Friday and told me I had a 4 cm Kidney Stone in my left kidney and my "presentation" was of a person passing a kidney stone. So they immediately

Ann R. DiMare

got me a bed and sent Jamie, the phlebotomist in to set up my IV line. After ten minutes of examining both arms and tying that rubber band around my arms in different locations, he admitted defeat and used the same right hand the nurses had used on Friday. Another phlebotomist came to draw blood. She went through the same exploration of the arms and decided to take 2 tubes from my left hand.

Next a PA (Physician's Assistant) told me she had reviewed my records and decided to do an Ultrasound and some X-rays but they would give me anti-nausea medication and pain killer medication via the IV to help me while I waited for the other two tests. The first dose of pain killer worked for about an hour and the nausea medication seemed to work better.

While doing the Ultrasound, they checked my right kidney, left kidney and stomach. The stone was blocking the flow of urine from my left kidney. They told me the medical term for that but I don't remember what it was. I gave a urine sample (still bloody) and they gave me more IV pain killer.

After another hours wait, they sent me for X-rays to determine where the stone was at this point. They took 4 films, 2 standing, 2 laying flat on my back. By now it was 11:30 PM and I still hadn't seen a doctor although the PA and the nurses were attentive.

Next they gave me a third dose of pain medication, took my vital signs and gave me discharge instructions. We left the hospital at 12:30 AM with a "hat" to urinate into, strainers to strain the urine and a cup to bring the stone back to my doctor for analysis. I was a bit lightheaded but Dick helped me to walk out.

We stopped at the pharmacy to fill my prescriptions. On the ride home from the pharmacy, I had my head out the car window as I thought for sure I was going to vomit. We were home at 1:00 AM. I ate one large strawberry, took my meds and went to bed.

I am now taking Ondansetron to stop the nausea, Tamsulosin to help the stone move quickly and Oxycodone for pain. They instructed me to call my PCP and my Urologist for follow up appointments.

The good news is I probably won't need the cystoscopy on June 28th. The bad news is my body is still producing kidney stones. I started producing them in 1977 a few months after Cara was born. This is my first one in 5 years. I asked about lithotripsy to crush the stone but that is not an option since the stone is only 4cms. They reserve lithotripsy for greater than 5 cms. I have had 4 lithotripsies in the last 10 years and have passed more many stones on my own. Since my past stones have been both calcium oxalate and uric acid stones, it's difficult to say what is causing them and what I could do to prevent them in the future. Passing stones for me has been more difficult than child birth. The lithotripsies were easy!

I did call my Urologist. Their computer is down so they will call me back to rebook my appointment as soon as the computer is up. So now I wait for the stone to pass and for the doctor's return call. All I can say is "Oh what a night!" I thank God the pain had nothing to do with the Cancer.

- Friday, June 18, 2010 9:48 AM, EDT

Yesterday I faxed my PCP the details of my experience at the ER on Wednesday. Her nurse called me to say the kidney stone was 4 mm not 4 cm and because it was so small, they referred me to the Urologist instead of telling me about it. While I don't agree that was the right thing to do, as I was worried about the bleeding, that is what they chose to do.

The PCP suggested I call the Chemotherapy Oncologist re: coming off the Coumadin since she didn't see the blood clot in the CT. I called Dr. Khatoon but she insisted I stay on the Coumadin until after the next CT scan (Sept. 27th).

Next I got a call from MWH (Dr. Gaonkar). He told me the X-rays showed the stone had moved from my kidney to my ureter. Remember at the ER, they did the X-rays at least an hour after the ultrasound so perhaps the saline was helping it to move.

I also heard from Dr. Rubenstein's office (Urologist). They made my appointment for 8:00 AM TODAY! I visited with Dr. Rubenstein. He said to surgically remove the kidney stone at this time would be risky because I am on the Coumadin. He suspects I would end up with more complications. So since the stone is so small, he wants to see if it will move on its own with the help of the meds I got in the ER. If it hasn't come out by June 28th (my next appointment with him) he will perform the cystoscopy to see where it is. I left a urine sample which he will test for bladder or kidney cancer. SCARY but true!!

He said the bleeding could have been from the Coumadin, kidney stone, radiation or "other". The other would be cancer!

I told the Urologist I was disappointed the doctors weren't all coordinating my care better and I assumed by sticking with all doctors associated with the MWH (Hallmark Healthcare) network, the doctors would all have access to my test results and information and would communicate better. I told him I don't like getting conflicting instructions and being left out of the information loop. Perhaps in the future, I will ask for copies of all my tests so I can review them myself!

In any case, I am now waiting again. I'm waiting for my next blood test on Monday to see if my Coumadin pills will be reduced. I'm waiting for a kidney stone to pass through my body. I'm waiting for the urine test results from today.

Happy Father's Day to all the dads!

• Saturday, June 26, 2010 11:11 AM, EDT

I'm still waiting and that is why I haven't done a journal entry since last week.

My PCP increased my Coumadin based on last Monday's blood work. I will see her again this Monday for another blood test. After seeing the PCP, I will go directly to the Urologist office for my cystoscopy. Am hoping it won't be painful. Although since I have been on pain killers all this week, perhaps I should just pop another one and continue the journey!

I am feeling much better about the CA since my last two CT scans showed NO CA and NO tumors in my abdomen or pelvis area. MY last CT scan also showed no blood clots so the next three months of Coumadin is just for "making sure" the clot doesn't come back. So really, all I am dealing with now is the fatigue and kidney stone. I must say even the Neuropathy has subsided since I am using the cream on a daily basis! I'm crawling my way back to good health.

Enjoy the weather and keep the prayers coming. Speaking of prayers, I went to the Padre Pio Foundation home site in Cromwell, CT this week with a group of people. What a wonderful place to pray. There are many statues there of Padre Pio, booklets about his life and memorabilia (bracelets, prayer cards, etc.) The priest who said the mass when the 56 of us arrived gave me a special blessing. I am confident I will return to good health with all the blessings I have in my life and the prayers from all of you! God bless you all and keep you safe until we meet again!

- Monday, June 28, 2010 5:33 PM, EDT

I had my blood test done this AM and will be staying on the same dose of Coumadin for the next two weeks then testing again. Based on all indications so far, it appears I will be coming off the Coumadin in September after my September 27th CT Scan (providing there is no recurrence of the blood clot).

343

And the good news is -- I went to my Urologist today for the cystoscopy. Since I have been without pain for two days, the doctor suspected I had passed the stone. Upon inspection, he confirmed the stone was not in my bladder and not in my urethra. That would mean, IF the stone were still in my body, it would be in the ureter tube and causing bleeding. Since I am not bleeding any more, the doctor believes the stone left my body without my seeing it or catching it. He said the CT scan indicated it was a calcium oxalate stone (first I heard about that). He wants to see me next March with another X-ray. If I have any pain or blood, I should see him ASAP.

And so, I feel like I am ready to celebrate and put the whole CA nightmare, kidney stone, blood clot and neuropathy behind me. I can handle the minor ailments I still have and will just need to work myself back to having more stamina/less fatigue. I'm anxious to come off the Coumadin so I can go back to eating salads!!!

Speaking of eating, I checked into what would be an appropriate diet given my type of kidney stones, the blood clot (avoid vitamin K), my hypothyroidism, my blood type and the cancer -- it appears the only thing I can ingest without causing problems is WATER!!

Thank you again to everyone for all your thoughts and prayers. They sustained me through a difficult time in my life.

- Monday, June 28, 2010 5:33 PM, EDT

I had my blood test done this AM and will be staying on the same dose of Coumadin for the next two weeks then testing again. Based on all indications so far, it appears I will be coming off the Coumadin in September after my September 27th CT Scan (providing there is no recurrence of the blood clot).

And the good news is ------ I went to my Urologist today for the cystoscopy. Since I have been without pain for two days, the doctor suspected I had passed the stone. Upon inspection, he confirmed the stone was not in my bladder and not in my uretha. That would mean, IF the stone were still in my body, it would be in the ureter tube and causing bleeding. Since I am not bleeding any more, the doctor believes the stone left my body without my seeing it or catching it. He said the CT scan indicated it was a calcium oxalate stone (first I heard about that). He wants to see me next March with another X-Ray. If however I have any pain or blood, I should see him ASAP.

And so, I feel like I am ready to celebrate and put the whole CA nightmare, kidney stone, blood clot and neuropathy behind me. I can handle the minor ailments I still have an will just need to work myself back to having more stamina/less fatigue. I'm anxious to come off the Coumadin so I can go back to eating salads!!!

Speaking of eating, I checked into what would be an appropriate diet given my type of kidney stones, the blood clot (avoid vitamin K), my hypothyroidism, my blood type and the cancer ----- it appears the only thing I can injest without causing problems is WATER!!

Thank you again to everyone for all your thoughts and prayers. They sustained me through a very difficult time in my life.

- Monday, August 2, 2010 4:45 PM, EDT

I haven't updated my journal in a while because I didn't appear to have any medical issues besides the neuropathy. Today, I woke up bleeding again but decided to go ahead with my plans. I was volunteering at an NFL Alumni Golf tournament. I did it last year and had a blast so decided to do it again. While at the Indian Ridge Country Club, the bleeding got worse so I called my Oncologist. She suggested I call my

Surgeon. He was out until August 10th so his nurse suggested I call my OB/GYN. He was on vacation for two weeks so his nurse suggested I call my Oncologist! I went full circle in a little over an hour. This time, the Oncologist suggested I call my Primary Care Physician. Since I was in the middle of talking to Gino Cappeletti, I asked her to just make me an appointment with my primary care doctor and to call me back. When she called me back she said Dr. Feygina said to, "Come right in". I left Andover and went to Dr. Feygina's office. After taking an urine sample (filled with blood) and examining me, she sent me to the hospital for an ultrasound and said to follow up with my Urologist. She believes I have a "kidney problem". She said, "Perhaps it is another stone". The nurse who did the test said she didn't see any kidney stones but she did see a blockage in my left kidney. So I made the appointment for this Friday at 9:45 AM as that is the first day my Urologist will be in this week. I guess many doctors take vacation the first week in August!

While I was at my PCPs office, she called my Oncologist and told her she wants to take me off the Coumadin so after a fairly lengthly conversation they decided I am done with Coumadin! It's ironic because, this AM I reordered my Coumadin thinking I would be on it until September!

So, now I wait again - until Friday or until I get pain. As of today, I am not in pain but am just bleeding!

Thank you to everyone who has been calling and emailing about my condition since they hadn't heard from me. I didn't mean to alarm anyone by not updating my journal. By the way, I am doing the final edit of my book and should be turning it over to the professional editor within the month.

- Friday, August 6, 2010 12:03 PM, EDT

I wonder for how long it is always going to be "something"!!

I went to my Urologist today to discuss my Ultrasound and my symptoms leading up to it. The doctor drew me a diagram showing my normal right kidney and my left kidney with a blockage. He then said in order to avoid "renal failure" and the constant scraping of my kidney wall when the urine pushes past the blockage, he suggests I have a stent put in my left kidney.

He had a cancellation for Monday so he was able to schedule me for the surgery at Mount Auburn Hospital at 2:00 on Monday. I need to be there by noon without anything (including water) in my stomach from midnight on. Thank goodness I am having company on Sunday with lots of yummy food. I can eat all night. Dr. R. then scheduled my pre-operative testing (blood, EKG, urine, etc.) for 2:30 this afternoon. If anyone has ever had a stent put in their kidney, I would love to know more so I can put my mind at ease.

For those of you who know Cambridge on a Friday afternoon, I'm guessing I will be home shortly before dusk! The commute is horrific. That's why I worked from 6:00 AM to 1:00 PM on Fridays!

• Monday, August 9, 2010 7:21 PM, EDT

I'm back!!! We left for Mt. Auburn Hospital at 10:30 AM. We arrived at 11:15 AM. I don't miss that commute to Cambridge!

As soon as I got there, the nurse took me in and prepared me for the surgery - IV, "johnny", blue bonnet, confirmation of name, birth date, etc. Nurse Anna was fabulous. She took my vital signs. Temp 97.6, BP 137/85, oxygen 96. She ordered me a baked stuffed lobster and some vodka for my IV but neither arrived in time for the surgery. I was visited by Dr. Rubenstein, a couple of Operating Room (OR) nurses and an anesthesiologist. The anesthesiologist gave me the antibiotic levaquin. At 1:40, they moved me to the OR room, put a heart monitor on me, a blood pressure cuff, an oxygen mask and a pulse monitor on my index finger. They must

347

have put something else in the IV because the next thing I knew, they were waking me up. Surgery started at 1:55 PM and finished at 3:05 PM. I was awake and alive once again. I was greatful and overjoyed!

Dr. Rubenstein installed a stent in my ureter tube and took another kidney stone out of my kidney. I believe that makes 13 kidney stones in my life (so far)!

After monitoring my vital signs a few more times, I was allowed to go "potty"! Unfortunately, I didn't produce enough to get released so I had 2 glasses of cranberry juice and two squares of graham crackers. After two more "potty" attempts and some post operative instructions, I was free to go home at 5:00 PM.

Dick got me a large bottle of vitamin water. I drank it very quickly. He dropped me off at the house before going to the pharmacy for my ciprofloxacin and tylenol with codeine. I will call Dr. Rubenstein tomorrow for a follow up visit in 2-3 weeks. He wants me to have a KUB (kidney, uretha, bladder) Xray prior to my appointment so I will schedule that as well. My understanding is Dr. Rubenstein will be removing the stent during my next office visit.

I'm grossly uncomfortable but not in severe pain. I will take my meds and go to bed. Tomorrow is another day and I'm confident it will be better than today.

My girlfriend Rita told me I was like a cat with nine lives. I'm starting to believe it. This was my forth major surgery and I am still alive. Thank you God!

• Tuesday, August 10, 2010 12:18 PM, EDT

I got very little sleep last night. It's difficult to sleep while sitting on the toilet. And that was the only place I felt comfortable!

The stent is pressing on my kidney, ureter, bladder and uretha. I have discomfort on my left side and enough pain that I am taking pain killers. I am drinking a lot of water. It seems to help a little but it's still very painful to urinate.

I am still working on my final edit of the book before shipping it to the professional editor. I keep getting new material so I wonder if it will ever get published. The next generation continues to have babies and I want to be sure to get everyone in the book as the book is a history book of my family as well. My cousin's daughter is due in December so I won't publish it until after that! Another cousin's son is having a baby in August but I already know her name.

The most exciting news for me is that I am getting new neighbors! Mary, my wonderful neighbor died in April. Her house went on the market last week. Logan, Deana and Sean are buying it! That's an Italian grandmother's dream!! Logan can visit his Nana any time he wants now! I will get to watch him ride his bike up and down the street. There is so much to live for and I'm thrilled to still be alive. I believe I have 5 more lives to go and hopefully, no more surgery.

My follow up with Dr. Rubenstein is August 25th. He plans to take the stent out at that time. September 27th is my next CT scan. WHEN they find I am still cancer free, my CTs will be scheduled for 6 months apart instead of 3 for the next year. I understand they go to once a year for the next 3 years! Tests I can deal with as long as I have good results! God Bless you all. Enjoy the rest of the day!

- Monday, August 16, 2010 11:57 AM, EDT

I have had a terrible week filled with no sleep, pain, discomfort, frequent urination and burning. I called my doctor on Friday. He asked me to go the weekend and call him back to let him know how I was doing. I called early this AM to report I had more of the same symptoms. He asked if I had a fever. Since there was no fever, he made me an appointment to see him this Wednesday to have the stent removed. He said it appeared my body was "rejecting" the stent. I can't tell you how relieved I was to hear I could have the stent out one week earlier than originally scheduled. I'm praying the pain will go away once the stent is removed and my body will start healing itself.

• Wednesday, August 18, 2010 12:30 PM, EDT

I had my stent removed today and am feeling so much better. I was instantly relieved once it was out. The stone was calcium oxalate so the doctor gave me a "low oxalate diet" to follow. Of the 40 items on the list of DO NOT EAT items, I eat 15 of them on a regular basis. It looks like I will be changing my diet forever! I had two stones this year in the same kidney, one in June and one in August. My follow up appointment is for December 10th.

I believe I am finally on the homestretch of my journey to wellness so will only update my journal after my doctor appointments or if something else goes wrong -- which I pray it won't.

Thank you all for your well wishes. I couldn't have done it without your support.

XOXOXO

• Friday, November 12, 2010 8:38 AM, EST

One year ago today (it was Friday the 13th last year), I had surgery to remove endometrial cancer from my body. Today, I am happy to say I am CANCER FREE despite the many side effects from the chemotherapy (blood clots, 2 kidney stones, a blocked kidney that required stent surgery, neuropathy, hair loss, etc.). Of the side effects, only the neuropathy remains. I am taking a med (Gabapentin) to relieve some of the pain from it. God heard our prayers and He answered them.

I am in FLA this month celebrating life with many of my friends. My nephew Michael visited from Oregon. My FAA friends Rita, Roberta, Donna, Pat, Teri and Deborah visited from Miami, Deerfield Beach, Naples, Kansas City, Chicago and Atlanta. Donna brought John Hughes. Teri brought her husband Randy and her mom Rose and Rita brought her mom Ann along. My brother Tony and his wife Teresa will be arriving soon. Today Roberta and I are heading to Rotunda West to visit Helen Papulis and her family. Dick and I will be celebrating Thanksgiving with his father, step-mom, sister and her family. Cara, Dave, Deana, Sean and Logan are coming down too so we can introduce Logan to Mickey Mouse and his other Disney friends. I have so much to be thankful for!

Logan has been my life-line to being physically active over the past year and I am happy to say he will be a big brother in early June!

Thank you for your continued prayers. When I met Teri's mom (whom I last saw 10 years ago), she told me she was praying for me. I am truly blessed to have such wonderful people in my life.

I wish you all a very HAPPY THANKSGIVING. I am humbled by your love and prayers.

Thank you.
Love,
Ann
XOXOX

8,807 VISITS FROM FAMILY AND FRIENDS

The following are excerpts from messages I received on CaringBridge.Com. I have included at least one message from each person who wrote. I appreciated every one of the 946 messages I received and continue to read them when I need cheering up.

Wednesday, November 4, 2009 9:51 AM, EST

I love that you said "I'll take the good with the bad"! When I e-published my CaringBridge after a year (when I was all better) the title was "Laugh, Sing and Eat Like a Pig." :-)

Dave deBronkart

Wednesday, November 4, 2009 9:55 AM, EST
I haven't stopped thinking about you. Please know that I'm here for you and if I can help in any way please let me know. I'm a good hugger and listener!!!
Be strong & Be a fighter! I LOVE YOU!
Joyce Misci
Revere, MA

Wednesday, November 4, 2009 9:00 AM, CST

I love you and pray for your complete recovery. Spoke to a friend at Bible Study Monday night, who is in her 70's. She had this same diagnosis in her 50's. It is amazing the strength we can muster when we fall completely in the arms of Jesus and let him carry us.
Teresa DiMare...your forever sister!
Roseburg, OR

Wednesday, November 4, 2009 9:02 AM, CST

Hang in there, Ann. My research indicates this form has good results when treated as you are doing. Anything I can do please let me know.

James Hallock
Waltham, MA

Wednesday, November 4, 2009 10:21 AM, EST

What a wonderful idea (Thanks Dave) I am so thrilled for you. When you are home recuperating you can make entries for us to read and rejoice in your recovery. I have also done some research and see with surgery and some follow up therapy there have been great results for curing this CA. I do know you will also be a survivor and we can laugh together on your next trip to Florida. Love you and am thrilled you are not only losing weight but are not crying - it only makes you weak!
Love Rita Kijek
Miami, FL

Wednesday, November 4, 2009 9:24 AM, CST

We are so glad you included us on your list of friends to be updated by caringbridge. Of course we were shocked and saddened by your diagnosis and wish you the best on your journey to recovery. You have lots of spunk, determination and grit that will serve you well while you undergo surgery and follow-up treatment. You have so many good friends in your corner, cheering you on and thinking good thoughts. We consider ourselves some of those friends and will keep you close to our hearts.
Barb & Jim Carey
Southport, NC

Wednesday, November 4, 2009 10:39 AM, EST

You know without question the prayers and well wishes of all the Smiths and Marinos are with you. I was so sad to receive this update, but deeply grateful that you want me to be a part of your journey to recovery.

With love and in friendship,
Cathy Marino
Winthrop, MA

Wednesday, November 4, 2009 10:45 AM, EST

I know you will be alright, you wouldn't have it any other way
and neither would we.
Paul & Michelle Campo
Methuen, MA

Wednesday, November 4, 2009 11:00 AM, EST

You are a strong woman and I am very confident that you will
get through this. Keep your chin up and only have positive
thoughts....you can do it!
Lots of Love
Judy Malloch
Revere, MA

Wednesday, November 4, 2009 11:10 AM, EST

Continued prayers are going out to you. Just let me know
what I can do and I will be there for you in a heartbeat. Stay
strong and continue to vent to the Big Guy above, he can truly
work miracles. My mother in law once told me that God never
dishes out more than one can handle to which I would look to
the sky and say but how much more can I take?? With His help
and guidance I got thru the rough times. Christine, Jeff and
Jen are also sending you their best and rooting for you. Love
you my dear neighbor and friend.
Priscilla Nathasingh
Saugus, MA

Wednesday, November 4, 2009 11:30 AM, EST

I am so proud of you. I can already see you are whipping this.
You are much stronger than your disease. God is blessing you
with healing and love from all of us.
Love, Roberta Stephens
Deerfield Beach, FL

Wednesday, November 4, 2009 11:33 AM, EST

Ann, There is no doubting that it is a long and difficult trip
upon which you are embarking. Some days it will take
superhuman strength to deal with the hurdles placed in your
path. I know you will be up to every challenge, especially with
the loving support of Dick, your family and all of us who are
your friends.
Tony Kijek
Miami, FL

Wednesday, November 4, 2009 10:34 AM, CST

You're the love of my life. I'm 100% confident you will beat this
disease so we can have another 50 great years together.
I will be with you every step of the way.
I love you.
Dick Orlando

Wednesday, November 4, 2009 11:21 AM, EST

You lost 7 pounds. You must take the good with the bad...the
humor is important too. You will need that the most in the
coming weeks. Be well, feel safe and try not to be too scared.
Sending you hugs, kisses and prayers daily. Get that nasty
cancer out of your system so we can rejoice. Hope is crucial.
Besides I see many great parties at your Mini-Mansion in the
future!!

Your Classmate Girlfriend,
Nancy (Taylor) O'Connor
Saugus, MA

Wednesday, November 4, 2009 10:48 AM, CST

News like this is always a big shocker to everyone. Thank you
for allowing us to share your grief with you. Your attitude
sounds terrific and I am sure you will do whatever you need
to do to beat this thing. We will keep you in our prayers every
day. So know you are not in this alone. We love ya!
Wes and Mary Jo Edwards
Litchfield, MN

Wednesday, November 4, 2009 11:50 AM, EST

Our journey together started in third grade and we have
overcome so many of life's hurdles. The woman I know and
love will beat this, I have no doubt!
Always in my heart and prayers,
Paula Smith
East Haven, CT

Wednesday, November 4, 2009 10:50 AM, CST

Annie, I second Rita's "what a great idea, thanks Dave." This
is a fantastic way to keep all of the people who love and care
about you up-to-date and in touch. I am looking forward to
many, many years of laughter and fun in the sun together.
You will beat this, you'll scare the hell out of it!!! Keep your
little Logan around you as much as possible; he will be the
best cure of all! John and I love you and are sending positive
vibes every day.
Donna Scheubert-Hughes
Streamwood, IL

Wednesday, November 4, 2009 9:08 AM, PST

Please remember that where the mind refuses to believe in disease, the body can follow. I am praying hard for your good health and happiness.
With love,
Carla DiMare
P.S. Dick's note to you brought a tear to my eye.

Wednesday, November 4, 2009 12:33 PM, EST

I'm so sorry to hear, at last we spoke you were heading to FLA and everything was great, I'm at a loss for words,
George Hebert

Wednesday, November 4, 2009 1:04 PM, EST

I heard about your illness today. Whatever is going on, Irwin and I love you very much and we are here for you in any way we can be. Love you,
Deborah and Irwin Husbands
Atlanta, GA

Wednesday, November 4, 2009 1:47 PM, EST

You are not alone we are here when you may feel a need for friendship. Our patron Saint Anthony has been called upon by our prayers to come to your side and rid you of your illness. A candle has been lit in your name and will be perpetual pending your recovery. Coming forward as you have is indicative of courage and bravery which is unsurpassed. Through our prayers we are sending you a flock of god's angels to be by your side.
Love your Godparents,
Rosemarie & Domenic Russo

Ann R. DiMare

Wednesday, November 4, 2009 2:48 PM, EST

I've been thinking about you constantly. I wish I wasn't so far
away but you know I would come if and whenever you need
me to. I am 100% confident that you are going to come out of
this fine. You are so strong, and your intelligence and faith will
keep your willpower going. We love you like family, the girls
love having an "Annie". Talk to you soon. Love,
Tina Orlando
Syracuse, NY

Wednesday, November 4, 2009 2:57 PM, EST

My prayers and thoughts are with you during this difficult
time. Hang in there and just know that they will fix you up
and put you on the road to recovery. Positive thinking is a very
powerful thing, so make sure your head is in that mode. We all
need maintenance now and again. Take care of yourself.
Love, Kisses and Prayers,
Suzanne Barker
Winthrop, MA

Wednesday, November 4, 2009 3:10 PM, EST

I was taken back when Tina told me the news the other day,
the girls and I are keeping you in our prayers. I hope you can
feel all of the love and prayers that are being sent your way.
With Love,
Kim Courcy and Family
Syracuse, NY

Wednesday, November 4, 2009 2:00 PM, CST

I was simply stunned to hear your news. This kind of thing
comes out of nowhere and changes lives in an instance.
Please know you are in my thoughts, and I have faith you will

find the courage to bear with the discomfort and uncertainty
you face at this time.
Robert Doutch
Stow, MA

Wednesday, November 4, 2009 2:26 PM, CST

Sorry to hear about your illness. Please take heart-your
surgery will be successful!!! Eileen and I will be thinking good
thoughts about you!!!
Good luck.
Mark Rosenthal
Milton

Wednesday, November 4, 2009 3:35 PM, EST

I'm literally speechless but you'll be in my prayers. Get well!
Peter Osgood
Cambridge, MA

Wednesday, November 4, 2009 2:35 PM, CST

You know Steve has been Stage 4 since 1998 - with each day
we know the Lord has carried us through it all, as HE will you.
My melanoma was a scare too - so we know how easy it is
to worry but we are "fixers" and "believers" and this action
with the caring page is testament to how brave and willing
to let God's loving care bring you through the tough days.
Treatment isn't easy. Keep me posted and know you have my
love and prayers each and every day. God Bless –
Rae Chappie
Spring Hill, FL

Wednesday, November 4, 2009 4:09 PM, EST

Hi Nana,

You are the best Nana in the world, I have so much fun when we are together!!!! Get well soon so we can go shopping and out to lunch!!!
Love,
Logan McGovern
Melrose, MA

Wednesday, November 4, 2009 5:04 PM, EST

So sorry this has happened in your life. I am thinking of you & sending positive energy for a full recovery. Take one day at a time...or one moment at a time....I learned this through Carina's 42 day nightmarish hospitalization & 5 surgeries. Sending love & the best of health to you for a complete recovery & a great prognosis—Joan Antonino

Wednesday, November 4, 2009 5:32 PM, EST

I am speechless (hard to believe) after reading your story. I can only offer you my love, support and prayers because I'm not close enough to give you a hug. Please know that you will be in my thoughts and I know that you will pull through this frightening time. Annie, you're a survivor! Think of all the people who love you and are keeping you close in their hearts. You know I'm your #1 fan!! Thanks for always being such a great friend. Lots of love,
Sandra Hershey
Alexandria, VA

Wednesday, November 4, 2009 5:48 PM, EST

I got an email from Rae and want to offer my prayers and support. I remember you from so many years ago and reconnected through facebook and our get together this summer. It was wonderful seeing you. Stay strong, stay positive and know you have many people who care about you and will be praying for your recovery. Always,

Anne-Marie (Inza) Altieri
Winthrop, MA

Wednesday, November 4, 2009 5:43 PM, EST

Well Annie, I didn't think that I was going to reach the end of the list of your caring family and friends. So many people behind you and supporting you every day. Now that the crying is out of the way you can move on to the next stage of accepting and dealing. This is where we come in! We being your family and friends. This is when we do our best work. We are here to lift you up and keep you up and that's where you are going to stay. You just need to keep the positive attitude and we will take care of the rest! Loving you more everyday!!
john costigan

Wednesday, November 4, 2009 6:51 PM, EST

Hi Cuz, Sending hugs and support, xoxoxox
Donna Cody

Wednesday, November 4, 2009 7:13 PM, EST

You are constantly in our thoughts and prayers. The outpouring of love and support from your friends and family is what will carry you through the difficult times ahead. Don't be afraid to lean on the people who love you most. You have always been a strong person and there is no doubt that your determination to beat this will shine through. Hugs and kisses from us to you!
Matt and Debbie Orlando
Methuen, MA

Wednesday, November 4, 2009 8:12 PM, EST

I hardly know what to say. I'm sending you a big hug...can you feel it? I know that being positive is very important, but remember, if you're feeling angry and confused about why this is happening, you have every right to have these feelings...you don't have to be upbeat all the time. You need time to just be.

I'm loving you and praying for you. Take sustenance from friends and family and take advantage of every wonderful offer of help and care. You know Sheila is watching over you, just like you watched over her. Love you lots

Sue Jarrell

Wednesday, November 4, 2009 7:38 PM, CST

Sister Annie, I Love you very much. Praying for a rapid recovery after the surgery.
Love Tony DiMare
Roseburg, OR

Wednesday, November 4, 2009 7:41 PM, CST

Your positive attitude will be one of the best treatments you can give yourself. You know you're not alone - God first and then all your many friends care about you and we're here to help you in any way possible. I'm glad you set this site up - it makes it so easy to communicate in one place to reach so many. Love you much and you're in my thoughts and prayers daily. Keep smiling and go ahead and cry whenever you feel like it. Tears are relaxing and cleanse the soul. Of course, loving on Logan will make you feel so much better.
Pat Larimore
Liberty, MO

Wednesday, November 4, 2009 8:51 PM, EST

I am shocked and saddened to hear you are going through this! You are a strong person and I have no doubt that everything will be fine. Know you are in my thoughts and prayers and not a moment will go by on Friday that I will not be thinking of you.

I will log in daily to check your progress and when you're up for company I would love to come and catch up.

Christine Risko

Brockton, MA

Wednesday, November 4, 2009 9:15 PM, EST

After the initial surprise of your news, I was so happy to see the caring bridge support you have from so many wonderful people. Although it may be a scary and uncertain time until after your surgery, try to stay positive and let the skill of your surgeon give you the best chance you have to become cancer free. All the prayers and well wishes can't hurt either. You are a kind and caring person. I believe in Karma so now it is time for the return of all the good deeds you have done for others. If there is anything I can do to help give me a call.
   Love, Karen Mendzela
   Londonderry, NH

Thursday, November 5, 2009 1:07 AM, HST

Aloha Ann, I had just finished reading about my friend who was miraculously cured by prayer and intercession of Father Damien who was just canonized as a Saint in Rome. I have prayed for you and will continue to pray and ask for your healing. The power of prayer is well noted. You are a wonderful and deserving person - "It's who you are and the way you live that count before God" John 4:23-24 - this is the prayer on my November 13th Scripture for the day. It appears that you might be annoyed at the date of your surgery but the 13th has always been lucky for me and especially November 13th -- my son's birthday -- so you

see the day and it's dates are what you make of them -- you are very dearly loved and a child of The Lord -- put yourself in His Hands... I will check in on you. Take Care, lean on the support that surrounds you, God Bless you and Keep you well.
Nancyann Asato
Waipahu, HI

Thursday, November 5, 2009 7:36 AM, EST

Just read about your diagnosis in my emails this morning. Needless to say, it still hasn't sunk in! Things like this change your life and the lives of those around you in an instant. I love your attitude though - you are so positive - I truly believe that's a big piece of fighting this. The energy that comes from all your family and friends who love and support you is flowing your way and will make a difference. Keep fighting - we all will too!

Love, Richard Abbott
Amesbury, MA

Thursday, November 5, 2009 9:28 AM, EST

I am deeply sorry to hear of what is happening in your life. I am sending so much love and healing energy your way. Stay the strong woman that you are!

Much love, Carina Antonino DiMare

Thursday, November 5, 2009 11:21 AM, EST

Just want you to know Frank and I love you and are praying for you and to let you know that we are here for you and Dick. Love you
Frank and Carmen Barbagallo
Methuen, MA

Thursday, November 5, 2009 1:30 PM, EST

Please know I will be thinking of you and waiting to hear good news. I'm sure the visiting line will be out the door and down the street with people wanting to wish you good wishes and a speedy recovery, myself included.

Susan Killoren

Woburn, MA

Thursday, November 5, 2009 12:31 PM, CST

Sending hugs and well wishes your way. This site is absolutely incredible, not only was it a great way to keep in touch with the family but also to hear day to day of how things were going so you do not get inundated with calls and emails. I know you will beat this, you are very thorough, if there is something to be read or done, you will do it, you are diligent. You also have a positive attitude and I think that is helpful in a time like this, just think when you do beat this you can print this journal and keep as a memoir of what you went through and a reminder that you are LOVED by so MANY. You have a GREAT Heart and will always be a great friend. Take care and be well.
Love always,
Cheryl McLeod
Cambridge, MA

Thursday, November 5, 2009 3:26 PM, CST

You're in both our prayers. Hope you're healing is fast and painless. Call any time you need someone to talk to. We'll be back from Virginia after your surgery. I'll keep in touch from there. All our best wishes!
Georgette & Kevin McGovern
Stoneham, MA

Thursday, November 5, 2009 6:57 PM, EST

Paula and I are so sorry that you are going through all this (as the t-shirts say, "cancer sucks!") but so relieved you have an excellent treatment plan in place. It sounds like you're in the best of medical hands and your attitude is one of pure fight--keep it up! We will keep you in our thoughts and prayers on your journey to health.

Love, Beverly Ballaro, Paula, & the boys
Lynnfield, MA

Thursday, November 5, 2009 8:09 PM, EST

You're in my thoughts and prayers. (I'm very sure you'll be fine... only the good die young !) and according to stories Dick tells you'll outlive him. Anyway, seriously, I will send you messages and keep in touch with your website (great idea). I want to wish you all the best during the journey and know we are all 100% behind you all the way. Keep the faith and stay positive.
Love, Janice Fisichelli
Pompano Beach

Thursday, November 5, 2009 8:24 PM, EST

I'm glad to see you are getting some good news. As I promised you, I said an extra prayer for you this morning. It is wonderful to see all the well wishes from people you have known for so many years.
Berl Winston
Swampscott, MA

Thursday, November 5, 2009 10:08 PM, EST

I'm so sorry to hear this news. It will be a challenge in the beginning, but after being in the middle of 2 cancer battles

with my parents, I find it is amazing how quickly we can adapt to our new circumstances and continue to live a full life. You will definitely get there too. You are a strong person and once the shock wears off you will feel even stronger. If you need anything at all please let us know! We love you,
Kim, Jim, Allison and Lori Paci
East Boston, MA

Friday, November 6, 2009 12:03 AM, EST

I can't believe this is happening to you. You are one of the strongest women I have ever met. I have no doubt you will beat this. I will pray for you daily and thank you for letting me into your life. Love to you and all of your family
Marie White
Lynn, MA

Friday, November 6, 2009 7:58 AM, EST

I will be thinking of you and praying for you... you are in my heart!! I'm glad you are eating better... although the food doesn't sound fantastic... but whatever it takes and whatever you can eat and keep down is great!!
Leslie Morales
NC

Saturday, November 7, 2009 3:21 AM, EST

Your facebook friends reach out to all of us for prayers. Here is mine.
Eating healthy can be a life choice. It requires changes and not everyone will be on board with the changes but you can do it! Read lots of nutrition books and take what fits for you from each of them. There are lots of varieties of Tofu so don't stop at the first few. I make chili with ground, browned

"protein" from the frozen food aisle of the regular grocery store....none of those who eat my chili have any idea it is good for them too! The regular grocery stores do offer some good healthy foods - you will become familiar with all those aisles that we just wander past.....hang in there.
Peggy Carr
Boston WHS'69

Saturday, November 7, 2009 2:09 PM, CST

John and I were very sorry to hear about your illness. It doesn't seem fair so soon after your retirement. Now is the time you should be living it up! We're glad to hear you have a grandson to cheer you. Our son Bill was a great comfort and diversion to my mother during her illness. We know if anyone can beat this thing, you can. You are young, strong, optimistic, intelligent and determined.
You will be in our daily prayers.
Love,
Jean and John Sigona
The Villages, FL

Sunday, November 8, 2009 7:22 PM, EST

Sherrie and I have joined your site and wish you a strong hand in the weeks ahead. I'm sure your inner strength and strong will can help the good days outweigh the bad. The blog entries on this site certainly give us a peek into what you're up to. Love and peace,
Jay, Sherrie, Anthony, Tianna, Nicholas, and Chloe DiMare
Hopkinton, MA

Sunday, November 8, 2009 7:42 PM, EST

You are in my thoughts and prayers. Let me know if I can help in any way. I am sending healing thoughts your way!

Susan Webb
Peabody, MA

Tuesday, November 10, 2009 4:02 PM, EST

Mary and I were saddened to hear about your illness. Keep
your spirits up and follow Bob Doutch's advice on asking
lots of questions so you get the right meds, etc. You are in
our thoughts and we trust your upcoming surgery will be
successful and your recovery rapid. Love,
Mary and Walt Maling
Cambridge, MS

Wednesday, November 11, 2009 7:48 AM, EST

With all the love and support coming your way, you will make
it through this! Stay positive. Please know you are in my
thoughts and prayers daily....sending lots of love for Friday.
Catherine Colton
Naples, FL

Wednesday, November 11, 2009 6:51 AM, CST

So sorry to hear the news. We know if anyone can beat the
damn thing, it's a fighter like you. You've always had your goals
and were determined to meet them. We are thinking of you.
Don and Ellen Ward
Wayland, MA

Wednesday, November 11, 2009 6:07 AM, PST

Hi auntie, missing you on the west coast. I'm praying for you
every day. I know you will make it through this. You are super
tough. love you. xo
Maximilian DiMare
San Francisco, CA

Wednesday, November 11, 2009 1:28 PM, CST

I was saddened to hear about your illness (and a bit angry too). It doesn't seem fair that this kind of thing all ways seems to hit one of "the good guys." I've always admired you for your courage and determination. I have even more admiration and respect for you now for your positive attitude and spirit. I know you'll fight through this and beat it, like you have with every other challenge in your life. Be strong, stay positive and keep the faith.
With love and prayers,
Dave Tammaro and the girls
Stoneham, MA

Thursday, November 12, 2009 10:32 AM, EST

Just want you to know I'm still sending prayers and tons of hope your way daily. It appears you have a large support group of friends (and characters) from the various stages of your life. It has to be comforting to read the wonderful, caring words your friends & family have expressed. You are loved! Be well!
Hugs & Kisses,
Nancy (Taylor) O'Connor
Saugus, MA

Thursday, November 12, 2009 12:54 PM, EST

So sorry to hear of your troubles. Please get well soon and recover quickly. I need my taxes done in Feb. Wishing you well and sending you lots of love your way.
Kris & Cathy Peachey
Peabody, MA

Thursday, November 12, 2009 10:55 AM, PST

Hello Ann, I think I figured out how to use this blog. It was great to talk with you and pray with you today. Be assured of our continued prayer and love.
Sal & Rhonda DiMare
Wenatchee, WA

Thursday, November 12, 2009 4:47 PM, EST

Prayers and love are with you. I will be with you in spirit tomorrow.
Jesus loves you and so do I.
Roberta Stephens
Deerfield Beach, FL

Thursday, November 12, 2009 6:44 PM, EST

God, hear my prayer,
And let my cry come to You.
Do not hide from me in the day of my distress
Turn to me and speedily answer my prayer.
Eternal God, Source of healing,
Out of my distress I call upon You.
Help me sense Your presence
At this difficult time.
Grant me patience when the hours are heavy;
In hurt or disappointment give me courage.
Keep me trustful in Your love.
Give me strength for today, and hope for tomorrow.
To your loving hands I commit my spirit
When asleep and when awake. You are with me; I shall not fear.
With love and in friendship,
Cathy Marino & Heathcliff (my four legged cancer survivor)

Thursday, November 12, 2009 6:33 PM, EST

Ann, my constant prayers are with you dear friend. Just got off the phone with Jen and she's sending prayers and her best to you. Christine and my sisters are also keeping you in their prayers. You are not going thru this journey alone. Dick, your wonderful family and your myriad of friends are all walking this journey with you, sending you all their love and prayers that there is no way you can't help but feel them in your soul. There's not a doubt in my mind come tomorrow, our wonderful maker The Lord God is going to be by your side protecting and watching over you. Keep your faith and trust in Him. Extra prayers for you tonight, first thing when I wake up tomorrow morning and thru the day. I will be here for you to help in any way I can. My love to you, Priscilla
Priscilla Nathasingh
Saugus, MA

Thursday, November 12, 2009 6:41 PM, EST

My thoughts are with you Sweetie. As you can imagine, Mom (Helen Papulis) and I were so disappointed we didn't get our visit with you and Roberta because of what you are dealing with. Please know I am praying for you along with all your family and friends!!! We love you very much and know the Good Lord is watching over you along with your Special Angel. I know you will come through this just fine and even stronger than ever. I have a strong faith and am a big believer in the power of prayer and love - you have these Sweetie so everything will be okay. You just concentrate on taking care of yourself - leave everything else in God's hands and the love and faith of your family and friends. God bless you Ann!! I look forward to your good health and seeing you in the future in Florida with Mom again. We will all go out to celebrate - My treat!! XOXOXOXO
Love, Annie Lukakis

Thursday, November 12, 2009 5:55 PM, CST

It was great talking with you the other day. I'll be thinking of you and praying for you and your family tomorrow especially. Keep the positive attitude and as I told you "the doctors will never forget you!" Look forward to your updates after the surgery and hope we can chat again soon.
Love & Prayers,
Mike and Ellen Conti

Thursday, November 12, 2009 7:15 PM, EST

You are well prepared and have a lot of Prayer Warriors on your side. I trust God and the people that He has put on your treatment team. I will be with you in heart while I will be out of touch next week.
Love and Prayers and Faith,
Dick Flynn
Concord, NC

Thursday, November 12, 2009 7:15 PM, CST

You have always been a Comforter and now along with God, your many friends and family stand ready to comfort you. This verse has always meant a lot to me:

II Corinthians 1:3 - Praise be to the God and Father of our Lord Jesus Christ, the Father of compassion and the God of all comfort, who comforts us in all our troubles, so that we can comfort those in any trouble with the comfort we ourselves have received from God.

We will be praying especially for you to feel His holy presence and comfort as you have surgery. I loved reading about your doctor - how comforting is that!

Love you,
Pat Larimore
Liberty, MO

Thursday, November 12, 2009 9:20 PM, EST

My prayers are with you for successful surgery and a speedy recovery. I will be in touch with the girls.
Love,
Robin Driscoll
Saugus, MA

Thursday, November 12, 2009 9:34 PM, CST

Our thoughts and prayers will be with you tomorrow. Of course, Dad and Jean send their love and well wishes too. Lots of Love from your hosts at the ChaCha Inn,

Darlene, Dan, Ciarcia Family
Malabar, FL

Friday, November 13, 2009 12:12 AM, CST

Mass and Communion this morning is for you, Ann.
Wes Edwards

Friday, November 13, 2009 7:06 AM, EST

I am sending you a lot of white light and praying with our angels for a speedy recovery and good news. I have been out of the Facebook loop, but you are much more than a fb friend to me. Think about the fun and laughter we had this summer at the golf events, you are every ones rock, so relax and let someone take care of you for a change...think positive thoughts as I am doing that for you... We will be on the golf course next summer, just imagine the green rolling hills, the

warmth of the sun shining on your face, please call when you are feeling up to it...knowing Annie she will be at it in no time..
Love, Karen Mustone

Friday, November 13, 2009 10:19 AM, CST

You have been in our thoughts and prayers every day.
Jim & Theresa Cosier
Hudson, NH

Friday, November 13, 2009 3:33 PM, CST

I pray that's things went as well as I feel they did!!
I just found you as new/old friend we have many more years for our friendship to grow.
Susan DePippo
Winthrop, MA

Friday, November 13, 2009 5:41 PM, EST

Jesus' healing light is surrounding you. Praise Him for your good news! I have been praying for you!

Love, Roberta Stephens
Deerfield Beach, FL
P.S. Dick, thank you.

Friday, November 13, 2009 5:07 PM, CST

Thank you God for all these blessings! Love and Prayers
Rae Gravel -Chappie

Friday, November 13, 2009 6:17 PM, EST

Dick, my cousin is so lucky to have such a loving partner to help her through this ordeal, thank you! So happy to hear

everything went as expected and know Ann will face her challenges with the great strength of character she has always shown. Please send her my love and kisses, xoxoxo
Cousin Donna Cody
North Reading, MA

Friday, November 13, 2009 6:48 PM, EST

Dick, you have been the most meaningful person on my mind next to Ann because i knew you would be responding for her. Annie is on the road to recovery and there are so many friends & family members to assist her! All of us together will give Annie what she needs. For us it begins right here. Annie is already where she needs to be. Love you Annie!
john costigan
Peabody, MA

Friday, November 13, 2009 7:08 PM, EST

I've been checking the website all afternoon hoping for an update and was so happy to hear the good news!! Thanks, Dick, for writing so soon, I'm sure you're exhausted too! My darling Ann Marie, just rest and let yourself be taken care of during this post-op time, I will see you soon and am thinking of you all the time.
Your Patricia Tuccelli
Winchester, MA

Friday, November 13, 2009 7:11 PM, EST

We are so pleased to hear that the surgery went so well today!! Thank you Dick for keeping us all posted! Annie, allow the love in your heart to wash through you , cleansing and healing all parts of your body. Your healing has already begun. We wish all the best health in the days to come. You will be in our prayers on your journey.

Love, Chris and Karen DiMare

Friday, November 13, 2009 8:46 PM, EST

Dick
I now know what Ann meant when she said that my Tony's updates on my health to all family and friends really helped. Thank you so much for doing this for us, it was great talking to you on the phone sorry I had to call but I am super hyper these days. I feel so happy for Ann that she has you just like I have Tony.
Love Rita Kijek

Friday, November 13, 2009 8:01 PM, CST

Dick's update was wonderful reading! I am delighted to hear the surgery went well. Please take it easy so that you can continue to heal!!
Pat Thomas-Fuller

Friday, November 13, 2009 9:44 PM, EST

Hi Birthday Sharer:
I think I was in a bit of shock when I heard the news, you looked and acted as you always have when I saw you last month. Know that along with your superior strength, our love and support are with you. Keep the fight, we know you will prevail!! With Love,
Cousin Paul, Donna, Andrew, Abby, Maddy DiMare
Marblehead, MA

Saturday, November 14, 2009 4:15 AM, EST

I am so glad to hear the surgery went well. You were in my thoughts and prayers all day yesterday and I continue to send healing thoughts and prayers your way. You are strong and I know

you will meet all challenges and continue on the path to health. Be sure to rest and allow the people who love you to care for you.
Susan Webb
Peabody, WA

Saturday, November 14, 2009 8:32 AM, CST

So happy to hear you're on the road to recovery! Our thoughts and prayers are with you. Love,
John & Wendy Carpenito
Saugus, MA

Saturday, November 14, 2009 1:03 PM, CST

Hi Ann, I hope you had a good night and feel better today. It was comforting for me to read Dicks lovely message about your day yesterday. You are in my thoughts all day. Don't you love the pulsating leggings! I wanted to take them home they felt so good. I am figuring out this care bridge, so I hope this message gets to you. What wonderful friends and family you have. Love
Alice Bell
Berwyn, PA

Sunday, November 15, 2009 8:10 AM, EST

Morning Annie... I am sending positive thoughts and hugs your way. I have been thinking of you so much..... I love you and pray for a quick recovery for you. My heart and prayers are with you. I love you lots. I feel in my heart that with time, everything will go well and you will be just fine! You are such a strong woman.... and I am so happy that we have reconnected and that you are in my life. Once again, I can't wait to get my plans all together and come and visit next summer and see you after so many years, give you huge hugs and kisses. And I hope to meet your wonderful family and meet this wonderful man in your life, Dick.

I love you
Leslie Morales
Charlotte, NC

Monday, November 16, 2009 7:55 AM, EST

Hey Cuz. Glad you got through the surgery OK. You were in my thoughts all day. You'll see a little more progress every day. Don't try to overdo...slow and steady wins the race. Hope to talk to you soon
Nella Noe

Monday, November 16, 2009 8:19 AM, EST

Dick, thanks so much for the wonderful updates. Okay "Lobster" now it's time to take it slow and easy. You are in my thoughts and prayers always.

Love,
Paula Smith (Marino)
East Haven, CT

Tuesday, November 17, 2009 7:56 AM, EST

Hi Ann, I'm praying for your speedy recovery and I know with a fighter like you, it won't be long! You'll be relaxing in your Ft. Lauderdale condo before you know it. God bless...

Marynia Mackiewicz

Tuesday, November 17, 2009 10:37 AM, EST

Gene and I send our love and wish you a speedy recovery! Love, Eileen and Gene Leonard

Tuesday, November 17, 2009 5:33 PM, EST

I just heard about your surgery. It seems that you are doing everything right and it's great that you can get back to your own home early. You are in my thoughts and my heart. Lots of (gentle) hugs.
Len Kurzweil
Newton, MA

Tuesday, November 17, 2009 6:16 PM, EST

Ellen and I are in a state of shock! We believe in the power of prayer! We have added you to our very short list of friends who because of an illness we offer remembrances for, pray for, offer masses for, offer communions for, send cards to etc. Starting this weekend, our prayers for the living, our mass intentions and our communions will be dedicated to you and to Jim Ballough. Love.
Joe and Ellen Petrie
Norwood, MA

Tuesday, November 17, 2009 9:06 PM, EST

Sorry to hear about your health issue. Fran and I will keep you in our thoughts and prayers. With Dick and Peaches for support you are ahead of the game. Don't get too organized and keep a few good books handy - safety manuals don't count. Our best wishes to you, Dick, and the family.
Joe and Fran McGann

Wednesday, November 18, 2009 12:19 PM, EST

I'm glad to hear your recovery is going well, many many hugs to you - I'm in Peabody quite alot now (yay!) so when you are ready for visitors I'll make a quick stop to hug you in person! Keep up the good recovery work :) Love,
Carrie Brown

Wednesday, November 18, 2009 12:47 PM, CST

ALL MY PRAYER'S ARE FOR YOUR FAST RECOVERY I KNOW
THE CHEF IS DOING HIS BEST TO MAKE ALL THE HURTS GO
AWAY HUGS FOR YOU BOTH
Beverley Cowan
Fort Lauderdale, FL

Wednesday, November 18, 2009 5:56 PM, EST

WHEN MY MOM TOLD ME YOU WERE GOING IN FOR CANCER
SURGERY, IT JUST HIT ME IN A WAY I CAN'T EXPLAIN. WHEN
FRANK AND I MET YOU OVER THE YEARS, WE WERE SO
TAKEN WITH YOUR CHARM AND PERSONALITY. YOU HAVE A
TWINKLE IN YOUR EYES THAT IS HARD TO MISS MAYBE THAT'S
WHY IT HIT ME SO. PLUS YOUR DICK'S GIRL AND WE WANT
EVERYTHING TO BE ALL RIGHT WITH YOU TWO. I SAY MY
PRAYERS EVERY NIGHT AND I HAVE INCLUDED YOU IN THEM.
I'M SO HAPPY THAT THE HYST. WENT WELL AND NOTHING
WAS FOUND. ANGELA TELLS ME IT'S JUST THE LYMPH NODES
LEFT.   HOPE FULLY, THEY WILL BE FINE AND YOU CAN
RECOVER PEACEFULLY. I'M THINKING OF BOTH OF YOU AT THIS
DIFFICULT TIME AND PRAY FOR A SPEEDY RECOVERY.
LOVE, DIANNE LUISTRO

Thursday, November 19, 2009 12:42 PM, EST

It was good to talk to Dick yesterday & find this wonderful
website. It will be easy to keep up with your progress. The
hardest part is waiting for Tuesday. I am praying every day
that the news will be good. With warmth, friendship, & love,
Angela Russotto

Thursday, November 19, 2009 9:06 PM, EST

Hey Cuz, I have been praying like I have never prayed before. Sounds like you are on a sturdy road to recovery. Just remember that the Lord and your mom and my mom are all watching over you. You can't lose with that combination.
Love, hugs and kisses,
Cousin Carlene (Noe) Lajoie
Londonderry, NH

Friday, November 20, 2009 10:05 AM, EST

I love you Auntie Annie! Dick, thanks for keeping such a detailed journal. I hope is as therapeutic for you as it is beneficial for all of us who love Auntie Annie (and you) so much. Let me know if there is anything I can do to help. Best,
Jake DiMare
Boston, MA

Friday, November 20, 2009 11:13 AM, EST

My heart goes out to you and your family during this time of need. I was stunned to learn of your illness. You looked so good at the Volpe Retiree luncheon. I will think of you every day. I figure if enough people focus their good energy towards someone that someone will benefit from their thoughts. You have good people around you who truly care about you and your well-being. That in itself is a blessing. I will continue to review your site and leave notes. All my love,
Deborah Cogill

Friday, November 20, 2009 10:48 AM, PST

Dear Anne, I know you will pull through this. You're such a strong women. I will pray for you. That little grandson of yours is a little doll. Can't wait till my little doll comes into this world. Be strong Anne.
Love, Patsy Abbott

Saturday, November 21, 2009 1:19 PM, CST

This note is from Emilie and Frank Collopy in Florida. My sister Angela has kept us posted on your situation and you have been in our prayers and thoughts. Take it slow and keep positive. Hope you have real good news on Tues. Love to you and Dick as well.
Francis Collopy

Saturday, November 21, 2009 5:14 PM, EST

So nice to hear your voice! It has been nice getting to witness Dick's affections for you and know you were being so well taken care of (I'm sure he loved you needing him so much!) Very happy progress has been made with no secondary infections etc and hoping for the best on Tuesday! Talk to you soon!!
Love Donna Cody xoxoxo
North Reading, MA

Sunday, November 22, 2009 10:50 PM, EST

Dear Anne, Your last update has blest my heart. Praise God that you are coming along and starting to feel - like a women again - P.J.'s - football - sleeping. What else could anyone ask.....JOKE!!!!! I know that you have been through hell and I know the Good Lord saw you through. Now, all you have to do is Trust In Him and each day we will pray God grants you healing and strength to recover each day as you gain strength in HIM, along the way - until your right back on your feet. After all Nana you have a lot of fun times ahead of you. So, do all that you have to do...get well and next year you will be able to take Logan for a sleigh ride in the snow.
Love you, Kathy & Russ Boyington
Revere, MA

Monday, November 23, 2009 9:58 AM, EST

I recently heard about your condition and was extremely saddened to hear the news. I was reading your journal and glad to hear you are through surgery and feeling better. Hopefully, the worst is now behind you and you will continue to get stronger every day. My prayers and thoughts are with you. Take Care,
Cousin David DiMare
Naples, FL

Monday, November 23, 2009 12:05 PM, CST

Glad you are back home and on the way to full recovery. You seem to be making excellent progress. Just take it easy and you will get there. We will be in Florida in March-we are hoping to see you there fully recovered and loving it. Take care.
Love,
Mark and Eileen Rosenthal

Monday, November 23, 2009 6:07 PM, EST

Keep your chin up and remember one day at a time and one step at a time. My prayers and thoughts are with you and you'll get thru tomorrow no matter what! Tell Dick & your family to have a great Turkey Day!
Love Kathy Tozza
Saugus, MA

Monday, November 23, 2009 7:31 PM, EST

Barbara and I are now back and caught up on all your journal entries. You were on my mind and in my heart the whole time. Things are sounding so good, and I await more good news tomorrow. May God continue to heal you through His might, support your through His strength, and comfort you through His love.
Dick Flynn
Concord, NC

Tuesday, November 24, 2009 6:21 AM, CST

God has blessed both of you with the love of each other and so many great friends and family members. But we all know that most of all he has blessed US with your love, beauty and caring hearts. We have shared so many laughs and made so many memories through our years of friendship and I cherish each and every one of them every day. As we all prepare for Thanksgiving you can truly see we are all thankful for your love and friendship through the years. You are both in our prayers as you work towards a full and speedy recovery. There is power in both love and prayer and with your partnership in this fight I know you will be back on your feet and relaxing in Florida in no time. You have come a long way in this battle and we all know you will win because of your strength, determination and the love in your hearts.

Your love and friendship has helped all of us pull through some rough times in our lives and we are all here pulling for you now. Love you and miss you very much. XOXOXOXOXOXOXOXOXOXOXO

Kenny Gardner, Janet & Christin

Tuesday, November 24, 2009 1:58 PM, EST

Your Godmother and I continue to hold you in our prayers. We have asked the "good" saints: Anthony, Jude and Christopher to help and escort you safely back home fully cleansed of illness. Dick, you have been, simply put, marvelous in your attentiveness to Anne, God Bless you!
Love, Ro & Dom Russo
Winthrop, MA

Tuesday, November 24, 2009 8:50 PM, EST

Phil and I were shocked to learn of your cancer. I'm so glad the surgery went well and it was localized. We'll be thinking of you at the next retiree's luncheon (we'll miss your smiling face) and send well wishes for a full and complete recovery!
Marilyn Mullane & Phil

Wednesday, November 25, 2009 7:07 AM, EST

This service is the best invention of technology EVER! I am pleased to read you good report. One day at a time - listen to she who has a real problem with that. Yet, each new report sounds more up and up and I pray that "up" you will be. I recall the exact words my mother said "Attitude is the essential part of recovery". So easy for me to say HANG IN THERE LADY so many, many prayers WILL BE ANSWERED - In God's time He makes all things possible! Think, reflect and WRITE... this is a must suggestion. When I faced (not cancer) but all of my heartaches. God just put a pen in my hand and the tear fell on paper and the start of recovery and going forward began..this has not been done - ONCE..everytime my heart breaks - give or take a month or so...God puts a pen in my hand. He writes the words that flow with the speed of approaching the healing. I have 2-3 or maybe 4 boxes of writings since my divorce and having to leave my children behind. Write Dear Ann, write what is going on inside you. write it all to Our Heavenly Father and He will fly the pages of heartbreak, fear and helpness - in His time... Anne, please try to do this - it is the gift I give to you - that was my salvation and yes, it was!!!! My SALVATION - through these writings my faith in God has grown and will grow as I face the trials of my life. Pls. consider my gift! My love is to you. Yes, I will as you count our many blessings and you just keep an eye fixed on God and a smile with glee on your Logan.
Kathy Boyington
Revere, MA

Wednesday, November 25, 2009 10:03 AM, EST

Theo and I send you our best and wish you a speedy recovery. Have a Happy Thanksgiving!

Joe Koziol

Wednesday, November 25, 2009 6:15 PM, EST

We're glad to hear your recovery is progressing in such a positive way! We are reading all of your updates and keeping you in our thoughts and prayers.
Love,
Beverly Ballaro, Paula, Pete, Jake, & Brian
Lynnfield, MA

Saturday, November 28, 2009 11:57 AM, EST

I understand you've just returned home from "the country club". Hopefully the weather cooperated and the cuisine was nourishing. Now you're on your road to recovery. May I suggest you read Lance Armstrong's book, "It's Not About The Bike"? You will find this to be truly encouraging and inspirational. Be well,

Ben Hogan

Wednesday, December 2, 2009 9:03 PM, EST

Sorry we haven't talked lately, I am so glad you have your daughters and their families and Dick with you. I've read your journal and am so proud of you. You are so strong and positive. You have always had the overcome attitude. You will overcome this too. God had always been your strength and your guide. The prayer Footprints come to mind and God can carry you right now.

*Your positive way, sense of humor, loving way with all, and your
determination will also with family and friends help you through
this time. Sorry to hear about Dicks father. You are in our
thoughts and prayers will talk soon. We LOVE you very much,*

Susan and Jahn Janetos
Dover, NH

Sunday, December 6, 2009 9:10 AM, EST

I am so glad you are continuing your recovery. I know it has
been a difficult journey and the days are long, but you are
a strong woman and you come through this stronger than
ever. I understand your connection with Logan because my
grandchildren also bring joy and love in to my life. I would
be lost without them. There is nothing in the world better
than the smile and touch of a little one. I know you have an
enhanced appreciation of those people who love and support
you. It is wonderful that you are continuing to maintain that
positive attitude which has sustained you in the past. I am
not a deeply religious person, but I will hold you in my heart
and I send you all my good wishes for the future. You will beat
this illness and you will be able to continue to watch your
beautiful grandson grow.
Love, Pam Sampson
P.S. I know I am a distant friend, but if you ever want to call
just to scream, vent, complain, cry or whatever, then call me
anytime. I am a licensed social worker now and I am happy to
be here for you any time. You are not alone.

Sunday, December 6, 2009 7:00 PM, CST

We've been really concerned about you. We somehow got
bumped off of your bridge. The last we heard was the day of
your surgery. So you can imagine our stress! And then She-
Who-Can-Save-to-Disk figured out how to get an update! And

so glad she did. It's wonderful to hear how you are progressing. We'll be keeping a close eye on you now. Going to visit Flossie on the 22nd...she'll be excited to hear of your progress!
Love ya, Jim Carey
Southport, NC

Monday, December 7, 2009 8:53 AM, CST

There's an over-the-counter lotion called "Sarna". I use it for eczema and friends/family have used it for poison ivy and shingles. Ice packs also help. It's hard not to scratch. it feels *soooo* good!
Kate McGann

Tuesday, December 8, 2009 11:50 AM, PST

You will survive chemo, if you have to do it. You are a female warrior! And you have what are likely the best doctors in the world on your side. Please keep thinking about what we talked about ... where the mind refuses to believe in disease, the body can follow. Praying for you, and looking forward to seeing you soon. With love,
Carla DiMare

Thursday, December 10, 2009 5:55 PM, CST

I know how difficult this period in your life is. You will survive and come through it with a greater appreciation of life, love and friends. What doesn't kill you makes you stronger...I truly believe that. You have so many friends who are rooting you on and sending love and prayers...I totally agree with John and Dick on their "hair theory". Hang in there. XXOO
Jan Vigoda

Monday, December 21, 2009 9:16 AM, EST

Hi Auntie, There's a thousand reasons I always remember
you but I would have to say the top of the list is the loving,
unselfish way you raised your family and provided Max and
I with a safe harbor when we needed it. Your home has been
the most welcoming one I have known in almost 35 years!! Let
me know if there is anything I can do.

Love, Jake DiMare

Friday, January 1, 2010 9:18 AM, EST

Thanks for the info on Caringbridge.org...wonderful . Florida
sounds nice and warm @ this time of year. 30 degrees this am
with black ice. Oh well.I am a New Englander..will be ok. Hope
you enjoyed your NY Eve...We had a quiet one but nice. Take
care. What is your health care plan on dealing with this CA?
Peace,
Brenda Lehman
Vineyard Haven, MA

Friday, January 1, 2010 5:27 PM, EST

Just wanted to see how you're doing, and hoping to hear
positive things. Your message from earlier today certainly
sounds like all is well right now and I'm glad to know that.
Continue on that path. We're praying for you!
Harvey Brand
Salem, MA

Wednesday, January 6, 2010 4:25 PM, EST

I got your response this morning and was in total shock. I am
praying for you and hope all will be OK. You are a fighter and
will get through this. I can't find my gun and badge, did you
and John take it? :>)
Harry Schaefer

Monday, January 11, 2010 12:21 PM, CST

I think your new cut looks great; you have not aged! Keep your spirits up, follow the instructions you are given, and you will be back down to Florida before you know it. Just wanted to let you know I was thinking of you and sending you positive thoughts from my cube! Have fun with the wigs; be daring!!
Joann Orsena

Tuesday, January 12, 2010 7:57 AM, EST

I am thinking of you always. Hope you recover very quickly so we can get together and see each other. We miss you.

Love Carol Ferrante

Tuesday, February 2, 2010 6:21 AM, EST

I have learned so much from your journals, thanks. It helps me understand a bit better what you are going through. You are an inspiration and you know I love ya!
Donna Cody
North Reading, MA

Tuesday, February 2, 2010 8:40 AM, EST

My Darling Gran Marie, I think the wig looks so cute!!! Really, I think it might be a style to try when your own hair grows back. Sorry to hear of the spasms again :(but glad to know you're heading south for some sun and rest. I don't know how you have the energy to do those returns but somehow I'm not surprised knowing you!!

I'll see you in two weeks for your Chemo finale - YEAH!! After that, we'll only meet in restaurants, on the Cape or maybe even FLA! Loads of Love to you and Dick, As Always,

Your Patricia Tuccelli
Winchester, MA

Saturday, February 27, 2010 1:20 PM, EST

SO good to get back in touch - even in this crazy, bizarre way.
YOUR site has been an inspiration to me - and will continue
to be so. So glad you are feeling better and are enjoying a
wonderful visit with family. I had a wonderful call from Karen
Cronin yesterday which was also a gift. So, many blessings
on our common journey, and I look forward to traveling and
sharing the survivor road together. Strong women rule. Many
prayers are coming from my way to your way!!
Lis Gordon

Saturday, March 13, 2010 9:03 AM, CST

Talk about a roller coaster! Well, the bad news is you have a
blood clot but the good news is you were hoping they'd find no
cancer and I'm assuming they did not. Is that right? My life verse
has been "All things work together for good to those who love
the Lord and are called according to his purpose." Romans 8:28.

I love you, friend! Here's an Irish Blessing for you:
May the road rise to meet you.
May the wind be always at your back.
May the sun shine warm upon your face.
And rains fall soft upon your fields.
And until we meet again,
May God hold you in the hollow of His hand.
May you live as long as you want,
And never want as long as you live.
Always remember to forget
The things that made you sad.
But never forget to remember
The things that made you glad.

Always remember to forget
The friends that proved untrue.
But never forget to remember
Those that have stuck by you.
Always remember to forget
The troubles that passed away.
But never forget to remember
The blessings that come each day.
May the saddest day of your future be no worse
Than the happiest day of your past.
Pat Larimore
Liberty, MO

Saturday, March 20, 2010 9:18 AM, EDT

So glad you're getting to enjoy Logan ! Pool time is wonderful
for both of you!
So sorry about the passing of your friend Leah...prayers for
you & her family.
I'm having a better day today...yesterday was a blur. We enjoy
your Sunny updates ! Hope every day , you're getting better :)
Take care, Your Island Friend, Brenda
Vineyard Haven

Saturday, April 17, 2010 10:29 AM, CDT

Just recently heard about your battle with cancer while
golfing with Don Ward, Lenny Kurzwiel, and Rich Gunderson in
Florida. Don mentioned you were posting on the Caring
Bridge site. Ann and I pray for your complete remission and
speedy recovery. There are many more years ahead for you to
enjoy. Stay positive and move forward believing in your ability
to overcome any of life's challenges and you will succeed in
overcoming them. We wish you a long and healthy life.
Tony & Ann Swierzbin

Saturday, August 7, 2010 12:07 PM, BST

My friend has cervical cancer which spread to the ureter tube area and was putting pressure on the sciatic nerve causing her considerable pain. She was also having discomfort urinating. They put in a stent about six months ago and she has had considerable relief and no complications. It seemed to be a relatively simple procedure and it certainly helped her. I hope this helps. You are in my prayers and I do know how it feels because last year I had my kidney removed because of a very aggressive kidney tumor.
Maria Doherty

Sunday, August 8, 2010 1:01 PM, EDT

My father had a stent to his left kidney which was narrowed causing him uncontrolled hypertension. His situation was emergent but we felt confident in his cardiologist who specializes in renal stents. He was not in the best physical condition at the time. Since the stent placement he has done wonderfully. He has subsequently had to have it re-opened, I believe three years later, but no other complications. His improved renal function has made it possible to overcome other health problems as well. It is very similar to a heart stent and he still takes plavix to prevent clots. Good luck with your procedure!
Mary Giannini

I received many emails, letters and cards from friends. This letter was from my girlfriend Patty after my last Chemotherapy Session:

Friday February 19, 2010 8:39 AM

My Dearest Annie,

394

I wanted to thank you again for my surprise Birthday gifts, I love and will use them all, and for the beautiful card I found in the bag when I got home.

But I also want to tell you again how proud I am of you and how you've managed this whole difficult time in your life. They always say it's not the challenges in life that matter but how you deal with them. You certainly get the Gold Medal for that!!! And I was even thinking how gracefully you've accepted the hair thing too which must be very hard, it just seems to be a non-issue for you now. Haha maybe it's easy because you know what a cute and perfect egg-head you have???

I've learned so much from you over the years, things you probably weren't even aware that made an impression on me for the better. You've taught me even more the last few months!! I'm sorry to hear on the bridge that you haven't felt well the last few days. I wish you didn't have taxes so you could just rest!! But, that's not My Gran Marie!

So, I look forward to our Birthday celebration after taxes, you choose the date, time and place.

Love, Love and more,

Your Patricia

REFERENCE MATERIALS USED

Family photo albums
Official Birth Certificates
Official Death Certificates
Official Marriage Certificates
Official Divorce Certificates
Family Tree Maker files, compiled by conversations with my aunts and uncles
Letters written by Father Domenic Silvestro
Letters written by my grandmother Anne DiMare
Letters I wrote to Ms. Louise Auger returned to me by her sister when she passed away
My mother's calendars
My calendars
My diaries
My Franklin Planners from 1990-2008
My mother's medical records
My medical records
My work records
AARP Magazine February 1, 2010

Ann DiMare lives in Saugus, MA with her fiancé Dick Orlando. She spends her time with her grandsons Logan and Mason and working on her tax business. She leaves this book to her descendents as a testimony to truth, faith, hope and love. Ann's favorite bible reading is from the First Letter of Paul to the Corinthians as it speaks of love. It reads:

CHAPTER 13

LOVE

If I speak with the tongues of men and of angels, I do not have love, I have become a noisy gong or a clanging cymbal. If I have the gift of prophecy, and know all mysteries and all knowledge; and if I have all faith, so as to remove mountains, but do not have love, I am nothing, and if I give all my possessions to feed the poor, and if I surrender my body to be burned, but do not have love, it profits me nothing.

Love is patient, love is kind and is not jealous; love does not brag and is not arrogant, does not act unbecomingly; it does not seek its own, is not provoked, does not take into account a wrong suffered, does not rejoice in unrighteousness, but rejoices with the truth;   bears all things, believes all things, hopes all things, endures all things. Love never fails;

but if there are gifts of prophecy, they will be done away; if there are tongues, they will cease; if there is knowledge, it will be done away. For we know in part and we prophesy in part; but when the perfect comes, the partial will be done away. When I was a child, I used to speak like a child, think like a child, reason like a child; when I became a man, I did away with childish things. For now we see in a mirror dimly, but then face to face; now I know in part, but then I will know fully just as I also have been fully known. But now **faith, hope, love,** abide these three; but the greatest of these is **love.**

Made in the USA
Las Vegas, NV
23 February 2025

18579564R00223